The **SSAT**
Course Book

MIDDLE & UPPER LEVEL

SUMMIT
EDUCATIONAL
GROUP

Focusing on the Individual Student

CONTENTS

TEST-TAKING FUNDAMENTALS

QUANTITATIVE

ARITHMETIC

VERBAL

SYNONYMS

ANALOGIES

READING COMPREHENSION

WRITING

ANSWER KEY

Preface

Since 1988, when two Yale University graduates started Summit Educational Group, tens of thousands of students have benefited from Summit's innovative, comprehensive, and highly effective test preparation. You will too.

Successful test-takers not only possess the necessary academic skills but also understand how to take the SSAT. Through your SSAT program, you'll learn both. You'll review and develop the academic skills you need, and you'll learn practical, powerful and up-to-date test-taking strategies.

The *Summit SSAT Course Book* provides the skills, strategies, and practice necessary for success on the SSAT. The result of much research and revision, the book is the most effective, innovative and comprehensive preparation tool available.

The book is separated into five main chapters. The first chapter – Test-Taking Fundamentals – gives students a solid foundation of SSAT information and general test-taking strategies. Some of the more important topics covered include question difficulty, scoring, and avoiding attractors.

The next four chapters correspond to the four main content strands of the SSAT – Quantitative, Verbal, Reading, and Writing. Each chapter is divided into manageable topic modules. Modules consist of the skills, strategies, and common question types for particular topics, several *Try It Out* questions, and several *Put It Together* questions. The questions progress in order of difficulty. At the end of each chapter, homework questions provide additional practice.

We are confident that you will not find a more complete or effective SSAT program anywhere.

We value your feedback and are always striving to improve our materials. Please write to us with comments, questions, or suggestions for future editions at:

edits@mytutor.com

Your program will give you the skills, knowledge, and confidence you need to score your best.

Good luck, and have fun!

SUMMIT
EDUCATIONAL
GROUP

Test-Taking Fundamentals

- About the SSAT
- Your Responsibilities
- SSAT Structure
- Scoring
- Knowing Your Limits
- Beating the SSAT
- Making Your Best Guess
- Using the Answer Choices
- General Tactics

About the SSAT

❑ The SSAT is used to determine acceptance into private or independent schools. The test is designed to measure students' academic potential and skills in relation to the rest of the private and independent school applicants. Because this group of test-takers is especially competitive and skilled, the test is designed to be highly challenging.

A student's performance on the SSAT is <u>not</u> designed to reflect the scores on typical school exams or grades.

The importance of this test is determined by each school's admission policies, so it is important to talk to your prospective schools as you plan your SSAT preparation.

❑ The SSAT is a "power" test, which means that its difficulty stems from how challenging its questions are rather than the challenge of a strict time constraint. Most students are able to move quickly enough to answer most of the questions on the SSAT, but the test has many tricks and traps to challenge them.

Over the course of this program, you are going to learn to recognize and overcome the SSAT's tricks and traps. You will master the SSAT by developing your test-taking abilities, working on fundamental SSAT skills, and practicing on real test questions.

❑ The SSAT is administered in two levels: the Middle Level and the Upper Level. Students who are currently in grades 5 through 7 take the Middle Level test, and students who are currently in grades 8 through 11 take the Upper Level test.

Your Responsibilities

❑ You will have about 1-2 hours of homework each session. You are expected to complete every assignment. Remember, your hard work will result in a higher score!

❑ Your scores on the verbal and reading portions of the test are determined in large part by your vocabulary and reading skill. Use flash cards, study the word groups, and read, read, read! The more you read and the more vocabulary you learn, the higher your score will be.

SSAT Structure

Writing Sample – 25 minutes

Quantitative – 30 minutes

MATHEMATICS																								
1	2	3	4	5	6	7	8	9	10	11	12	13	14	15	16	17	18	19	20	21	22	23	24	25
EASY					→				MEDIUM						→				DIFFICULT					

Reading Comprehension – 40 minutes

READING PASSAGES																																							
1	2	3	4	5	6	7	8	9	10	11	12	13	14	15	16	17	18	19	20	21	22	23	24	25	26	27	28	29	30	31	32	33	34	35	36	37	38	39	40
NOT IN ORDER OF DIFFICULTY																																							

Verbal – 30 minutes

SYNONYMS																													
1	2	3	4	5	6	7	8	9	10	11	12	13	14	15	16	17	18	19	20	21	22	23	24	25	26	27	28	29	30
EASY					→				MEDIUM						→				DIFFICULT									

ANALOGIES																													
31	32	33	34	35	36	37	38	39	40	41	42	43	44	45	46	47	48	49	50	51	52	53	54	55	56	57	58	59	60
EASY					→				MEDIUM						→				DIFFICULT									

Quantitative – 30 minutes

MATHEMATICS																								
1	2	3	4	5	6	7	8	9	10	11	12	13	14	15	16	17	18	19	20	21	22	23	24	25
EASY					→				MEDIUM						→				DIFFICULT					

❑ An official SSAT contains an additional section, not shown above, known as the "Experimental Section." This is used as a trial for new test questions, and your results are <u>not</u> used to calculate your score.

The Experimental Section contains 16 questions and is 15 minutes long. It can contain any type of question from the SSAT.

Scoring

- ❑ The SSAT scoring method is a complex system that is designed to best reflect each student's standing within the very competitive group of SSAT students.

- ❑ Every question on the SSAT is worth one raw score point. Therefore, the easiest question is worth just as much as the most difficult question. There are no points for skipped questions. Each incorrect answer results in a ¼ point deduction from the points that have been earned. The total number of correct answers, minus the total penalty for incorrect answers, is the *raw score*.

  Your raw score is converted to a *scaled score* for each section. The raw score for each SSAT section is scaled to adjust for varying difficulty among the different editions of the test. The SSAT is scaled on a bell curve so that the majority of students achieve middling scores.

  For the Upper Level test, the scaled score for each section falls between 500 and 800. For the Middle Level test, the scaled score falls between 440 and 710. You will also receive a total scaled score, which is the sum of the section scores.

  In addition, you will receive two percentile scores for each section that tell how you performed with respect to other students of the same gender in your grade. Your *national percentile score* tells you how your scores compare to those of students nationally. For example, a national percentile score of 70 means you scored as well as or better than 70% of students. Your *SSAT percentile* tells you how your scores compare to those of independent school students. For example, a score of 55 means you did as well as or better than 55% of independent school students who also took the SSAT.

  In general, your **SSAT percentile is the most important score**. Relative to the national percentile, the SSAT percentile might seem quite low. This is because the SSAT percentile is being compared only to other SSAT students, which is a very competitive and well-educated group. Within this group, achieving a high rank requires a great level of skill and preparation.

- ❑ Your writing sample is not scored, but is sent directly to the admissions committees of the schools to which you apply. Many schools consider your writing skills as a factor for admission and may want to see how well you write under test conditions.

Knowing Your Limits

❑ Put your time and energy into the problems you are most capable of answering. If you struggle with difficult problems or with finishing sections in time, spend more of your time on the easy and medium problems and less time on the difficult problems. Here's why:

- Because your percentile scores reflect your <u>grade level</u> performance, you may not need to answer every question to score well. If you are at the lower end of the grade spectrum, this means you may be able to omit several questions and still score well.

- You'll minimize mistakes on difficult questions, which often contain attractor or trap answers.

- You'll be less hurried, and you'll make fewer careless mistakes.

❑ Push your limits.

As you prepare for the SSAT, try to learn from the questions that give you trouble. Note your mistakes and make sure that you don't repeat them. Pay attention to the questions that are the most difficult and note what makes them so challenging and how to solve them.

As your skills improve, you will be able to answer more and more of the questions on the SSAT. You will learn to recognize tricks and traps and work with more speed and confidence.

Beating the SSAT

❑ Never leave an easy problem blank.

On an easy problem, an answer that instinctively seems right usually is. When the test writers construct a standardized test, they keep in mind the average student. They want the average student to answer the easy problems correctly and the difficult problems incorrectly.

Do not make the early problems harder than they really are. If all else fails, go with your hunch.

❑ Avoid attractors.

The test writers predict potential mistakes by students and include those mistakes as answer choices. In other words, they set traps for the unsuspecting student. We call these answer choices "attractors." Attractors show up most often on medium and difficult problems.

Try the following Synonym question, and look for attractors.

> EXHAUSTIVE:
> (A) tired
> (B) polluted
> (C) thorough
> (D) extreme
> (E) excessive
>
> This is a difficult synonym. Notice how (A) and (B) attract your attention because both *tired* and *polluted* seem related to *EXHAUSTIVE*. It's easy to think of exhausted or exhaust, as in car exhaust. But *EXHAUSTIVE* has a different meaning: *thorough*. The correct answer is (C).

TRY IT OUT

Try to spot the attractor answer choices in the following problems.
Consider how a student might mistakenly choose each attractor answer.

1. $\dfrac{3}{4} + \dfrac{1}{3} =$

    (A) $\dfrac{1}{4}$

    (B) $\dfrac{4}{7}$

    (C) 1

    (D) $1\dfrac{1}{12}$

    (E) $1\dfrac{1}{3}$

2. Sword is to sheath as arrow is to

    (A) bull's eye
    (B) dart
    (C) gun
    (D) quiver
    (E) heart

Making Your Best Guess

❑ If you can certainly eliminate at least two answers, you should guess from the remaining answer choices. The more answers you can eliminate, the greater advantage you have.

Once you have eliminated an answer, cross it out in the test booklet. This prevents you from wasting time looking at eliminated answers over and over.

Note: Be careful using the guessing strategy on the difficult problems. When you eliminate an answer, be absolutely sure you have a legitimate reason for doing so. Once you've eliminated all the answers you can, guess from the remaining answer choices.

Assume you don't know how to solve the following math problem.
Which answer choices should you eliminate and why?
(Hint: The figure is drawn to scale.)

$x°$

$150°$

In the figure above, $x =$

(A) 110
(B) 90
(C) 80
(D) 60
(E) 45

To prove to yourself that eliminating answer choices and guessing helps your score, cover the answers at the bottom of the page and try the following exercise.

Educated Guessing

On the following 20 questions, assume you have correctly eliminated answer choices B and D. Try to guess the right answer for each question by filling in an oval for each.

1. Ⓐ ⊗ Ⓒ ⊗ Ⓔ
2. Ⓐ ⊗ Ⓒ ⊗ Ⓔ
3. Ⓐ ⊗ Ⓒ ⊗ Ⓔ
4. Ⓐ ⊗ Ⓒ ⊗ Ⓔ
5. Ⓐ ⊗ Ⓒ ⊗ Ⓔ
6. Ⓐ ⊗ Ⓒ ⊗ Ⓔ
7. Ⓐ ⊗ Ⓒ ⊗ Ⓔ
8. Ⓐ ⊗ Ⓒ ⊗ Ⓔ
9. Ⓐ ⊗ Ⓒ ⊗ Ⓔ
10. Ⓐ ⊗ Ⓒ ⊗ Ⓔ
11. Ⓐ ⊗ Ⓒ ⊗ Ⓔ
12. Ⓐ ⊗ Ⓒ ⊗ Ⓔ
13. Ⓐ ⊗ Ⓒ ⊗ Ⓔ
14. Ⓐ ⊗ Ⓒ ⊗ Ⓔ
15. Ⓐ ⊗ Ⓒ ⊗ Ⓔ
16. Ⓐ ⊗ Ⓒ ⊗ Ⓔ
17. Ⓐ ⊗ Ⓒ ⊗ Ⓔ
18. Ⓐ ⊗ Ⓒ ⊗ Ⓔ
19. Ⓐ ⊗ Ⓒ ⊗ Ⓔ
20. Ⓐ ⊗ Ⓒ ⊗ Ⓔ

\# RIGHT   _____

$-1/4 \times$ (# WRONG)   _____

= RAW SCORE   _____

Unless you were extremely unlucky, you probably received a positive raw score (versus zero if you had chosen to leave these questions blank), and, of course, a higher raw score means a higher scaled score and percentile rank.

Answers to above exercise:

1. C   2. A   3. E   4. A   5. A   6. C   7. E   8. C   9. A   10. E
11. A   12. C   13. E   14. E   15. C   16. E   17. A   18. C   19. E   20. A

Using the Answer Choices

❑ On a multiple-choice test, the answer choices can provide you with further ammunition to solve the problem. Don't get stuck trying to find an answer with a certain method. If you can't solve the problem in the forward direction, try to solve in the reverse direction by using the answer choices.

Megan ate $\frac{1}{3}$ of her jellybeans, and then threw five away. If she had 25 jellybeans left, how many did she start with?

(A) 32
(B) 35
(C) 40
(D) 45
(E) 50

Take answer (B) and step through the problem. If Megan had 35 jellybeans and ate $\frac{1}{3}$ of them, she would eat $11\frac{2}{3}$ jellybeans. It is unlikely that she would eat a fraction of a jellybean, so you should look for an answer choice which is evenly divisible by 3. Answer (D) 45, might work. If she ate $\frac{1}{3}$ of 45 (15) and then threw 5 away, she would have 25 left. (D) is correct.

TRY IT OUT

Use your answer choices to find the correct answer.

1. If $2x^2 - 3x + 6 = 15$, then x equals

    (A) 2
    (B) 3
    (C) 4
    (D) 6
    (E) 9

SUMMIT
EDUCATIONAL
GROUP

Ratify is to repeal as

(A) inhabit is to repeat
(B) decay is to depress
(C) violate is to frighten
(D) disperse is to reject
(E) adore is to detest

This might seem impossible if you don't know what ratify and repeal mean. If you use your answer choices, however, you can figure it out.

Look at each answer choice, keeping in mind that any correct analogy pair must have a clearly defined relationship between the two words.

Inhabit and repeat aren't connected at all. Eliminate (A).

There's no relationship between these words. Eliminate (B).

The words sound good together, but you can't define a relationship between them. It can't be (C).

The words don't relate. Eliminate (D).

Adore means not to detest. This is a good possibility.

Pick (E). This word pair forms the most concise and clear relationship of all the answer choices. And as we'll see in the Analogies chapter, the correct word pair must always form a concise and clear relationship.

General Tactics

❑ Focus on one question at a time.

The SSAT is timed, so it's normal to feel pressure to rush. Resist the temptation to think about the 10 questions ahead of you or the question you did a minute ago. Relax and focus on one question at a time. Believe it or not, **patience** on the SSAT is what allows you to work more quickly and accurately.

❑ Carefully read and think about each question.

Before you jump to the answers, start scribbling things down, or do calculations, make sure you understand exactly what the question is asking.

❑ In SSAT problems (especially math problems), every bit of information is important and useful.

❑ Write in your test booklet.

When you're ready to solve the problem, use the space in your test booklet. Cross out incorrect answers, write down calculations to avoid careless errors, summarize reading passages, etc. Write down whatever will help you solve the problem.

❑ Memorize the format and instructions before you take the test. At test time, you can skip the instructions and focus on the problems.

Chapter Review

❑ General Test-Taking

Your SSAT preparation will focus on learning strategies and strengthening core skills.

Your responsibilities include doing 1-2 hours of homework per session and learning as much vocabulary as you can.

Except for the Reading Comprehension, groups of questions progress from easy to difficult.

❑ Answering Questions

Put your time and energy into the problems you're most capable of answering.

Don't leave easy problems blank. If an answer seems right, it probably is.

Beware of attractors on medium and difficult problems.

Educated guessing will raise your score.

Use the answer choices to help you solve the problems.

SUMMIT
EDUCATIONAL
GROUP

Quantitative

- General Information
- Plugging In
- Solving Backwards
- Choosing Numbers
- Math Tips

General Information

❑ Format/Directions

The quantitative section of the SSAT has two sections with 25 questions each. The questions go from easy to difficult.

❑ Directions are as follows:

> Following each problem in this section, there are five suggested answers. Work each problem in your head or in the blank space provided at the right of the page. Then look at the five suggested answers and decide which one is best.
>
> <u>Note</u>: Figures that accompany problems in this section are drawn as accurately as possible EXCEPT when it is stated in a specific problem that its figure is not drawn to scale.
>
> Sample Problem:
>
>   4,412
> −2,826
>
> (A) 1,586
> (B) 1,596
> (C) 1,696
> (D) 2,586
> (E) 2,686
>
>

SSAT Structure

Writing Sample – 25 minutes

Quantitative – 30 minutes

MATHEMATICS																								
1	2	3	4	5	6	7	8	9	10	11	12	13	14	15	16	17	18	19	20	21	22	23	24	25
EASY					→				MEDIUM					→				DIFFICULT						

Reading Comprehension – 40 minutes

READING PASSAGES																																							
1	2	3	4	5	6	7	8	9	10	11	12	13	14	15	16	17	18	19	20	21	22	23	24	25	26	27	28	29	30	31	32	33	34	35	36	37	38	39	40
NOT IN ORDER OF DIFFICULTY																																							

Verbal – 30 minutes

SYNONYMS																													
1	2	3	4	5	6	7	8	9	10	11	12	13	14	15	16	17	18	19	20	21	22	23	24	25	26	27	28	29	30
EASY					→				MEDIUM					→				DIFFICULT										

ANALOGIES																													
31	32	33	34	35	36	37	38	39	40	41	42	43	44	45	46	47	48	49	50	51	52	53	54	55	56	57	58	59	60
EASY					→				MEDIUM					→				DIFFICULT										

Quantitative – 30 minutes

MATHEMATICS																								
1	2	3	4	5	6	7	8	9	10	11	12	13	14	15	16	17	18	19	20	21	22	23	24	25
EASY					→				MEDIUM					→				DIFFICULT						

Plugging In

❏ Some SSAT math questions can be solved quickly by using the answer choices.

Questions involving algebraic equations can often be solved by plugging in the answer choices for a variable.

> If $7x - 3 = 46$, then $x =$
>
> (A) 0
> (B) 1
> (C) 5
> (D) 7
> (E) 9
>
>
> If you start with (C), you get $7(5) - 3 = 46$, or $32 = 46$ (not a true statement). So, x must be bigger than 5, because 32 is too small.
>
> Eliminate (A) and (B), because these will make your quantity smaller.
>
> Try (D) and (E).
>
> The correct answer is (D) because $7(7) - 3 = 46$.

❏ When plugging in, start with answer choice (C).

Since numerical answer choices are presented in either ascending or descending order, choice (C) will be in the middle. If (C) isn't right, you might be able to tell if you need a larger or smaller number. By starting in the middle, you can reduce the number of answer choices you plug in, which will save you time.

TRY IT OUT

Solve the following equations by plugging in:

1. If $2 \times (N+5) = 100$, then $N =$

   (A) 10
   (B) 25
   (C) 40
   (D) 45
   (E) 50

   _____

2. What is L if $12 \times L \times 2 = 24$?

   (A) -14
   (B) 0
   (C) $\dfrac{1}{24}$
   (D) 1
   (E) 24

   _____

3. If $\dfrac{500}{25} + \dfrac{70}{25} + \dfrac{A}{25} = 23$, what is A?

   (A) 0
   (B) 2
   (C) 5
   (D) 15
   (E) 25

   _____

4. Which value of N does NOT satisfy $\dfrac{N}{4} + \dfrac{2}{3} > \dfrac{1}{6}$?

   (A) 2
   (B) 1
   (C) 0
   (D) -1
   (E) -2

Solving Backwards

❑ Many word problems can be solved by using the answer choices to work backward. This may be easier than trying to set up an algebraic equation.

Out of 73 black and white socks in a drawer, there are 23 more white socks than there are black socks. How many white socks are there?

(A) 23
(B) 25
(C) 45
(D) 48
(E) 50

Now go to the answer choices.

Start with (C).

If there are 45 white socks, there are 22 black socks (45 − 23 = 22). This gives a total of 67 socks. Since 67 is less than 73, we know there must be more than 45 white socks. So your choices are (D) or (E).

Let's try (E).

If there are 50 white socks, there are 27 black socks (50 − 23 = 27). This gives 77 total socks. Incorrect.

The answer must be (D), but let's check it.

48 white socks means there are 25 black socks (48 − 23 = 25).
48 + 25 = 73. (D) is correct.

❑ Use the answer choices as a guide for how to solve questions.

❑ Some questions are so complicated that it is hard to put all of the information together. It often helps to look at what the question is asking you for and then to consider what you need to do to find that information.

TRY IT OUT

Use the answer choices to solve the following word problems:

1. There are 5 times as many pairs of white socks as there are
    pairs of black socks in Jason's drawer. If the total number of
    pairs of socks equals 36, then how many pairs of white socks
    are in the drawer?

    (A) 3
    (B) 6
    (C) 15
    (D) 18
    (E) 30

2. George and Bessie both collect stamps. If George has 22
    stamps and Bessie 38 stamps, how many stamps must George
    purchase from Bessie if they are to have the same number of
    stamps in their collections?

    (A) 4
    (B) 8
    (C) 16
    (D) 18
    (E) 26

3. 24 feet of fence enclose Dan's rectangular yard. What's the
    yard's width, if the width is $\frac{1}{3}$ of the length?

    (A) 3 feet
    (B) 6 feet
    (C) 9 feet
    (D) 18 feet
    (E) 64 feet

Choosing Numbers

❏ Some questions may seem difficult because they feel too abstract. You can make some questions more concrete and easier to solve by giving values to variables.

❏ When a question has expressions for answer choices, try choosing numbers for the variables. Make up values and test them out to see which answer choice works.

> Nate bought a burger for *B* dollars and a soda for *S* dollars. He paid with a $5 bill. What was the amount of change, in dollars, that Nate received?
>
> (A) $B + S + 5$
> (B) $B - S + 5$
> (C) $B - (S + 5)$
> (D) $5 - (B + S)$
> (E) $5 - (B - S)$
>
>
>
> First, choose values for *B* and for *S*.
>
> Let's make *B* = $3 and *S* = $1.
>
> According to the question, if the burger costs $3 and the soda costs $1, Nate should receive $1 in change.
>
> Let's check the answer choices. We'll plug in the values we chose for *B* and *S* and see which results in $1 in change:
>
> (A) $\$3 + \$1 + \$5 = \$9$
> (B) $\$3 - \$1 + \$5 = \$7$
> (C) $\$3 - (\$1 + \$5) = -\$3$
> ✓ (D) $\$5 - (\$3 + \$1) = \$1$
> (E) $\$5 - (\$3 - \$1) = \$3$
>
> The correct answer is (D), because when we plug in the numbers we chose, we get the right result.

❏ Depending on the question and the numbers you choose, you might have more than one answer work. If this happens, try different numbers and test those answers again.

PUT IT TOGETHER

1. If n is greater than 1, which of the following is greatest?

    (A) $2n+1$

    (B) $n+2$

    (C) $n+1$

    (D) n

    (E) $\dfrac{n}{n}+2$

2. John is x years old and Paul is 8 years older than John. If in 4 years Paul will be twice as old as John, then how old is John now?

    (A) 4

    (B) 8

    (C) 12

    (D) 16

    (E) 20

3. The price of gasoline was C cents at the beginning of the month. What was the price, in cents, after it went down 3 cents, doubled, and then went up 7 cents?

    (A) $C-10$

    (B) $C-4$

    (C) $C+8$

    (D) $2C+1$

    (E) $2C+4$

4. Olivia paid for a tool with a $100 bill. She received D dollars in change. Which of the following expressions tells how many dollars she paid for the tool?

    (A) $\dfrac{100D}{2}$

    (B) $\dfrac{D}{100}$

    (C) $\dfrac{100}{D}$

    (D) $100-D$

    (E) $D-100$

Math Tips

❑ Pay attention to units. Information in a question might be in one unit (such as feet or seconds) while the answer is in another unit (such as yards or minutes).

Know how to convert the following units:

12 inches = 1 foot

3 feet = 1 yard

100 centimeters = 1 meter

1,000 meters = 1 kilometer

60 seconds = 1 minute

60 minutes = 1 hour

❑ If the first answer choice you check is correct, check another answer choice. If more than one answer choice seems right, you may have misunderstood the question or there may be the option to choose "all of the above."

❑ The answer choice "It cannot be determined from the information given" is **rarely** the correct answer. If a question seems impossible, it is best to reread the question and try to solve it in a different way.

Chapter Review

❏ Format/Directions

Questions get harder as you go. The last question in a Quantitative section is much more difficult and takes much longer to solve than the first question, but they are both worth just one point. Pace yourself; work patiently and carefully.

❏ Plugging In

Use answer choices to help you solve problems.

When plugging in, start with answer choice (C).

❏ Solving Backwards

Consider what information the question asks for and think of what you must do to find that information.

Answer choices can sometimes be clues for what type of answer you should get.

❏ Choosing Numbers

In complex equations or word problems, choose values for variables or unknown numbers. This can make abstract problems easier to handle.

SUMMIT
EDUCATIONAL
GROUP

Arithmetic

- ❑ Addition, Subtraction, Multiplication, and Division
- ❑ Odd and Even Integers
- ❑ Positive and Negative Numbers
- ❑ Divisibility and Remainders
- ❑ Multiples and Factors
- ❑ Fractions
- ❑ Decimals and Place Value
- ❑ Rounding and Estimation
- ❑ Decimals
- ❑ Percents
- ❑ Ratios
- ❑ Proportions
- ❑ Exponents
- ❑ Roots
- ❑ Order of Operations
- ❑ Averages
- ❑ Probability
- ❑ Ordering and Sequences
- ❑ Charts and Graphs

Arithmetic

❑ Over half of SSAT math is arithmetic. Mastering arithmetic skills will help you solve arithmetic problems as well as algebra and geometry problems.

❑ In this chapter, you will:

- learn arithmetic vocabulary including integers, multiples, and divisibility.

- review basic arithmetic concepts like adding, subtracting, multiplying, and dividing.

- review the rules regarding fractions, decimals, and percents.

- learn how to apply these concepts to the types of multiple choice questions that appear on the SSAT.

Vocabulary

❑ An **integer** is any positive or negative whole number or zero.

$$\{...,-3,-2,-1,0,1,2,3,...\}$$

❑ A **digit** is any whole number from 0 to 9.

$\{0,1,2,3,4,5,6,7,8,9\}$ is the set of all digits.

❑ A **prime number** is an integer greater than 1 that is divisible only by 1 and itself.

2 is the smallest prime number. It is also the only prime number that is even.

2,3,5,7,11, and 13 are examples of prime numbers.

❑ A **sum** is the result of an addition.

❑ A **difference** is the result of a subtraction.

❑ A **product** is the result of a multiplication.

❑ A **quotient** is the result of a division.

A **dividend** is the number being divided in a division.

A **divisor** is the number dividing in a division.

$$\text{divisor} \overline{)\,\text{dividend}}^{\displaystyle \text{quotient}}$$

❑ A **base** is a number being raised to an exponent.

An **exponent** is the number of times you multiply a base by itself.

❑ **Consecutive numbers** are whole numbers that increase or decrease incrementally by 1.

$\{31,32,33,34\}$ and $\{-2,-1,0,1,2,3,4,5\}$ are sets of consecutive numbers.

Addition, Subtraction, Multiplication, and Division

❑ On SSAT math problems, you will have to calculate sums, differences, products, and quotients. Occasionally, you will have to deal with large numbers.

Work carefully and methodically. If you rush, you are likely to make careless mistakes.

❑ Make sure your answer makes sense. Use logic to check your work.

For instance, if you are multiplying two positive whole numbers and you get an answer that is smaller than the original numbers, you might have made a mistake.

❑ Memorize the following rules.

0 times any number equals 0.

0 divided by any number equals 0.

$$91 \times 0 = 0 \qquad\qquad 0 \div 10 = 0$$

1 times a number equals the number.

Any number divided by 1 equals the number.

$$2,345 \times 1 = 2,345 \qquad\qquad 999 \div 1 = 999$$

Any number divided by itself equals 1.

$$1,023 \div 1,023 = 1$$

To multiply any number by a power of 10 (10, 100, 1000, etc.), move the decimal place to the right by the number of zeros.

$$93 \times 100 = 9,300 \qquad\qquad 6.34 \times 10,000 = 63,400$$

To divide any number by a power of 10, move the decimal place to the left by the number of zeros.

$$26 \div 10 = 2.6 \qquad\qquad 2,435 \div 100 = 24.35$$

TRY IT OUT

1. $11,324 + 89,376 =$

2. $1,001 + 9,999 =$

3. $50 + 1,000 + 100 + 0 =$

4. $6,003 + 9 + 8 =$

5. $10 + 100 + 1,000 + 10,000 =$

6. $6,923 - 3,110 =$

7. $10,294 - 10,294 =$

8. $1,100 - 100 =$

9. $20,000 - 7,000 =$

10. $115 - 30 =$

11. $7 \times 3 =$

12. $27 \times 23 =$

13. $289 \times 100 \times 1 =$

14. $5 \times 4 \times 3 \times 2 \times 1 \times 0 =$

15. $9,999 \times \dfrac{1}{10} =$

16. $286 \div 13 =$

17. $412 \div 1 =$

18. $0 \div 989 =$

19. $34,776 \div 100 =$

20. $\dfrac{99}{99} =$

PUT IT TOGETHER

1. Jeremy has 5 marbles and Evan has 19. How many
    marbles must Evan give to Jeremy if they are to have the
    same number?

    (A) 4
    (B) 7
    (C) 9
    (D) 14
    (E) 28

---

2. If $9+9+9+9+9+9+9 = 7 \times \square$, what is the value of
    $\square$?

    (A) 7
    (B) 9
    (C) 16
    (D) 56
    (E) 63

---

3. If $46 + 78 = (10 \times 2) + (1 \times \square) + (100 \times 1)$, then $\square =$

    (A) 2
    (B) 4
    (C) 14
    (D) 24
    (E) 124

---

4. $8\overline{)648} =$

    (A) $\dfrac{600}{8} \times \dfrac{40}{8} \times \dfrac{8}{8}$

    (B) $\dfrac{6}{8} \times \dfrac{4}{8} \times \dfrac{8}{8}$

    (C) $\dfrac{600}{8} + \dfrac{40}{8} + \dfrac{8}{8}$

    (D) $\dfrac{64}{8} + \dfrac{8}{8}$

    (E) $\dfrac{6}{8} + \dfrac{4}{8} + \dfrac{8}{8}$

$$
\begin{array}{r}
4 \\
89\overline{)37\square} \\
35\square \\
\hline
20
\end{array}
$$

5. In the division problem shown above, what digit is represented by $\square$?

   (A) 0
   (B) 4
   (C) 6
   (D) 8
   (E) 9

---

8   6   7   5   3

6. The five digits shown above can form a three-digit number and a two-digit number by using each digit once. Of the pairs of numbers that can be formed, which three-digit number divided by the two-digit number will have the smallest quotient?

   (A) $358 \div 67$
   (B) $358 \div 76$
   (C) $653 \div 78$
   (D) $876 \div 35$
   (E) $876 \div 53$

---

7. For which of the following would the result be greater if the number 50 is used instead of 60?

   I. $60 - 100$

   II. $100 - 60$

   III. $\dfrac{100}{60}$

   (A) I only
   (B) II only
   (C) III only
   (D) II and III only
   (E) I, II, and III

Odd and Even Integers

❑ An **odd number** is an integer that is not divisible by 2.

$$\{...-5,-3,-1,1,3,5,...\}$$

❑ An **even number** is an integer that is divisible by 2.

$$\{...-6,-4,-2,0,2,4,6,...\}$$

❑ Even and odd integers follow certain rules when added, subtracted, or multiplied.

It can be helpful to memorize these rules. You may also test a few numbers to remember the rules when you need to.

even ± even = even

$0+4=4$	$8-2=6$

even ± odd = odd

$4+3=7$	$9-4=5$

odd ± odd = even

$7-5=2$	$3+1=4$

even × even = even

$6\times6=36$	$2\times4=8$

even × odd = even

$4\times3=12$	$2\times1=2$

odd × odd = odd

$7\times11=77$	$3\times5=15$

TRY IT OUT

1. Which of the following could be the result of adding two even integers?

   {1, 3, 4, 6, 11, 17, 23, 99, 400}

2. Which of the following could be the result of subtracting two odd integers?

   {–3, 0, 1, 5, 12, 18, 100, 101}

3. Which of the following could be the result of multiplying two odd integers?

   {0, 1, 3, 4, 8, 11, 21, 24, 90}

PUT IT TOGETHER

1. If x and y are both odd integers, which of the following is NOT an odd integer?

   (A) xy
   (B) $3xy$
   (C) $x-y$
   (D) $2x-y$
   (E) $2x+y$

$18 \times K$

2. For which of the following values of K will the product above be an odd number?

   (A) 9
   (B) 2
   (C) 1
   (D) 0
   (E) 0.5

---

3. If x is an even integer, which of the following must also be even?

   I. $x+1$
   II. $x+2$
   III. $2x$
   IV. $3x$

   (A) II and III only
   (B) II and IV only
   (C) III and IV only
   (D) II, III, and IV only
   (E) I, II, III, and IV

Positive and Negative Numbers

❑ A **positive number** is any number that is greater than 0.

$$\{1, 3, 2.4, \frac{6}{7}\}$$

❑ A **negative number** is any number that is less than 0.

$$\{-3.5, -57, -\frac{1}{2}, -.273\}$$

❑ Negative numbers follow certain rules when being added, subtracted, multiplied, or divided.

Adding a negative number is the same as subtracting a positive number.

$$4 + (-3) = 4 - 3 \qquad\qquad 0 + (-5) = 0 - 5$$

Subtracting a negative number is the same as adding a positive number.

$$4 - (-3) = 4 + 3 \qquad\qquad 0 - (-5) = 0 + 5$$

A negative number multiplied or divided by a negative number gives a positive number.

$$(-10) \times (-2) = 20 \qquad\qquad (-12) \div (-4) = 3$$

A negative number multiplied by a positive number (or vice versa) gives a negative number.

A negative number divided by a positive number (or vice versa) gives a negative number.

$$(-10) \times (2) = -20 \qquad\qquad (12) \times (-4) = -3$$

TRY IT OUT

1. $-5+2=$

2. $-3+4=$

3. $-1+8=$

4. $-9+9=$

5. $6+(-5)=$

6. $1+(-2)=$

7. $-5-7=$

8. $-1-4=$

9. $14-(-9)=$

10. $-8-(-4)=$

11. $-1-(-9)=$

12. $3\times(-5)=$

13. $-20\div2=$

14. $(-2)\times(-6)=$

15. $(-60)\div(-15)=$

PUT IT TOGETHER

1. If the positive number N is multiplied by a number less than 0, the product <u>must</u> be

(A) less than N
(B) 0
(C) greater than 0
(D) greater than N
(E) It cannot be determined from the information given.

Divisibility and Remainders

❏ A number is **divisible** by another number if it can be evenly divided by that number with no remainder.

> 25 is divisible by 5 because $25 \div 5 = 5$ with no remainder.
>
> 25 is not divisible by 6 because $25 \div 6 = 4$ with a remainder of 1.

❏ When a number does not divide evenly into another number, the number that remains at the end of the division is called the **remainder**. The remainder is always less than the divisor.

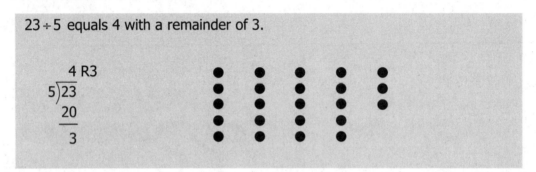

> 23 ÷ 5 equals 4 with a remainder of 3.
>
> $$\begin{array}{r} 4\ R3 \\ 5\overline{)23} \\ \underline{20} \\ 3 \end{array}$$

You can check your answer by multiplying the divisor by the quotient and adding the remainder. This should equal the original dividend.

$$(\text{divisor} \times \text{quotient}) + \text{remainder} = \text{dividend}$$

> 23 ÷ 5 equals 4 with a remainder of 3.
>
> $(5 \times 4) + 3 = 23$

TRY IT OUT

1. Is 8 divisible by 2?

2. Is 36 divisible by 8?

3. What is the remainder when 30 is divided by 7?

4. What is the remainder when 30 is divided by 6?

5. What is the remainder when 7 is divided by 30?

PUT IT TOGETHER

1. Heather wants to buy shirts for her 15 employees. There
    are 4 shirts in each package. How many packages of shirts
    must she buy in order for each employee to have a shirt?

    (A) 3
    (B) 4
    (C) 5
    (D) 11
    (E) 60

---

2. When x is divided by 6, the remainder is 5. Which of the
    following could have remainder 1 when divided by 6?

    (A) $x-3$
    (B) $x-2$
    (C) $x-1$
    (D) $x+1$
    (E) $x+2$

$$\begin{array}{r} 4\ R3 \\ 741\overline{)2,96\square} \end{array}$$

3. In the division problem above, what digit is represented
    by $\square$?

    (A) 1
    (B) 3
    (C) 4
    (D) 7
    (E) 9

Multiples and Factors

❑ A **multiple** is the product of a particular number and another number.

> 4, 8, 12, and 20 are all multiples of 4:
>
> $4 = 4 \times 1$ $8 = 4 \times 2$ $12 = 4 \times 3$ $20 = 4 \times 5$

❑ A **factor** of a number is a number that divides evenly into that number.

> 6 is a factor of 24 because 6 divides evenly into 24.
>
> 6 and 4 are called a pair of factors, because $6 \times 4 = 24$.

❑ To find the **prime factorization** of a number, factor the number until all factors are prime. The prime factorization of a number is the product of its prime factors.

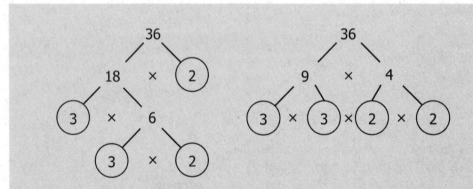

The prime factorization of 36 is $3 \times 3 \times 2 \times 2$.

Note: no matter which two factors you start with, you'll get the same result.

TRY IT OUT

1. List all the pairs of factors of 32.

2. List all of the pairs of factors of 63.

3. List 5 multiples of 2.

4. List 3 multiples of 12.

5. Find the prime factorizations of 24, 84, and 100.

PUT IT TOGETHER

1. In a group of eight friends, each friend is given the same number of tickets, with no tickets left over. Which of the following could be the total number of tickets given out?

    (A) 12
    (B) 30
    (C) 52
    (D) 60
    (E) 96

2. A crate holds 2 dozen bottles in each layer, and there are three layers in each crate. If a warehouse contains only full crates of bottles, which of the following could be the number of bottles in the warehouse?

    (A) 120
    (B) 140
    (C) 146
    (D) 206
    (E) 216

3. If $\frac{x}{4}$ is a whole number, then x could be

    (A) 1
    (B) 6
    (C) 10
    (D) 12
    (E) 13

Fractions

❑ Fractions are used to represent portions of a whole. Fractions are written as $\frac{PART}{WHOLE}$. Fractions also represent divisions, with the part divided by the whole.

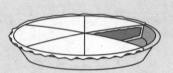

The pie above is divided into 6 equal parts.

One part, or $\frac{1}{6}$ of the pie, is missing. Five parts, or $\frac{5}{6}$ of the pie, are left.

❑ The **numerator** is the top part of a fraction. The **denominator** is the bottom part.

❑ An **improper fraction** has a numerator that is greater than or equal to the denominator.

❑ A **mixed number** is made up of a whole number and a fraction. It is equal to the sum of the whole number and the fraction.

$$1\frac{3}{8} = 1 + \frac{3}{8}$$

❑ To convert a mixed number to an improper fraction, rewrite the whole number as a fraction with the same denominator. Then, add the two fractions.

Convert $2\frac{3}{5}$ to an improper fraction:

$$2\frac{3}{5} \implies 2 + \frac{3}{5} \implies \frac{10}{5} + \frac{3}{5} \implies \frac{13}{5}$$

❑ To convert an improper fraction to a mixed number, divide the numerator by the denominator. The whole number of the dividend will be the whole number and the remainder will be the numerator of the fraction.

$$\frac{17}{5} \implies 5\overline{)17} \implies 3\text{ R}2 \implies 3\frac{2}{5}$$

TRY IT OUT

Convert mixed numbers to improper fractions:

1. $1\dfrac{1}{4}$

2. $6\dfrac{2}{3}$

3. $5\dfrac{6}{7}$

Convert improper fractions to mixed numbers:

4. $\dfrac{3}{2}$

5. $\dfrac{8}{3}$

6. $\dfrac{19}{4}$

Solve:

7.   If half a number is 5, what is the whole number?

8.   If one third of a number is 4, what is the whole number?

9.   If $\dfrac{4}{9}$ of a number is 7, what is $\dfrac{8}{9}$ of the number?

10. If $\dfrac{3}{4}$ of a number is 15, what is $\dfrac{1}{4}$ of the number?

11. If $\dfrac{4}{7}$ of a number is 40, what is the whole number?

12. If there are 300 calories in a $\dfrac{2}{3}$-cup serving of granola, how many calories are there in a 1-cup serving?

PUT IT TOGETHER

1. $\left(4\times\frac{1}{4}\right)+\left(3\times\frac{1}{3}\right)=$

    (A) 0
    (B) $\frac{4}{7}$
    (C) 1
    (D) $\frac{7}{4}$
    (E) 2

2. When a cake is cut into 8 even slices instead of 12 even slices, which of the following must be true?

    (A) each slice will be smaller
    (B) some slices will have difference sizes
    (C) there will be 4 more slices
    (D) each slice will be larger
    (E) 2 of the slices will be twice as large

3. When 30 gallons of water were poured into an empty tank, the water filled $\frac{2}{3}$ of the tank's total capacity. What is the tank's total capacity in gallons?

    (A) 20
    (B) 40
    (C) 45
    (D) 60
    (E) 75

4. If n is greater than 1, then $\frac{1}{n}$ must be

    (A) less than 0
    (B) less than 1
    (C) greater than 1
    (D) greater than n
    (E) between 1 and n

5. If x and y are not equal to zero, what is the value of

$$\frac{6x}{6x} - \frac{3y}{3y}?$$

(A) –1
(B) 0
(C) 1
(D) 2
(E) It cannot be determined from the information given.

---

6. If $\frac{m}{n} = 1$, and m and n are non-zero integers, which of the following must be true?

(A) m is greater than n
(B) n is greater than m
(C) $m = y - 1$
(D) $m = 1$
(E) $m = n$

---

7. If $\frac{2}{3}$ of a number is 18, then $\frac{4}{3}$ of the number is

(A) 6
(B) 9
(C) 27
(D) 36
(E) 72

---

8. A jug that is $\frac{3}{5}$ full contains 15 ounces of liquid. How many ounces of liquid does the jug hold when it's full?

(A) 9
(B) 10
(C) 24
(D) 25
(E) 45

Reducing Fractions

❑ In general, fractions should be written in their reduced forms. To reduce fractions, divide the top and bottom by a common factor. Continue to divide by common factors until the top and bottom have no more common factors.

Reduce $\dfrac{12}{30}$.

2 is a common factor of 12 and 30. Divide both 12 and 30 by 2.

$$\frac{12 \div 2}{30 \div 2} = \frac{6}{15}$$

3 is a common factor of 6 and 15. Divide both 6 and 15 by 3.

$$\frac{6 \div 3}{15 \div 3} = \frac{2}{5}$$

There is no factor that divides into 2 and 5, so $\dfrac{2}{5}$ is reduced completely.

❑ The Lowest Common Denominator of a group of fractions is the smallest number that each of the denominators will divide into. Finding a common denominator is the first step in adding or subtracting fractions. Finding a common denominator also lets you compare the relative sizes of fractions.

What is the LCD of $\dfrac{3}{4}$, $\dfrac{1}{2}$, $\dfrac{2}{3}$? Arrange the fractions from smallest to largest.

The LCD is 12. 12 is the smallest number that 2, 3, and 4 will divide into.

Rewriting the fractions with the LCD, we get:

$$\frac{3 \times 3}{4 \times 3} = \frac{9}{12} \qquad \frac{1 \times 6}{2 \times 6} = \frac{6}{12} \qquad \frac{2 \times 4}{3 \times 4} = \frac{8}{12}$$

Fractions arranged from smallest to largest:

$$\frac{1}{2} = \frac{6}{12}, \quad \frac{2}{3} = \frac{8}{12}, \quad \frac{3}{4} = \frac{9}{12}$$

TRY IT OUT

Reduce the following fractions:

1. $\dfrac{14}{21}$

2. $\dfrac{26}{30}$

3. $\dfrac{45}{100}$

4. $\dfrac{28}{63}$

Find the lowest common denominator for each group of fractions, and arrange the fractions from smallest to largest:

5. $\dfrac{3}{8}, \dfrac{4}{3}, \dfrac{1}{3}$

6. $\dfrac{2}{5}, \dfrac{3}{8}, \dfrac{3}{4}$

7. $\dfrac{7}{30}, \dfrac{1}{6}, \dfrac{4}{5}, \dfrac{8}{15}$

8. $\dfrac{1}{2}, \dfrac{2}{3}, \dfrac{3}{7}, \dfrac{4}{5}$

PUT IT TOGETHER

1. Which of the following is greater than $\frac{2}{3}$?

    (A) $\frac{1}{2}$

    (B) $\frac{3}{4}$

    (C) $\frac{3}{5}$

    (D) $\frac{4}{7}$

    (E) $\frac{5}{8}$

---

2. All of the following are true EXCEPT

    (A) $\frac{1}{2} < \frac{3}{5}$

    (B) $\frac{1}{3} < \frac{2}{5}$

    (C) $\frac{3}{4} < \frac{3}{5}$

    (D) $\frac{7}{8} < \frac{8}{9}$

    (E) $\frac{4}{7} < \frac{5}{8}$

---

3. If $\frac{1}{2}$ of a number is 200, then $\frac{2}{5}$ of the number is

    (A) less than 200
    (B) greater than 200
    (C) greater than the number
    (D) equal to 200
    (E) equal to the number

4. $2\dfrac{2}{3}$ is equal to how many sixths?

    (A) 4
    (B) 8
    (C) 10
    (D) 14
    (E) 16

Adding and Subtracting Fractions

❑ To add fractions, first adjust the fractions so they have a common denominator. Then add the numerators only and keep the common denominator.

$$\frac{1}{3}+\frac{1}{2}=$$

lowest common denominator = 6.

$$\frac{1\times 2}{3\times 2}=\frac{2}{6} \text{ and } \frac{1\times 3}{2\times 3}=\frac{3}{6}.$$

So, $\frac{1}{3}+\frac{1}{2}$ ⟹ $\frac{2}{6}+\frac{3}{6}$ ⟹ $\frac{2+3}{6}$ ⟹ $\frac{5}{6}$

❑ To subtract fractions, first adjust the fractions so they have a common denominator. Then subtract the numerators only.

$$\frac{3}{4}-\frac{1}{3} \quad ⟹ \quad \frac{9}{12}-\frac{4}{12} \quad ⟹ \quad \frac{5}{12}$$

When subtracting fractions, it often helps to convert mixed numbers to improper fractions before subtracting.

TRY IT OUT

1. $\dfrac{1}{3} + \dfrac{1}{3}$

2. $\dfrac{1}{2} + \dfrac{1}{3}$

3. $\dfrac{1}{2} + \dfrac{1}{6}$

4. $\dfrac{1}{12} + \dfrac{2}{3}$

5. $\dfrac{3}{10} + \dfrac{5}{6}$

6. $\dfrac{1}{3} + \dfrac{1}{6} + \dfrac{4}{9}$

7. $1\dfrac{1}{3} + \dfrac{1}{6}$

8. $5\dfrac{1}{3} + 2\dfrac{1}{2}$

9. $\dfrac{2}{3} - \dfrac{1}{3}$

10. $\dfrac{1}{2} - \dfrac{1}{4}$

11. $\dfrac{2}{5} - \dfrac{1}{10}$

12. $\dfrac{5}{12} - \dfrac{1}{3}$

13. $\dfrac{6}{7} - \dfrac{1}{2}$

14. $7 - \dfrac{1}{3}$

15. $2\dfrac{1}{2} - 1\dfrac{1}{2}$

16. $3\dfrac{1}{3} - 1\dfrac{5}{6}$

17. $4\dfrac{3}{5} - 2\dfrac{1}{5}$

PUT IT TOGETHER

1. $300 - 2\frac{8}{9} =$

    (A) $299\frac{1}{9}$

    (B) $298\frac{8}{9}$

    (C) $298\frac{1}{9}$

    (D) $297\frac{8}{9}$

    (E) $297\frac{1}{9}$

2. $3\frac{1}{6} + 1\frac{5}{6} + 5\frac{5}{6} =$

    (A) $9\frac{5}{6}$

    (B) 10

    (C) $10\frac{1}{6}$

    (D) $10\frac{5}{6}$

    (E) $11\frac{1}{6}$

3. $17\left(\frac{6}{51} - \frac{2}{17}\right) =$

    (A) 16
    (B) 4
    (C) 2
    (D) 1
    (E) 0

4. If $\dfrac{1}{3} + \dfrac{x}{12} = 1$, then $x =$

   (A) 8
   (B) 6
   (C) 4
   (D) 3
   (E) 2

5. If $\dfrac{4}{16} + \dfrac{1}{4} = \dfrac{x}{20}$, then $x =$

   (A) 5
   (B) 10
   (C) 15
   (D) 20
   (E) 40

Multiplying and Dividing Fractions

❑ To multiply fractions, multiply straight across.

First, convert mixed numbers to improper fractions.

If possible, cross-simplify before multiplying. To cross-simplify, look for common factors between the numerator of your first fraction and the denominator of your second fraction, or between the denominator of your first fraction and the numerator of your second fraction.

$$1\frac{4}{5} \times \frac{1}{6} \implies \frac{9}{5} \times \frac{1}{6} \implies \frac{\overset{3}{\cancel{9}}}{5} \times \frac{1}{\underset{2}{\cancel{6}}} \implies \frac{3}{5} \times \frac{1}{2} \implies \frac{3 \times 1}{5 \times 2} \implies \frac{3}{10}$$

Remember, you should only cross-simplify when fractions are being <u>multiplied</u>.

❑ Two numbers are **reciprocals** if their product is 1.

> The reciprocal of 4 is $\frac{1}{4}$ because $4 \times \frac{1}{4} = 1$.

To find the reciprocal of a fraction, "flip" the fraction by switching its numerator and denominator.

> The reciprocal of $\frac{2}{5}$ is $\frac{5}{2}$.

❑ To divide fractions, multiply by the reciprocal of the divisor.

$$\frac{1}{3} \div \frac{1}{2} \implies \frac{1}{3} \div \frac{1}{2} \implies \frac{1}{3} \times \frac{2}{1} \implies \frac{2}{3}$$

TRY IT OUT

1. $\dfrac{2}{3} \times \dfrac{1}{7}$

2. $\dfrac{1}{3} \times \dfrac{3}{5}$

3. $\dfrac{4}{5} \times \dfrac{1}{2}$

4. $\dfrac{3}{4} \times \dfrac{8}{15}$

5. $\dfrac{3}{7} \times \dfrac{14}{15}$

6. $\dfrac{3}{4} \times 16$

7. $5 \times \dfrac{5}{6}$

8. $\dfrac{7}{8} \times 24$

9. $\dfrac{1}{2} \div \dfrac{1}{3}$

10. $\dfrac{2}{5} \div \dfrac{1}{5}$

11. $\dfrac{2}{3} \div \dfrac{5}{6}$

12. $\dfrac{3}{7} \div \dfrac{9}{14}$

13. $4\dfrac{1}{3} \div \dfrac{5}{6}$

14. $2\dfrac{2}{7} \div \dfrac{4}{7}$

15. $12 \div \dfrac{2}{5}$

16. $14 \div \dfrac{2}{7}$

PUT IT TOGETHER

1. All of the following are equal EXCEPT

    (A) $1 \times \dfrac{2}{4}$

    (B) $\dfrac{4}{1} \times \dfrac{3}{6}$

    (C) $3 \times \dfrac{1}{6}$

    (D) $\dfrac{15}{6} \times \dfrac{1}{5}$

    (E) $\dfrac{2}{3} \times \dfrac{3}{4}$

2. $\dfrac{\frac{1}{3}}{\frac{1}{3}} =$

    (A) $\dfrac{1}{9}$

    (B) $\dfrac{1}{6}$

    (C) $\dfrac{2}{9}$

    (D) $\dfrac{2}{3}$

    (E) 1

3. Which of the following products is greatest?

    (A) $\dfrac{1}{3} \times \dfrac{1}{6}$

    (B) $\dfrac{1}{4} \times \dfrac{1}{5}$

    (C) $\dfrac{1}{7} \times \dfrac{1}{4}$

    (D) $\dfrac{1}{8} \times \dfrac{1}{2}$

    (E) $\dfrac{1}{5} \times \dfrac{1}{5}$

4. A piece of fabric that is $4\frac{1}{2}$ feet long can be cut into how many pieces that are each 3 inches long?

(A) 12
(B) 13
(C) 14
(D) 17
(E) 18

5. Which of the following is a way to compute the product $2\frac{1}{3}\times15$?

(A) $(2\times15)+\left(\frac{1}{3}\times15\right)$

(B) $\left(\frac{1}{3}\times2\right)+\left(\frac{1}{3}\times15\right)$

(C) $15\times2\times\frac{1}{3}$

(D) $2+\left(\frac{1}{3}\times15\right)$

(E) $(2\times15)+\left(2\times\frac{1}{3}\right)$

$$\frac{1}{4}\;\square\;\frac{1}{2}=N$$

6. Which of the following symbols, when used in place of the box in the equation shown above, will result in the greatest value of N?

(A) −
(B) +
(C) ×
(D) ÷
(E) The value of N will be the same for each of the symbols

Decimals and Place Value

❑ **Decimals** are a way of writing fractions whose denominators are powers of 10.

$$\frac{4}{10} = .4 \qquad \frac{36}{1,000} = .036$$

❑ Be sure to know the names for the different places.

In the number 237.614,

2 is in the *hundreds* place.
3 is in the *tens* place.
7 is in the *units* (or *ones*) place.
6 is in the *tenths* place.
1 is in the *hundredths* place.
4 is in the *thousandths* place.

❑ It might help to think of money when working with decimals and place value.

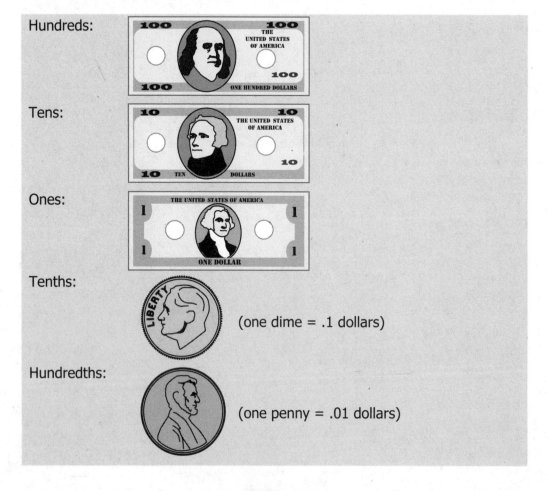

Hundreds:

Tens:

Ones:

Tenths: (one dime = .1 dollars)

Hundredths: (one penny = .01 dollars)

TRY IT OUT

1. What digit is in the <u>hundredths</u> place in the number 536.187?

2. What digit is in the <u>hundreds</u> place in the number 536.187?

PUT IT TOGETHER

1. Which digit in the number 2,148.93 has the LEAST value?

    (A) 1
    (B) 2
    (C) 3
    (D) 4
    (E) 9

2. Which of the following is the number: *three-hundred twelve and sixty-four thousandths*?

    (A) 3,012.64
    (B) 3,012.064
    (C) 312.64
    (D) 312.064
    (E) 0.31264

3. How many <u>thousandths</u> are in 0.2?

    (A) 0.02
    (B) 2
    (C) 20
    (D) 200
    (E) 2000

4. How many <u>tenths</u> are in $5\frac{1}{2}$?

    (A) 52
    (B) 55
    (C) 505
    (D) 520
    (E) 550

Rounding and Estimation

❑ To round a number, look at the digit to the right of the place you're rounding to. If that digit is greater than or equal to 5, round up; if that digit is less than 5, round down.

> Round 942.637 to the nearest:
>
> hundredth = 942.64
>
> tenth = 942.6
>
> whole number = 943
>
> hundred = 900
>
> thousand = 1,000

TRY IT OUT

1. Round 1.5 to the nearest whole number.

2. Round 1.54 to the nearest tenth.

3. Round 2.227 to the nearest hundredth.

4. Round 23.358 to the nearest whole number.

5. Round 351 to the nearest hundred.

6. Round 351 to the nearest ten.

7. Round 99.99 to the nearest tenth.

8. Which of the following is closest to $3,315 \div 3.3$?

   (A) 10   (B) 100   (C) 110   (D) 1,000   (E) 1,100

9. Which of the following is closest to $78,826 \div 2.09$?

   (A) 30,000   (B) 35,000   (C) 40,000   (D) 45,000   (E) 400,000

PUT IT TOGETHER

1. What will be the approximate price for 4 plates if they
    cost $1.47 each?

    (A) $5
    (B) $6
    (C) $7
    (D) $8
    (E) $9

2. Which sum is closest to $19 + 27 + 71$?

    (A) $20 + 30 + 70$
    (B) $20 + 20 + 70$
    (C) $20 + 90$
    (D) $40 + 70$
    (E) $30 + 70$

$$\frac{309}{1,256} =$$

3. The resulting quotient of the calculation shown above is
    closest to which of the following?

    (A) $\dfrac{2}{3}$

    (B) $\dfrac{1}{2}$

    (C) $\dfrac{1}{3}$

    (D) $\dfrac{1}{4}$

    (E) $\dfrac{1}{5}$

4. When 6,513 is divided by 407, the result is closest to which of the following?

    (A) 12
    (B) 13
    (C) 14
    (D) 15
    (E) 16

5. Peter spent a total of $28\frac{3}{4}$ hours working on a project, and he earned \$12.11 per hour. Of the following, which is closest to the total amount he earned for his work on the project?

    (A) \$400
    (B) \$360
    (C) \$300
    (D) \$250
    (E) \$240

Decimal Operations

❏ To **add or subtract decimals**, line up the decimal points. Place the decimal point for your answer beneath the other decimal points. Do this **before** you add or subtract. Then add or subtract as you would any other set of numbers.

$$342 + 1.93 + 12.46 \implies \begin{array}{r} 342.00 \\ 1.93 \\ + \ 12.46 \\ \hline 356.39 \end{array}$$

❏ To **multiply decimals**, multiply the numbers as you would any other numbers. Then count the total number of decimal places in the numbers you are multiplying. Place the decimal in the product this many places from the right.

$$23.6 \times 1.9 = ? \implies \begin{array}{r} 236 \\ \times \ 19 \\ \hline 2124 \\ 2360 \\ \hline 4484 \end{array} \implies 4484.0 \implies 44.84$$

23.6 has one decimal place and 1.9 has one decimal place, so there is a total of two decimal places. Therefore, we place the decimal in the product two places from the right.

❏ To **divide by a decimal**, follow these steps:

1. Move the decimal point in the divisor to the right until you have a whole number.

2. Move the decimal point in the dividend the same number of places to the right.

3. Place a decimal point directly above the new decimal point in the dividend.

4. Divide.

$$.25\overline{)10.5} \implies .25\overline{)10.50} \implies 25\overline{)1050.0} \implies 25\overline{)1050.0}^{42.0}$$

TRY IT OUT

1. $1.0003 + 5.2 + 12.62 =$

2. $30.39 + 50.61 + 2 =$

3. $10 - 2.35 =$

4. $150.55 - 54 =$

5. $\dfrac{5}{10} + \dfrac{45}{100} =$

6. $14 \times .7 =$

7. $14 \times .07 =$

8. $28.1 \times .9 =$

9. $1.4 \times .001 =$

10. $2.9 \times 1,000 =$

11. $.27 \times 12.2 =$

12. $\dfrac{9}{10} \times 100 =$

13. $.4\overline{)16}$

14. $.04\overline{)1.6}$

15. $.52\overline{)1.0452}$

16. $.001\overline{).16}$

17. $2.8\overline{)84.56}$

PUT IT TOGETHER

1. $0.0050 \times 10.00 =$

   (A) 5
   (B) 0.5
   (C) 0.05
   (D) 0.005
   (E) 0.0005

---

2. Half of the members in a group of 32 members contribute
   $0.15 each to a charity. How much was the total
   contribution of these members?

   (A) $48
   (B) $24
   (C) $4.80
   (D) $2.40
   (E) $0.48

Percent-Decimal Conversion

❑ Percents can be thought of as hundredths.

19% ⟹ 19 hundredths ⟹ 0.19

❑ To change a percent to a decimal, move the decimal point two places to the left.

24% ⟹ 24.0% ⟹ 0.24

4% ⟹ 04.0% ⟹ .04

❑ To change a decimal to a percent, move the decimal point two places to the right.

0.92 ⟹ 0.920 ⟹ 92.0%

1.43 ⟹ 1.430 ⟹ 143.0%

❑ Memorize the common percent-decimal equivalents

1% = .01	10% = .1	100% = 1.0
25% = .25	50% = .50	75% = 0.75
20% = .20	40% = 0.40	60% = 0.60
80% = 0.80	$33\frac{1}{3}\% = .\overline{3}$	$66\frac{2}{3}\% = .\overline{6}$

TRY IT OUT

Express the following decimals as percents:

1. .63

2. 2.07

3. .04

4. 0.1256

5. .0005

Express the following percents as decimals:

6. 73%

7. 119%

8. $7\frac{1}{2}\%$

9. .75%

10. 2.1%

PUT IT TOGETHER

1. All of the following are equal EXCEPT:

    (A) .3
    (B) $\dfrac{3}{10}$
    (C) $\dfrac{300}{1000}$
    (D) .300
    (E) 3%

Percent-Fraction Conversion

❑ Percents are a way of expressing fractions with a denominator of 100.

To change a percent to a fraction, put the percent over 100 (without the percent sign) and reduce.

$$25\% \implies 25 \text{ out of } 100 \implies \frac{25}{100} \implies \frac{1}{4}$$

❑ To change a fraction to a percent, change the fraction to an equivalent fraction with a denominator of 100.

Convert $\frac{3}{5}$ to a percent.

$$\frac{3}{5} \implies \frac{3}{5} \times \frac{20}{20} \implies \frac{60}{100} \implies 60\%$$

❑ You can also change a fraction into a decimal by dividing the numerator by the denominator. Then change the resulting decimal to a percent.

Convert $\frac{4}{20}$ to a percent.

$$\frac{4}{20} \implies 20\overline{)4.00}^{\,.20} \implies .20 = 20\%$$

❑ Memorize the common percent-fraction equivalents

$$1\% = \frac{1}{100} \qquad\qquad 10\% = \frac{1}{10} \qquad\qquad 100\% = \frac{1}{1}$$

$$25\% = \frac{1}{4} \qquad\qquad 50\% = \frac{1}{2} \qquad\qquad 75\% = \frac{3}{4}$$

$$20\% = \frac{1}{5} \qquad\qquad 40\% = \frac{2}{5} \qquad\qquad 60\% = \frac{3}{5}$$

$$80\% = \frac{4}{5} \qquad\qquad 33\tfrac{1}{3}\% = \frac{1}{3} \qquad\qquad 66\tfrac{2}{3}\% = \frac{2}{3}$$

TRY IT OUT

Convert the following percents to fractions:

1. 40%

2. 68 %

3. 8%

4. 140%

5. 1001%

Convert the following fractions to percents:

6. $\frac{1}{10}$

7. $\frac{1}{4}$

8. $\frac{3}{5}$

9. $1\frac{1}{5}$

10. $\frac{5}{7}$

PUT IT TOGETHER

1. Which of the following is NOT equal to $1,600\times0.4$?

   (A) $1,600\times\frac{4}{10}$

   (B) $1,600\times\frac{4}{100}$

   (C) $1,600\times\frac{2}{5}$

   (D) 16×40

   (E) 160×4

2. If 20 out of 25 students in a class went on a field trip, what percent of the students went on the trip?

   (A) 95%
   (B) 80%
   (C) 75%
   (D) 25%
   (E) 20%

3. $\frac{1}{5}$ percent =

   (A) 0.002
   (B) 0.02
   (C) 0.2
   (D) 2
   (E) 20

Solving Percent Problems

☐ Method 1: **"Is over of"** calls for a proportion. One side of the proportion is the percentage written as a fraction. The other side is a fraction in which the numerator is the number that comes after the word "is" and the denominator is the number that comes after the word "of."

$$\frac{\text{is}}{\text{of}} = \frac{\text{percent}}{100}$$

40% of what number is 16?

40% **of** what number **is** 16?

denominator   numerator

$$\frac{40}{100} = \frac{16}{x}$$ ⇨ Cross-multiply to solve: $40x = 1600$ ⇨ $x = 40$

Note: "cross-multiplying" is covered later in the Proportions lesson.

☐ Method 2: **Translation** calls for translating the words in the question directly to a math equation.

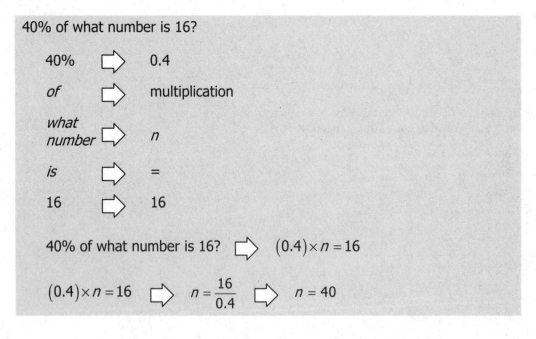

40% of what number is 16?

40%	⇨	0.4
of	⇨	multiplication
what number	⇨	n
is	⇨	=
16	⇨	16

40% of what number is 16? ⇨ $(0.4) \times n = 16$

$(0.4) \times n = 16$ ⇨ $n = \dfrac{16}{0.4}$ ⇨ $n = 40$

TRY IT OUT

1. What is 40% of 12?

2. What is 25% of 250?

3. What is 8% of 16?

4. What is 150% of 30?

5. 12 is what percent of 24?

6. What percent of 48 is 36?

7. 50 is what percent of 40?

8. What percent of 210 is 70?

9. 10% of what number is 20?

10. 80% of what number is 5?

11. $33\frac{1}{3}\%$ of what number is 10?

12. 250% of what number is 5?

PUT IT TOGETHER

1. If 20 percent of N is 30, then 10 percent of the same
    number is

    (A) 10
    (B) 12
    (C) 15
    (D) 18
    (E) 20

2. 110 is 50% of what number?

    (A) 50
    (B) 55
    (C) 155
    (D) 200
    (E) 220

3. Stefan wants to buy 2 sandwiches that have a regular
    price of N dollars each. The shop that sells the sandwiches
    has a deal in which the second sandwich is half the
    regular price. If he buys the two sandwiches, what percent
    of the regular price of two sandwiches will he pay?

    (A) 25%
    (B) 50%
    (C) 75%
    (D) 100%
    (E) 125%

4. In a school club, 60% of the student members are girls. If
    there are 24 boys in the club, how many students are in
    the club?

    (A) 64
    (B) 60
    (C) 48
    (D) 40
    (E) 36

5. If 20 percent of a number is equal to x, which of the following is equal to 10 percent of twice the same number?

(A) $4x$

(B) $2x$

(C) x

(D) $\dfrac{x}{2}$

(E) $\dfrac{x}{4}$

6. The price of a computer is decreased by 50%. If this new price is increased by 50%, what will be the percent change from the original price of the computer to the final price?

(A) 25%
(B) 40%
(C) 50%
(D) 60%
(E) 100%

7. Harriet currently has $12,600 in her savings account. If her account receives 5 percent interest per year, how much did she have in her account one year ago?

(A) $13,230
(B) $13,200
(C) $12,030
(D) $12,000
(E) $11,970

Ratios

❑ When two quantities are compared by dividing one quantity by the other, the comparison is called a **ratio**.

   A ratio may be written as "X:Y" or "X/Y" or "X to Y."

❑ A ratio can be thought of as a comparison of parts.

In a fruit basket, there are 3 oranges to every 2 apples.

The ratio of apples to oranges is 2:3.

If there are only apples and oranges in the basket, the ratio of apples to the whole basket is 2:5 and the ratio of oranges to the whole basket is 3:5.

❑ A ratio doesn't necessarily represent the actual number of things.

If the ratio of boys to girls in a class is 1:3, it means that for every boy in the class, there are 3 girls.

The ratio of boys to total students is 1:4.

The ratio of girls to total students is 3:4.

If there are 20 students in the class, 5 of the students are boys and 15 of the students are girls. You can figure this by multiplying both terms in the ratio by 5.

TRY IT OUT

Express the following as ratios:

1. $4 to $7

2. 40 cm to 1m

3. 10 in. to 3 ft.

Solve the following word problems:

4. A class has 18 girls and 12 boys. What is the ratio of girls to boys?

5. A class has 15 girls and x boys. The ratio of girls to boys is 3:2. How many boys are in the class?

6. A basket has apples and oranges. The ratio of apples to oranges is 1:4. If there are 24 oranges in the basket, how many of pieces of fruit are in the basket?

PUT IT TOGETHER

1. The ratio of 2 to 3 is the same as the ratio of all of the following EXCEPT

   (A) 6 to 8
   (B) 10 to 15
   (C) 12 to 18
   (D) 16 to 24
   (E) 18 to 27

2. Hannah runs half as fast as she rides her bicycle. If she runs to the library in 30 minutes, how many minutes does it take her to ride her bicycle to the library?

   (A) 15 minutes
   (B) 30 minutes
   (C) 40 minutes
   (D) 45 minutes
   (E) 60 minutes

3. The ratio of boys to girls in a classroom is 4 to 3. If there are 28 children in the classroom, how many are girls?

   (A) 7
   (B) 12
   (C) 16
   (D) 21
   (E) 24

4. In a basket of fruit, there are 32 apples for every 48 oranges. What is the ratio of apples to oranges?

   (A) 2:5
   (B) 3:5
   (C) 2:3
   (D) 3:2
   (E) 5:2

5. Justin has the same number of $5 bills as $10 bills. If the
    value of his $5 bills plus the value of his $10 bills equals
    $120, how many $5 bills does Justin have?

    (A) 6
    (B) 8
    (C) 12
    (D) 40
    (E) 80

6. Gregory plants 16 trees in an orchard with an area of
    4,000 square feet. He should only have two trees for every
    800 square feet. How many trees should he remove from
    the orchard?

    (A) 3
    (B) 4
    (C) 5
    (D) 6
    (E) 11

Proportions

❑ A proportion is a statement that two ratios are equivalent.

❑ The quickest way to solve proportions is usually to **cross-multiply**. With both ratios written as fractions, multiply the numerator of each ratio by the denominator of the other, and set the products equal to each other.

In other words, $\dfrac{a}{b} = \dfrac{c}{d}$ is a proportion if $ad = bc$.

> Jon eats 2 hard-boiled eggs every 5 minutes. At this rate, how many hard-boiled eggs will Jon eat in 30 minutes?
>
> Let x = the number of hard-boiled eggs Jon will eat in 30 minutes.
>
> Now set up a proportion:
>
> $$\frac{2 \text{ eggs}}{5 \text{ minutes}} = \frac{x \text{ eggs}}{30 \text{ minutes}}$$
>
> Cross-multiply:
>
> $$\frac{2}{5} = \frac{x}{30} \implies \frac{2}{5} \diagup\!\!\!\!\times \frac{x}{30} \implies 5 \cdot x = 2 \cdot 30 \implies 5x = 60 \implies x = 12$$

❑ Proportions can sometimes be solved by finding common denominators.

$$\frac{6}{15} = \frac{x}{10} \implies \frac{6}{15} \cdot \left(\frac{2}{2}\right) = \frac{x}{10} \cdot \left(\frac{3}{3}\right) \implies \frac{12}{30} = \frac{3x}{30} \implies x = 4$$

TRY IT OUT

Solve for *n*:

1. $\dfrac{n}{2} = \dfrac{4}{1}$

2. $\dfrac{5}{6} = \dfrac{n}{12}$

3. $\dfrac{2}{3} = \dfrac{8}{n}$

4. $\dfrac{n}{10} = \dfrac{8}{5}$

5. $\dfrac{5}{n} = \dfrac{6}{10}$

Solve the following word problems:

6. If a dealer buys 24 pairs of shoes for $300, how much does he pay for a shipment of 36 pairs of shoes at the same rate?

7. If Frank gives Kelly 5 roses every 2 hours, how many roses does he give her during one day?

8. A map is drawn to a scale of 10 miles = 1 inch. What distance is represented by 2.5 inches?

9. A motorist used 8 gallons of gasoline to travel 160 miles. At the same rate, how many gallons of gas does the motorist need to travel 80 miles?

PUT IT TOGETHER

1. If $\dfrac{4}{3n} = \dfrac{1}{9}$, then $n =$

   (A) 12
   (B) 16
   (C) 18
   (D) 24
   (E) 36

2. If 10 biscuits cost \$2, then, at the same rate, a dozen biscuits will cost

   (A) \$2.20
   (B) \$2.40
   (C) \$2.80
   (D) \$3.00
   (E) \$3.60

3. Barry solved 2 math problems in 30 minutes. At the same rate, how long will it take him to solve 11 math problems?

   (A) 2 hours 15 minutes
   (B) 2 hours 30 minutes
   (C) 2 hours 45 minutes
   (D) 3 hours
   (E) 3 hours 15 minutes

4.   On a blueprint, a line 4 inches long represents 32 feet. On this blueprint, how many inches represent 80 feet?

(A) 10
(B) 12
(C) 14
(D) 15
(E) 16

Exponents

❏ An exponent tells you how many times to multiply a number by itself.

$$4^3 = 4 \times 4 \times 4 \qquad 2x^5 = 2 \cdot x \cdot x \cdot x \cdot x \cdot x \qquad (7y)^3 = 7y \cdot 7y \cdot 7y$$

❏ Know the following properties of exponents:

Any base raised to an exponent of 0 equals 1.

$$3^0 = 1 \qquad\qquad 21^0 = 1$$

A base with an exponent of 1 is equal to the base.

$$7^1 = 7 \qquad\qquad 100^1 = 100$$

A number greater than 1 raised to a power greater than 1 becomes larger.

$$2^4 = 16 \qquad\qquad 3^2 = 9$$

When a fraction is raised to an exponent, apply the exponent to both the numerator and the denominator.

$$\left(\frac{1}{2}\right)^2 = \frac{1}{4} \qquad\qquad \left(\frac{2}{3}\right)^2 = \frac{4}{9}$$

A positive fraction less than 1 raised to a power greater than 1 becomes smaller.

$$\left(\frac{1}{4}\right)^2 = \frac{1}{16} \qquad\qquad \left(\frac{1}{3}\right)^4 = \frac{1}{81}$$

A negative number raised to an even power becomes positive.

$$(-1)^2 = 1 \qquad\qquad (-4)^4 = 256$$

A negative number raised to an odd power remains negative.

$$(-1)^5 = -1 \qquad\qquad (-2)^3 = -8$$

TRY IT OUT

Simplify:

1. $2^0 =$

2. $2^1 =$

3. $2^2 =$

4. $2^3 =$

5. $(-2)^1 =$

6. $(-2)^2 =$

7. $(-2)^3 =$

8. $(-2)^4 =$

9. $(-1)^{100} =$

10. $(-1)^{101} =$

11. $\left(\dfrac{1}{3}\right)^2 =$

12. $\left(\dfrac{2}{3}\right)^3 =$

Solve:

13. If $x^2 = 9$, then $x =$

14. If $x^3 = 64$, then $x =$

15. If $x^3 = -8$, then $x =$

16. If $x^5 = -1$, then $x =$

17. If $x^2 = \dfrac{1}{100}$, then $x =$

18. If $5^x = 125$, then $x =$

PUT IT TOGETHER

1. Which of the following is true?

    (A) $2^2 = 4^4$
    (B) $2^2 > 4^4$
    (C) $2^4 < 4^2$
    (D) $2^4 = 4^2$
    (E) $2^4 > 4^2$

Multiplying and Dividing Numbers with Exponents

❑ To multiply two numbers with the same base, add the exponents.

$x^a \cdot x^b = x^{a+b}$

$m^2 \times m^4 \implies (m \cdot m) \cdot (m \cdot m \cdot m \cdot m) \implies m \cdot m \cdot m \cdot m \cdot m \cdot m \implies m^6$

$2^2 \times 2^5 = 2^{2+5} = 2^7$ $t \times t^4 = t^{1+4} = t^5$

Note: $3^2 + 3^4$ does not equal 3^6

❑ To divide two numbers with the same base, subtract the exponents.

$x^a \div x^b = x^{a-b}$

$m^5 \div m^2 \implies \dfrac{m \cdot m \cdot m \cdot m \cdot m}{m \cdot m} \implies \dfrac{m \cdot m \cdot m}{1} \implies m^3$

$\dfrac{3^5}{3^2} = 3^{5-2} = 3^3$ $\dfrac{b^6}{b^5} = b^{6-5} = b^1$

Note: $x^5 - x^2$ does not equal x^3

❑ To raise a power to a power, multiply the exponents.

$\left(x^a\right)^b = x^{ab}$

$\left(m^2\right)^3 \implies \left(m^2\right) \cdot \left(m^2\right) \cdot \left(m^2\right) \implies m \cdot m \cdot m \cdot m \cdot m \cdot m \implies m^6$

$\left(2^3\right)^7 = 2^{3 \times 7} = 2^{21}$ $\left(d^3\right)^5 = d^{3 \times 5} = d^{15}$

❑ Pay special attention to parentheses when dealing with exponents. Each "piece" inside the parentheses must be raised to the exponent.

$\left(5x^2\right)^3 \implies (5)^3 \cdot \left(x^2\right)^3 \implies 125 \cdot x^6 \implies 125x^6$

TRY IT OUT

Simplify:

1. $2^2 \times 2^3 =$

2. $x^4 \cdot x^3 =$

3. $\dfrac{7^3}{7^2} =$

4. $\dfrac{x^{12}}{x^2} =$

5. $\left(6^3\right)^2 =$

6. $\left(x^{11}\right)^4 =$

7. $\left(4x^3\right)^2 =$

PUT IT TOGETHER

1. $\left(3x^2 y\right)^3 =$

   (A) $3x^2 y^3$
   (B) $3x^5 y^3$
   (C) $9x^6 y^3$
   (D) $27x^5 y^3$
   (E) $27x^6 y^3$

Roots

❑ A **square root** (also known as a **radical**) is an exponent of 2 in reverse.

A number's square root is the number which, when multiplied by itself, gives you the original number.

$$\sqrt{81} = 9 \text{ because } 9 \times 9 = 81.$$

$$\sqrt{x} \cdot \sqrt{x} = x \text{ because } \sqrt{x^2} = x.$$

❑ To simplify a square root, factor out any square factors. It helps to separate the number in the radical into the product of multiple radicals.

$$\sqrt{50} \quad \Rightarrow \quad \sqrt{25 \times 2} \quad \Rightarrow \quad \sqrt{25} \times \sqrt{2} \quad \Rightarrow \quad 5\sqrt{2}$$

❑ A **cubic root** is an exponent of 3 in reverse.

$$\sqrt[3]{8} = 2 \text{ because } 2 \times 2 \times 2 = 8.$$

$$\sqrt[3]{-27} = -3 \text{ because } (-3) \times (-3) \times (-3) = -27.$$

❑ You can save time on roots problems by memorizing common roots.

$$\sqrt{1} = 1 \qquad\qquad \sqrt[3]{1} = 1$$

$$\sqrt{4} = 2 \qquad\qquad \sqrt[3]{8} = 2$$

$$\sqrt{9} = 3 \qquad\qquad \sqrt[3]{27} = 3$$

$$\sqrt{16} = 4 \qquad\qquad \sqrt[3]{64} = 4$$

$$\sqrt{25} = 5$$

$$\sqrt{36} = 6$$

$$\sqrt{49} = 7$$

$$\sqrt{64} = 8$$

$$\sqrt{81} = 9$$

TRY IT OUT

Simplify the following radicals:

1. $\sqrt{16}$

2. $\sqrt{49}$

3. $\sqrt{\dfrac{1}{9}}$

4. $\sqrt{\dfrac{4}{9}}$

5. $\sqrt{x^2}$

6. $\sqrt{x^4}$

7. $\sqrt{4x^{10}}$

8. $\sqrt[3]{1000}$

9. $\sqrt[3]{64}$

10. $\sqrt[3]{-1}$

11. $\sqrt[3]{-125}$

12. $\sqrt[3]{\dfrac{1}{8}}$

13. $\sqrt{8}$

14. $\sqrt{12}$

15. $\sqrt{80}$

16. $\sqrt{32}$

PUT IT TOGETHER

1. $\sqrt{41}$ is closest to what number?

    (A) 3
    (B) 4
    (C) 5
    (D) 6
    (E) 7

---

2. $\sqrt{3} \times \sqrt{3} =$

    (A) 1
    (B) $\sqrt{6}$
    (C) 3
    (D) 9
    (E) 30

Order of Operations

❑ To simplify a problem with multiple operations, you need to follow the order of operations.

1. Parentheses: ( )

2. Exponents: 3^2

3. Multiplication: 2×4

4. Division: $6 \div 2$

5. Addition: $5 + 6$

6. Subtraction: $9 - 6$

Simplify:

$$3 \times (10 - 2) - 7 + 4^2 =$$

$= 3 \times 8 - 7 + 4^2$	(parentheses)
$= 3 \times 8 - 7 + 16$	(exponents)
$= 24 - 7 + 16$	(multiplication)
$= 17 + 16$	(addition / subtraction)
$= 33$	(addition)

Just remember "**P**lease **E**xcuse **M**y **D**ear **A**unt **S**ally" or the word **PEMDAS** and you'll remember the order of operations.

Note: Addition does not necessarily come before subtraction. When you get to the addition and subtraction part of the simplification, move from left to right through the expression.

TRY IT OUT

Simplify:

1. $9 \times 2^2 + 3 - \left(2^3 - 6\right) =$

2. $15 \div 3 + 2 \times (2 - 1)^2 =$

3. $12^2 + 4^3 - \dfrac{6^2}{3} =$

4. $\left(7 - (2 + 2 + 2)\right)^2 =$

PUT IT TOGETHER

1. $4 \times (2 + 2 \times 4) =$

    (A) 16
    (B) 20
    (C) 32
    (D) 40
    (E) 64

    ---

2. The expression $\sqrt{49} \times \left(3n^2 + n^2\right) - 2$ is equal to

    (A) $28n^2 - 2$
    (B) $26n^2$
    (C) $21n^4 - 2$
    (D) $11n^4 - 2$
    (E) $9n^2$

Averages

❑ To find the average of a list of numbers, find the sum of the numbers and divide by the number of terms.

Average = Sum ÷ Number of Terms

> Joanne's test scores were 73, 90, 82, 85, and 80. What was her average test score?
>
> $$\frac{73+90+82+85+80}{5} = \frac{410}{5} = 82$$

❑ To solve some SSAT average problems, you need to use this formula in reverse, solving for the sum when you are given the average.

Sum = Average x Number of Terms

> The average weight of a group of 10 men is 150 lbs. One of these men weighs 200 lbs. What is the average weight of the other men?
>
> First, find the total weight of the group: $10 \times 150 = 1,500$
>
> Now, find the total weight for the other 9 men: $1,500 - 200 = 1,300$
>
> Now, find the average: $\frac{1,300}{9} = 144.44$ lbs.

TRY IT OUT

1. What is the average of 12 and 20?

2. What is the average of 50, 100, and 150?

3. John is 12 years old, Sarah is 10 years old, Mark is 8 years old, and Tom is 6 years old. What is the average age of the 4 children?

4. The Minnesota Wild hockey team won 25 games the first season, 42 games the second season, and 50 games the third season. What is the average number of games won by the Minnesota Wild over those three seasons?

5. Karen sold 5 chocolate bars on Monday, 9 chocolate bars on Tuesday, 4 chocolate bars on Wednesday, none on Thursday, and 7 chocolate bars on Friday. What is the average number of chocolate bars Karen sold each day?

6. A basketball player averages 20 points per game for the first 8 games. After 9 games, his average is 18 points per game. How many points did he score in the ninth game?

7. Jill scores an average of 3 runs per game for the first 10 games of the softball season. After 12 games, her average is 4 runs per game. How many runs did she score in the last two games?

8. Michael's average grade for 7 math tests is 92. After the eighth test his average is 87. What was his grade on the eighth math test?

9. After working for 6 weeks, Susan's average weekly salary is $160. For the first 3 weeks her average salary was $150. What was her average weekly salary for the last 3 weeks?

10. The average age of a group of 7 children is 10. If the youngest child is 3, and the oldest child is 12, what is the average age of the other 5 children?

PUT IT TOGETHER

1. Four people have spent an average of $9 each in supplies
    for a class project. If they contribute a total of $7 more for
    supplies to complete the project, how many dollars in all
    will be spent on the project?

    (A) $64
    (B) $63
    (C) $54
    (D) $44
    (E) $43

2. The average age of two girls is 19 and the average age of
    three boys is 9. What is the average age of all five people?

    (A) 16
    (B) 15
    (C) 14
    (D) 13
    (E) 12

3. After four tests, Kevin had an average of 77 points per
    test. After the fifth test, his average was 80 points per test.
    How many points did Kevin score on the fifth test?

    (A) 98
    (B) 92
    (C) 89
    (D) 78
    (E) 72

4. Three people buying a present together each pay $10.
    How much would each person pay if a fourth person
    shared the cost of the present?

    (A) $2.50
    (B) $3.00
    (C) $6.00
    (D) $7.50
    (E) $9.00

5. Which of the following <u>must</u> be true of the numbers m
    and n if m is greater than n and the two numbers have an
    average of 100?

    (A) $100 - m = 100 - n$
    (B) $m = 100 - n$
    (C) $m = 100 + n$
    (D) $m - n = 50$
    (E) $m + n = 200$

6. If the average of three consecutive whole numbers is 24,
    what is the largest number?

    (A) 7
    (B) 8
    (C) 9
    (D) 24
    (E) 25

Probability

❑ Probability is the chance of something happening.

The probability of an event occurring is the ratio of the number of ways the event can happen to the total number of possible events.

In a bag of marbles, there are 2 black marbles, 3 gray marbles, and 4 white marbles. If a marble is chosen randomly from the bag, what are the chances that the marble is black?

Number of black marbles: 2

Total number of marbles: 9

Probability of choosing black: 2 to 9

In the dartboard shown below, the gray portions are twice the size of the white portions. If a dart is thrown randomly at the dartboard, what are the odds that it hits a gray part of the board?

Ratio of gray area to white area: 2 to 1

Ratio of gray area to total area: 2 to 3

Probability of hitting a gray part: 2 to 3

TRY IT OUT

1. Jonathan has 3 pennies, 2 nickels, and a quarter in his pocket. If he picks one coin at random, what is the probability that it is a penny?

2. There are 10 male students and 6 female students in a classroom. If one person is chosen at random, what is the probability that it will be a male?

3. A box contains red, white, and blue chips. 18 of the chips are white. 10 of the chips are red. 2 of the chips are blue. What is the probability of NOT drawing a red chip?

PUT IT TOGETHER

1. According to the chart, if a brown car is randomly chosen, what are the chances it will be chosen from lot 2?

NUMBER OF CARS OF EACH COLOR
IN THREE LOTS

Car Color	Lot 1	Lot 2	Lot 3
White	12	9	0
Blue	4	0	6
Brown	3	6	1

(A) $\frac{1}{7}$

(B) $\frac{1}{6}$

(C) $\frac{2}{5}$

(D) $\frac{3}{5}$

(E) $\frac{2}{3}$

2. There are 30 wrapped prizes in a bag. 12 of the prizes are toys, 6 are candy, 4 are gift certificates, and the rest are books. If Jessica takes a prize without looking in the bag, what are her chances of choosing a book?

(A) 2 in 15
(B) 1 in 5
(C) 4 in 15
(D) 1 in 4
(E) 1 in 3

3. If the 12 men and 20 women in the final drawing for a
    raffle each have an equal chance of winning, what is the
    probability that the winner will be a man?

    (A) 1 in 2
    (B) 1 in 4
    (C) 1 in 5
    (D) 2 in 5
    (E) 3 in 8

Ordering and Sequences

❑ To compare the relative sizes of decimals, line up the decimal points.

> List the following numbers from smallest to largest: 0.27, 2.85, 28.6, 0.271.
>
> Arrange the numbers vertically and keep the decimal points in one line:
>
> 0.27
> 2.85
> 28.6
> 0.271
>
> Since 28.6 is the only number with a tens place, it is the largest.
> 2.85 is the next largest.
> 0.27 is the same as 0.270, which is smaller than .271.
>
> So, from smallest to largest, the numbers go: 0.27, 0.271, 2.85, 28.6

❑ To compare the relative sizes of fractions, find the lowest common denominator and compare the numerators.

❑ **Consecutive numbers** are whole numbers that increase or decrease incrementally by 1.

> $\{4,5,6\}$ and $\{9,8,7,6,5\}$ are both sets of consecutive numbers.
>
> $\{n,n+1,n+2,n+3\}$ is also a set of consecutive numbers.

❑ Sequences and patterns can often be solved by recognizing trends or by writing out the numbers.

> The price of a single doughnut is $0.79, and the price of each additional doughnut is 2 cents less than the previous one. If Doug buys 5 doughnuts, what is the price of his fifth doughnut?
>
> 1st = $0.79, 2nd = $0.77, 3rd = $0.75, 4th = $0.73, 5th = $0.71

TRY IT OUT

1. List the following from largest to smallest:
    4.23, 33.1, 33.01, 4.1937, .00936.

2. List the following from largest to smallest: $\dfrac{2}{3}, \dfrac{3}{5}, \dfrac{5}{12}, \dfrac{7}{10}$

3. Donna is taller than Theodore but shorter than William.
    Theodore is taller than Fred but shorter than Regina. Who
    is shortest?

4. The sum of a pair of consecutive numbers is 39. What is
    the smaller of the two numbers?

PUT IT TOGETHER

1. Which of the following numbers is the smallest?

    (A) 0

    (B) $-\dfrac{1}{10}$

    (C) 1

    (D) $\dfrac{1}{10}$

    (E) -1

    _____

2. Buck is younger than Jim but older than Maddie. Maddie is older than Graham. Who is youngest?

    (A) Buck
    (B) Graham
    (C) Jim
    (D) Maddie
    (E) It cannot be determined from the information given.

    _____

3. A history textbook has a picture on the third page and on every second page after the third. No other pages in the book have pictures. Which of the following is the number of a page that will have a picture?

    (A) 11
    (B) 12
    (C) 14
    (D) 20
    (E) 30

4. On a shelf, gems are placed in this repeating pattern: pink, blue, green, yellow, red; pink, blue, green, yellow, red; etc. If the first gem is pink, what will be the color of the 63rd gem on the shelf?

(A) blue
(B) green
(C) pink
(D) red
(E) yellow

---

5. The sum of three consecutive numbers is 204. What is the largest of the three numbers?

(A) 615
(B) 206
(C) 69
(D) 67
(E) 66

Charts and Graphs

❑ Before looking at a chart or graph question, take a moment to interpret the information presented.

❑ Note the title, labels, and units used in graphs and charts.

Pay attention to the scale on line graphs and bar graphs, because they might not begin at zero.

❑ Check your answer by reviewing the chart or graph. The figure can help you visualize the information to make sure that your answer makes sense.

TRY IT OUT

1. How many more rock records than jazz records are there in the collection?

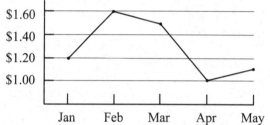

VINYL RECORD COLLECTION
Each ⊙ represents 4 records

Blues	⊙ ⊙ ◖
Jazz	⊙ ⊙ ⊙
Rock	⊙ ⊙ ⊙ ⊙ ◖
Classical	⊙ ◖

2. The number of rock records is how many times the number of classical records?

3. According to the graph, what was the average stock price for the 5 months from January to May?

HONEST JOE'S AUTO SHACK
Average Monthly Stock Price

4. According to the graph, in which month was there the greatest change in the average price of the stock compared to the previous month?

5. If 50 people saw the film, how many of the viewers were 21 or younger?

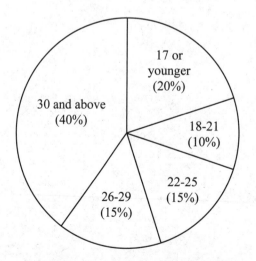

AGE DISTRIBUTION OF
VIEWERS AT A SCI-FI FILM

17 or younger (20%)
18-21 (10%)
22-25 (15%)
26-29 (15%)
30 and above (40%)

6. If the total number of viewers aged 22-29 was 12, how many viewers saw the film?

PUT IT TOGETHER

Questions 1-2 refer to the graph in Figure 1.

WHERE THE MONEY GOES
WHEN BUYING FOOD

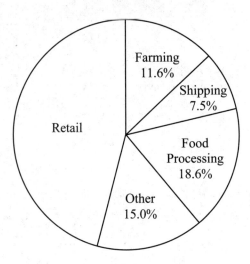

Figure 1

1. According to the chart, the retailer receives how many cents per dollar for food?

    (A) 47.3
    (B) 48.3
    (C) 57.3
    (D) 58.3
    (E) It cannot be determined from the information given.

2. According to the chart, if a farmer earns $1,000 for a shipment of food, which of the following is closest to the amount that the food processors would earn for the shipment?

    (A) $2,000
    (B) $1,800
    (C) $1,600
    (D) $1,400
    (E) $1,000

3. Every month, Ashley budgets $200 for extra expenses. She spends $100 at restaurants (*R*), $60 on clothing (*C*), and the rest on miscellaneous items (*M*). Which of the following graphs is the best representation of how Ashley budgets her monthly expenses?

    (A)

    (B)

    (C)

    (D)

    (E)

Questions 4-6 are based on the graph in Figure 2.

4. The average annual spending on food in 1990 was approximately how much less than in 2000?

   (A) $2,200
   (B) $2,100
   (C) $1,200
   (D) $1,000
   (E) $800

5. The annual expense with the lowest amount in 2010 was how much in 1990?

   (A) $1,200
   (B) $1,400
   (C) $1,600
   (D) $1,800
   (E) $3,200

6. According to the graph, which of the following experienced the greatest increase in annual spending from 2000 to 2010?

   (A) Food
   (B) Shelter
   (C) Health
   (D) Clothing
   (E) Transportation

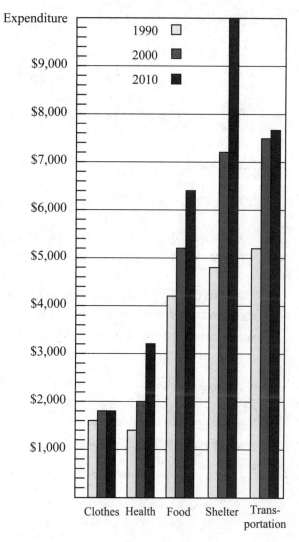

AVERAGE ANNUAL SPENDING
PER U.S. HOUSEHOLD

Figure 2

Chapter Review

❑ Addition, Subtraction, Multiplication, and Division

Be careful and methodical when calculating sums, differences, products, and quotients. Know all the special rules (e.g., multiplication by 1, etc.).

Make sure your answers make sense. Use logic to check your work.

❑ Fractions

Know how to add, subtract, multiply, divide, reduce and compare fractions.

To convert a mixed number to an improper fraction, rewrite the whole number as a fraction with the same denominator. Then, add the two fractions.

To convert an improper fraction to a mixed number, divide the numerator by the denominator. The whole number of the dividend will be the whole number and the remainder will be the numerator of the fraction.

❑ Decimals

To round a number, look at the digit to the right of the place you're rounding to. If that digit is greater than or equal to 5, round up; if that digit is less than 5, round down.

❑ Percents

To change a percent to a decimal, move the decimal point two places to the left.

To change a decimal to a percent, move the decimal point two places to the right.

To change a percent to a fraction, put the percent over 100 (without the percent sign) and reduce.

To change a fraction to a percent, change the fraction to an equivalent fraction with a denominator of 100.

Memorize common percent-decimal-fraction equivalents.

❑ **Exponents and Roots**

Know the basic behavior of exponents and roots.

$$x^a \times x^b = x^{a+b}$$

$$\left(x^a\right)^b = x^{a \times b}$$

$$\frac{x^a}{x^b} = x^{a-b} \quad \text{and} \quad x^{-a} = \frac{1}{x^a}$$

$$\sqrt{ab} = \sqrt{a} \times \sqrt{b}$$

$$\sqrt{\frac{a}{b}} = \frac{\sqrt{a}}{\sqrt{b}}$$

❑ **Order of Operations**

Know the proper order of operations. Use the word PEMDAS to help you remember.

❑ **Averages**

$$\frac{\text{Sum}}{\text{Number of Terms}} = \text{Average}$$

$$\text{Average} \times \text{Number of Terms} = \text{Sum}$$

❑ **Ordering and Sequences**

To compare the relative sizes of decimals, line up the decimal points.

To compare the relative sizes of fractions, find the lowest common denominator and compare the numerators.

Sequences and patterns can often be solved by recognizing trends or by writing out the numbers.

Arithmetic Practice

Addition, Subtraction, Multiplication, and Division

1. $1,000 - 32 =$

    (A) 1032
    (B) 972
    (C) 971
    (D) 970
    (E) 968

2. John's term paper is 10,000 words long. If he has typed only 1,564 of those words so far, how many words does he have left to type?

    (A) 8,336
    (B) 8,436
    (C) 8,454
    (D) 8,546
    (E) 9,536

Odd and Even Integers

3. Which of the following is an odd integer that is between 3 and 8 and between 6 and 11?

    (A) 5
    (B) 6
    (C) 6.5
    (D) 7
    (E) 8

4. If N is the sum of two odd integers, then which of the following is always true?

    (A) N is positive
    (B) N is negative
    (C) N is even
    (D) N is odd
    (E) N is greater than both numbers

Positive and Negative Numbers

5. $-2 \times 7 \times -3 \div -6 =$

(A) −7
(B) −6
(C) −2
(D) 2
(E) 7

---

6. The temperature at 5 a.m. was 6 degrees below zero. If the temperature rose 11 degrees by 1 p.m., then the temperature at 1 p.m. was

(A) 17 degrees above zero
(B) 8 degrees above zero
(C) 5 degrees above zero
(D) 1 degree below zero
(E) 17 degrees below zero

Divisibility and Remainders

7. Eric has 24 checkers. If he divides the checkers into 3 equal groups, how many checkers are in each group?

(A) 5
(B) 6
(C) 7
(D) 8
(E) 9

---

8. If $7 \div 5 = d$ with a remainder of 2, what is d?

(A) 0
(B) 1
(C) 2
(D) 5
(E) 7

---

9. If x is divisible by 4, which of the following statements must always be true?

(A) $x + 2$ is divisible by 2
(B) $x + 2$ is divisible by 3
(C) $x + 2$ is divisible by 4
(D) $x + 2$ is divisible by 5
(E) $x + 2$ is divisible by 6

Multiples and Factors

10. Mrs. Flynn bought 5 dozen cookies for her students. Mrs. Flynn has 20 students in her class. What is the greatest number of cookies that each student may have if the cookies are shared equally?

    (A) 3
    (B) 5
    (C) 7
    (D) 12
    (E) 20

11. After all the tickets for a show had been sold, $140 had been collected. If all the tickets were sold for the same price, which of the following CANNOT be the price for one ticket?

    (A) $1.40
    (B) $2.00
    (C) $6.00
    (D) $7.00
    (E) $10.00

12. Alex has three times as many dresses as skirts. Which of the following could be the sum of Alex's dresses and skirts?

    (A) 6
    (B) 7
    (C) 10
    (D) 12
    (E) 15

Fractions

13. $10\frac{1}{4} - 2\frac{3}{4} =$

    (A) 8.25
    (B) 8
    (C) 7.75
    (D) 7.5
    (E) 7.25

14. $56 - 7\frac{2}{5} =$

    (A) $48\frac{2}{5}$

    (B) $48\frac{3}{5}$

    (C) $49\frac{2}{5}$

    (D) $49\frac{3}{5}$

    (E) $64\frac{2}{5}$

15. $1 + \frac{1}{2}$ is greater than which of the following?

    (A) $\frac{2}{2}$

    (B) $\frac{3}{2}$

    (C) $\frac{4}{2}$

    (D) $\frac{5}{2}$

    (E) $\frac{6}{2}$

16. $\frac{1}{4} \times 48 \times \frac{1}{3} \times 12 =$

    (A) 12
    (B) 16
    (C) 40
    (D) 48
    (E) 56

Place Value

17. What is the hundreds digit in the number 67,675?

    (A) 600
    (B) 70
    (C) 6
    (D) 7
    (E) 5

18. Which of the following is 90,603?

    (A) nine thousand six hundred three
    (B) nineteen thousand sixty-three
    (C) ninety thousand six hundred three
    (D) nine hundred thousand sixty-three
    (E) nine hundred thousand six hundred three

19. What is the units digit of $5 \times 5 \times 5$?

    (A) 0
    (B) 1
    (C) 3
    (D) 5
    (E) 7

Rounding and Estimation

20. What is the best estimate for $9,887 \times 1,001$?

    (A) 99,000
    (B) 980,000
    (C) 990,000
    (D) 9,800,000
    (E) 9,900,000

21. Which of the following is closest to 0.24×105?

    (A) 2 times 10.5
    (B) half of 100
    (C) half of 210
    (D) $\frac{1}{4}$ of 100
    (E) $\frac{1}{4}$ of 111

Decimals

22. $0.1 + 0.01 + 0.001$ is equal to

    (A) .101
    (B) .101001
    (C) .1
    (D) .111
    (E) .3

___

23. Which of the following is closest to 5?

    (A) 4.9
    (B) 5.1
    (C) 5.01
    (D) 5.001
    (E) 5.0001

___

24. $0.0035 \times 4.00 =$

    (A) 140
    (B) 14.0
    (C) 1.4
    (D) 0.0140
    (E) 0.00140

___

Percents

25. If Eliza has eaten 3 of the 10 cookies her father made, what percent of the cookies has she eaten?

    (A) 20%
    (B) 25%
    (C) 30%
    (D) 31%
    (E) 33%

___

26. Fred sells cars for Wreck-A-Week. There are 30 cars in the Wreck-A-Week lot. If Fred sold 20% of the cars in the lot, how many cars did he sell?

    (A) 6
    (B) 10
    (C) 12
    (D) 20
    (E) 24

27. 4 is 20% of

(A) 5
(B) 10
(C) 16
(D) 18
(E) 20

Ratios

28. There are twice as many goldfish as guppies in Sue's fish tank. If there are only goldfish and guppies in the fish tank, then which could be the total number of fish in the tank?

(A) 5
(B) 10
(C) 15
(D) 20
(E) 25

29. At a dude ranch, there are three times as many horses walking around as there are humans. If there are 8 human legs at the ranch, how many horses are there?

(A) 12
(B) 24
(C) 32
(D) 48
(E) 96

Proportions

30. Frederick is bicycling 3 miles every 20 minutes. At that rate, how many miles does he bicycle in 2 hours?

(A) 6
(B) 12
(C) 15
(D) 18
(E) 24

31. In a recent university poll, there were 4.5 teachers for every 60 students. If there are 12,000 students, how many teachers are there?

    (A) 9
    (B) 90
    (C) 900
    (D) 9,000
    (E) 90,000

Exponents

32. 2.5^3 is closest to which of the following?

    (A) 8
    (B) 9
    (C) 10
    (D) 12
    (E) 15

Square Roots

33. What is the square root of 25?

    (A) 2.5
    (B) 4
    (C) 5
    (D) 50
    (E) 625

34. Which of the following does NOT equal 100?

    (A) 10^2
    (B) 10×10
    (C) 1×100
    (D) $1,000 \div 10$
    (E) $\sqrt{1,000}$

Order of Operations

35. $2(4-6)-(-8+2)\div 3 =$

    (A) −10
    (B) −6
    (C) −2
    (D) $\frac{2}{3}$
    (E) 6

Averages

36. The Huskies scored an average of 70 points in their first two games. For the next three games, they averaged 50 points. What was the total number of points scored in those five games?

    (A) 600
    (B) 290
    (C) 240
    (D) 180
    (E) 120

37. The average age of the 10 members of the basketball team is 28. The average age of the 30 members of the sewing club is 60. What is the average age of all the members of the basketball team and the sewing club?

    (A) 56
    (B) 52
    (C) 50
    (D) 48
    (E) 46

Probability

38. If the first number picked in a BINGO game is odd, which of the following rows is most likely to have that number?

    (A) 2   4   8   7   6

    (B) 11 19 18 12 13

    (C) 21 24 30 27 24

    (D) 31 38 37 33 35

    (E) 42 40 46 44 48

---

39. In a class of 30 students, 18 are female and 12 are male. If a student is chosen at random to be a teacher's assistant, what is the probability that a female is chosen?

    (A) $\frac{1}{5}$

    (B) $\frac{1}{3}$

    (C) $\frac{2}{5}$

    (D) $\frac{3}{5}$

    (E) $\frac{2}{3}$

Ordering and Sequences

40. Susan is twice as old as Bobby. Bobby is twice as old as William. If William is 5 years old, how old is Susan?

    (A) 25
    (B) 20
    (C) 15
    (D) 10
    (E) 5

41. Ed is 2 inches taller than Ernie. Ernie is 2 inches shorter than Andrew. If Andrew is 59 inches tall, how tall is Ed?

    (A) 59 inches
    (B) 57 inches
    (C) 55 inches
    (D) 53 inches
    (E) 51 inches

42. The smallest of 5 consecutive odd integers is 21. What is the average of the 5 integers?

    (A) 19
    (B) 22
    (C) 23
    (D) 25
    (E) 30

Charts and Graphs

43. In which category was the percent of students enrolled in 1990 most nearly equal to the percent of students enrolled in 2010?

    (A) Biology
    (B) Business
    (C) Education
    (D) Engineering
    (E) Social Science

44. The percent of students studying business in 1980 was approximately how many times the percent of students studying education in 2010?

    (A) 2
    (B) 3
    (C) 4
    (D) 5
    (E) 13

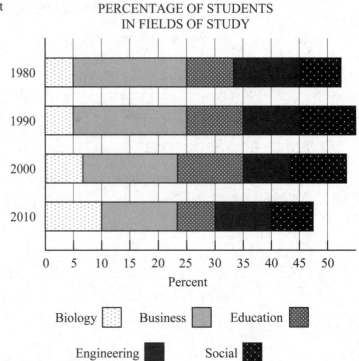

PERCENTAGE OF STUDENTS
IN FIELDS OF STUDY

Arithmetic Practice
Middle Level

1. 3 friends painted a house together and earned a total of $600. If they split the earnings evenly, how much money did each friend get?

    (A) $50
    (B) $125
    (C) $150
    (D) $200
    (E) $300

2. $5,010 - 1,777 =$

    (A) 2,233
    (B) 3,233
    (C) 3,333
    (D) 3,343
    (E) 4,343

3. Which of the following is a true statement?

    (A) $10 \div 0 = 1$
    (B) $10 \div 1 = 1$
    (C) $10 \times 1 = 1$
    (D) $10 \div 10 = 1$
    (E) $10 \times 0 = 10$

4. A furniture factory makes stools with 3 legs and stools with 4 legs. At the end of one day, the number of 3-legged stools made is 16 and the number of 4-legged stools made is 12. Which is the total number of stool legs used by the factory at the end of that day?

    (A) 96
    (B) 86
    (C) 48
    (D) 28
    (E) It cannot be determined from the information given.

5. In the figure above, what fraction of the fish have dark-colored tails?

    (A) $\frac{1}{12}$

    (B) $\frac{1}{9}$

    (C) $\frac{1}{6}$

    (D) $\frac{1}{3}$

    (E) $\frac{1}{2}$

6. Which of the following is NOT prime?

    (A) 3
    (B) 8
    (C) 13
    (D) 17
    (E) 31

7. John can do 50 jumping jacks in one minute. Jane can do 1 more jumping jack per minute than John can. How many jumping jacks can Jane do in two minutes?

    (A) 50
    (B) 100
    (C) 101
    (D) 102
    (E) 200

8. Fred went to bed at 9:00 PM and got up for school at 6:00 AM. How many hours did he sleep?

   (A) 2
   (B) 3
   (C) 6
   (D) 9
   (E) 12

9. Mary has to sell one carton of candy bars for her youth group fundraiser. She sold one-half of the candy bars in the carton and then ate two of them. If a carton contains 24 candy bars, how many does Mary have left to sell?

   (A) 13
   (B) 12
   (C) 11
   (D) 10
   (E) 8

10. $\dfrac{7}{8} - \dfrac{1}{4} = ?$

    (A) 1
    (B) $\dfrac{5}{8}$
    (C) $\dfrac{3}{8}$
    (D) $\dfrac{1}{4}$
    (E) $\dfrac{1}{8}$

11. There are 6 packages of hamburger in the freezer. Each package weighs 1.5 pounds. How many pounds of hamburger are in the freezer?

    (A) 1.5 pounds
    (B) 4 pounds
    (C) 6 pounds
    (D) 7.5 pounds
    (E) 9 pounds

12. Which of the following is NOT true?

(A) $\frac{1}{2} = \frac{2}{4}$

(B) $\frac{1}{2} = \frac{3}{6}$

(C) $\frac{1}{2} = \frac{4}{8}$

(D) $\frac{1}{2} = \frac{5}{10}$

(E) $\frac{1}{2} = \frac{6}{11}$

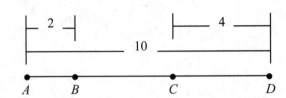

13. According to the figure above, what is the length of AC?

(A) 4
(B) 6
(C) 8
(D) 10
(E) 12

14. $\frac{1}{7} \times \frac{1}{4} = ?$

(A) $\frac{1}{28}$

(B) $\frac{1}{11}$

(C) $\frac{2}{11}$

(D) $\frac{4}{7}$

(E) $\frac{7}{4}$

15. Peter and Pam went to the supermarket. Peter bought $\frac{1}{2}$ pound of bologna. Pam bought $\frac{3}{4}$ pound of bologna. How much bologna did they buy?

(A) $1\frac{1}{4}$ pounds

(B) 1 pound

(C) 2 pounds

(D) $\frac{2}{3}$ pound

(E) $\frac{3}{8}$ pound

16. $\frac{1}{2} \times \frac{1}{2} \times \frac{1}{2} = ?$

(A) $\frac{3}{2}$

(B) $\frac{3}{6}$

(C) $\frac{1}{8}$

(D) $\frac{1}{6}$

(E) $\frac{1}{4}$

17. Jamie invited 20 friends to her birthday party. If $\frac{3}{5}$ of her guests are girls, how many of her guests are girls?

(A) 4
(B) 6
(C) 8
(D) 10
(E) 12

18. Karen has 9 quarters. If she buys 3 candy bars at 50 cents each, how many quarters does she have left?

(A) 0
(B) 1
(C) 2
(D) 3
(E) 4

19. Marty has 80 dimes. If he exchanges them for one-dollar bills, how many dollar bills will he receive?

(A) 4
(B) 5
(C) 6
(D) 7
(E) 8

20. John gave half of his candy bar to his little brother. John then ate half of what was left. What fraction of the candy bar did John eat?

(A) $\frac{3}{4}$

(B) $\frac{2}{3}$

(C) $\frac{1}{2}$

(D) $\frac{1}{3}$

(E) $\frac{1}{4}$

21. One can of beans weighs 14 ounces. How much will 5 cans of beans weigh?

(A) 90 ounces
(B) 80 ounces
(C) 70 ounces
(D) 60 ounces
(E) 50 ounces

22. $4 \times 3 \times 2 \times 1 \times 0 = ?$

(A) 24
(B) 10
(C) 5
(D) 1
(E) 0

23. Krista has 7 marbles and Jose has 15 marbles. How many marbles must Jose give Krista for each one to have the same number of marbles?

(A) 4
(B) 7
(C) 8
(D) 10
(E) 15

---

24. $3 \times \frac{2}{3}$ equals

(A) $10 \times \frac{2}{5}$

(B) $\frac{2}{3} \times \frac{3}{2}$

(C) $\frac{3}{2} \times \frac{4}{3}$

(D) $\frac{10}{5} \times \frac{5}{3}$

(E) $\frac{1}{3} \times \frac{6}{3}$

---

25. $\dfrac{12+8+4}{2 \times 4 \times 8} =$

(A) $\frac{3}{8}$

(B) $\frac{2}{5}$

(C) $\frac{3}{2}$

(D) $\frac{12}{7}$

(E) 6

---

26. A $15 pair of earrings is on sale for 20% off. What is the sale price of the earrings?

(A) $3
(B) $10
(C) $12
(D) $13
(E) $14

27. A building has 47 floors, the first 7 of which are below the lobby. If an elevator starts on the third floor and goes 6 floors up, which of the following best describes where the elevator is now?

(A) 2 floors below the lobby
(B) the lobby
(C) 1 floor above the lobby
(D) 2 floors above the lobby
(E) 9 floors above the lobby

---

28. Pat buys a piece of licorice 150 inches long. If she plans to give away all of the licorice by giving each of her 5 friends an equal piece, how long should she cut each piece?

(A) 60 feet
(B) 30 feet
(C) 10 feet
(D) 5 feet
(E) 2.5 feet

---

29. $.1 \times 10 \times .2 \times 5 =$

(A) .5
(B) 1
(C) 1.5
(D) 10
(E) 50

---

30. What is the best estimate for $\dfrac{759,987}{1,998}$?

(A) 40
(B) 280
(C) 400
(D) 500
(E) 4,000

31. Which of the following is equal to $2\overline{)178}$?

    (A) $\dfrac{178}{2}$

    (B) $178 \div 2$

    (C) $\dfrac{100}{2} + \dfrac{70}{2} + \dfrac{8}{2}$

    (D) 89

    (E) All of the above.

---

32. All the following are greater than $\dfrac{1}{2}$ except

    (A) $\dfrac{13}{25}$

    (B) $\dfrac{19}{39}$

    (C) $\dfrac{22}{43}$

    (D) $\dfrac{25}{49}$

    (E) $\dfrac{29}{54}$

---

33. If 30 percent of N is equal to $30, what is the value of N?

    (A) $1
    (B) $10
    (C) $100
    (D) $1,000
    (E) $10,000

---

34. If $\dfrac{1}{3}$ of a number is greater than 15, the number must be:

    (A) greater than 45
    (B) equal to 45
    (C) less than 45
    (D) equal to 5
    (E) less than 5

35. The price of gas dropped from $1.52 / gallon to $1.02 / gallon. This decrease is closest to what percent?

(A) 10%
(B) 13%
(C) 15%
(D) 33%
(E) 40%

36. 977 runners began a marathon. If 30% of the runners did not finish, what is the best estimate of those who finished the race?

(A) 270
(B) 300
(C) 600
(D) 700
(E) 937

37. Matt paid an additional $4.50 in tax for a meal that cost $45.00. What was the percent tax?

(A) 1%
(B) 2%
(C) 5%
(D) 10%
(E) 11%

38. 36 is less than $\frac{3}{4}$ of a number. The number must be

(A) less than 27
(B) less than 48
(C) equal to 108
(D) greater than 48
(E) greater than 72

39. All of the students at Small Town High play baseball, basketball, or both. If there are 23 students on the baseball team, 12 students on the basketball team, and 5 students on both, how many students go to Small Town High?

    (A) 16
    (B) 17
    (C) 28
    (D) 30
    (E) 40

40. 201.86×9.75 is closest to which of the following?

    (A) 200
    (B) 450
    (C) 1,800
    (D) 2,000
    (E) 2,100

41. Which is the largest fraction?

    (A) $\dfrac{4}{7}$

    (B) $\dfrac{5}{9}$

    (C) $\dfrac{7}{15}$

    (D) $\dfrac{9}{19}$

    (E) $\dfrac{10}{21}$

42. At 4 a.m., the temperature was 12 degrees below 0. By 1 p.m., the temperature had risen 27 degrees. What was the temperature at 1 p.m.?

    (A) 27 above zero
    (B) 15 above zero
    (C) 15 below zero
    (D) 39 above zero
    (E) 39 below zero

43. Which of the following is the largest?

(A) 60% of 125
(B) 30% of 125
(C) 30% of 375
(D) 60% of 250
(E) 30% of 250

---

44. If the average of 7 consecutive whole numbers is 8, what is the largest number?

(A) 11
(B) 15
(C) 16
(D) 28
(E) 56

---

45. Between 7 a.m. and 9:30 a.m., Carl makes 8 deliveries. If Carl keeps up this rate (with the exception of a lunch break between 1:00 p.m. and 1:30 p.m.), how many total deliveries will he make before finishing work at 3 p.m.?

(A) 21
(B) 24
(C) 27
(D) 29
(E) 30

---

46. 75% of the 19,950 people who ride the subway drink coffee. The rest don't. What is the best approximation of those who DON'T drink coffee?

(A) 3,000
(B) 5,000
(C) 15,000
(D) 17,000
(E) 18,000

47. Donald Mac's restaurant has served 2.7 million customers. If King Burger's restaurant has served 220,000 fewer customers, how many customers has King Burger served?

    (A) 490,000
    (B) 2,480,000
    (C) 2,520,000
    (D) 2,920,000
    (E) 4,900,000

48. When Kelly drives to work, she has two travel expenses: parking and paying tolls. She must pay $1.50 in tolls each way (going to work and returning home) and $6 for parking. For every $42 Kelly spends in parking, how much does she spend on tolls?

    (A) $10.50
    (B) $21.00
    (C) $23.00
    (D) $63.00
    (E) $67.50

49. A contractor has 25 stories left to build on a building, which is now 13 stories less than the building next door to it. When finished, the new building will have

    (A) 12 more stories than the building next door
    (B) 38 fewer stories than the building next door
    (C) 12 fewer stories than the building next door
    (D) 38 more stories than the building next door
    (E) 25 more stories than the building next door

Arithmetic Practice
Upper Level

1. Six boys are in line from shortest to tallest, each boy
    facing the back of the next taller boy. Ted is 4.07 feet tall.
    The heights of the other five boys are given below. How
    tall is the boy immediately in front of Ted?

    (A) 4 ft
    (B) 4.1 ft
    (C) 4.7 ft
    (D) 4.75 ft
    (E) 5 ft

2. The Summit School needs 150 pens. If pens are sold in
    boxes of 12, how many boxes of pens should The Summit
    School order?

    (A) 15
    (B) 14
    (C) 13
    (D) 12
    (E) 11

3. On average, Marin sells 100 pizza pies a day, and makes a
    profit of $2.75 on each pie. If her profits are cut to $2.50,
    how many more pizza pies will Marin have to sell in
    order to make the same daily profit as before?

    (A) 450
    (B) 50
    (C) 25
    (D) 15
    (E) 10

4. $\frac{1}{4} \times \frac{1}{3} \div \frac{1}{6} = ?$

(A) $\frac{1}{2}$

(B) $\frac{1}{3}$

(C) $\frac{1}{4}$

(D) $\frac{1}{6}$

(E) $\frac{1}{12}$

---

5.   In a class of 40 students, 25 take home economics and 25 take woodworking. If everyone in the class takes either home economics, woodworking, or both, how many take both?

(A) 5
(B) 10
(C) 15
(D) 20
(E) 25

---

6.   At 5 p.m., Chauncy realized that she had to return a book to the library by 5:30 p.m. If the library is 20 miles away, what must her average speed be in order to make it to the library by 5:30 p.m.?

(A) 40 m.p.h.
(B) 35 m.p.h.
(C) 30 m.p.h.
(D) 25 m.p.h.
(E) 20 m.p.h.

---

7.   Of the following, 50% of 3.75 is closest to

(A) 3.00
(B) 2.50
(C) 2.25
(D) 1.80
(E) 1.50

8.   Which of the following is closest to 20 percent of $7.90?

   (A) $1.40
   (B) $1.50
   (C) $1.60
   (D) $1.80
   (E) $2.00

9.   A basketball player made 27 baskets in 12 games. How many baskets will the player make in 32 games if she continues to make baskets at the same rate?

   (A) 30
   (B) 45
   (C) 47
   (D) 72
   (E) 88

10. If $\dfrac{x}{100}$ is equal to 0.6, then x is equal to which of the following?

   (A) 0.006
   (B) 0.06
   (C) 6
   (D) 60
   (E) 600

11. List A contains all whole numbers between 9 and 13. List B contains all whole numbers between 11 and 14. Which of the following is a number in both lists?

   (A) 11
   (B) 11.5
   (C) 12
   (D) 12.5
   (E) 13

12. What is the best approximation of $2,097 \times 3,098$?

   (A) 600,000
   (B) 840,000
   (C) 6,500,000
   (D) 8,000,000
   (E) 8,400,000

13. No more than 7 clowns can get into a taxi at one time. If there are 39 clowns, how many taxis will they need?

(A) 1
(B) 5
(C) 6
(D) 7
(E) 14

14. 0.332×12 is closest to which of the following?

(A) $\dfrac{1}{3}$ of 10

(B) $\dfrac{1}{3}$ of 20

(C) $\dfrac{2}{3}$ of 10

(D) $\dfrac{2}{3}$ of 20

(E) $\dfrac{3}{10}$ of 10

15. Mr. Collins received apples from 7 of his students. If each of the students gave him the same number of apples, which of the following could be the total number of apples he received?

(A) 6
(B) 8
(C) 11
(D) 28
(E) 33

16. $50 - 4\dfrac{5}{9} =$

(A) $44\dfrac{4}{9}$

(B) $44\dfrac{7}{9}$

(C) $45\dfrac{2}{9}$

(D) $45\dfrac{4}{9}$

(E) $45\dfrac{8}{9}$

17. If the cafeteria is 200 feet long and the tables are 7 feet long, how many tables will fit end to end along the length of the cafeteria?

(A) 28
(B) 29
(C) 30
(D) 88
(E) 89

18. $125 \times .101 =$

(A) 1.2512
(B) 1.2625
(C) 12.625
(D) 125.125
(E) 126.25

19. 30% of the leaves in a pile were put in bags. If 300 leaves were put into bags, how many leaves were in the pile?

(A) 390
(B) 700
(C) 900
(D) 1,000
(E) 10,000

20. At 7 p.m., the water was 15 inches from the top of the sink. If the water rises at 1 inch per minute, how high is the water at 7:20 p.m.?

(A) 14 inches from the top of the sink.
(B) 10 inches from the top of the sink.
(C) 5 inches from the top of the sink.
(D) 1 inch from the top of the sink.
(E) It has overflowed the sink.

21. Sally is thinking of the number 8.17. She will give a prize to the friend whose guess is closest to 8.17. The guesses are listed below. Which guess wins the prize?

(A) 8
(B) 9
(C) 8.1
(D) 8.2
(E) 8.8

22. 35 percent of 19,889 is closest to which of the following?

   (A) 660
   (B) 6,100
   (C) 7,000
   (D) 8,500
   (E) 9,000

---

23. One pitcher of lemonade has 64 fluid ounces in it. Another pitcher has 52 fluid ounces in it. How many ounces must be poured from one pitcher to the other pitcher in order to make the amount of lemonade in each equal?

   (A) 6
   (B) 8
   (C) 10
   (D) 12
   (E) 22

---

24. With 6 weeks remaining before the fundraising deadline, Lisa has raised $57 more than Charlie has. For Charlie to raise as much money as Lisa, he must raise an average of at least how much more money per week than Lisa?

   (A) $9
   (B) $9.33
   (C) $9.50
   (D) $24
   (E) $84

---

25. Rounded to the nearest hundredth, what does $16 - 11\frac{7}{9}$ equal?

   (A) 0
   (B) 0.22
   (C) 0.89
   (D) 1.11
   (E) 4.22

26. Because of some great investments, Harry's income in 1998 was $8 million. This was 20 times his income in 1980. What was his income in 1980?

    (A) $4,000
    (B) $40,000
    (C) $80,000
    (D) $160,000
    (E) $400,000

27. Jack sold 9 cars, which was more than $\frac{1}{3}$ of the number of cars that were in his lot. The number of cars in his lot must have been

    (A) less than 3
    (B) greater than 3
    (C) equal to 12
    (D) less than 27
    (E) greater than 27

28. Which fraction is less than $\frac{1}{3}$?

    (A) $\frac{6}{15}$
    (B) $\frac{23}{66}$
    (C) $\frac{1000}{2999}$
    (D) $\frac{12}{39}$
    (E) $\frac{500}{900}$

29. All the following are equal to $\frac{2}{3}$ EXCEPT

(A) $\frac{1}{4} \times \frac{16}{6}$

(B) $\frac{4}{15} \times \frac{15}{6}$

(C) $\frac{4}{6} \times \frac{100}{10}$

(D) $\frac{2}{7} \times \frac{21}{9}$

(E) $\frac{1}{8} \times \frac{16}{3}$

30. If 3 of every 10 people have red hair, how many redheads will there be in a group of 15,000 people?

(A) 1,500
(B) 3,000
(C) 4,500
(D) 5,000
(E) 45,000

31. Jackie paid $2.40 in sales tax for her dress. If the sales tax was 6 percent, what was the price of the dress?

(A) $2.40
(B) $4.00
(C) $14.40
(D) $40.00
(E) $42.00

32. 2,222.2 is how many times the value of 22.222?

(A) $\frac{1}{100}$

(B) $\frac{1}{10}$

(C) 10
(D) 100
(E) 1,000

33. Bessie has 5 plots in her garden, and each plot has at least one flower. If no two plots have the same number of flowers, what is the smallest possible number of flowers in the garden?

    (A) 10
    (B) 15
    (C) 25
    (D) 50
    (E) 100

34. Patrick has 30 math problems to do from 6 p.m. to 9 p.m. By 6:20 p.m., he has finished 5 problems. If he continues to work at this rate, how much time will he have to spare when he has finished all 30 problems?

    (A) $\frac{1}{3}$ hr.
    (B) 1 hr.
    (C) $1\frac{2}{3}$ hrs.
    (D) 2 hrs.
    (E) He will not have enough time to finish before 9 p.m.

35. Matt's long distance call to France cost $4.95. The call was billed as follows: $1.25 for each of the first two minutes and $0.60 for every minute after that, except for the last minute, which is $1.25. How long did Matt's phone call last?

    (A) 3 minutes
    (B) 4 minutes
    (C) 5 minutes
    (D) 6 minutes
    (E) 7 minutes

36. What is the best estimate for 298×450?

    (A) 135,000
    (B) 150,000
    (C) 1,250,000
    (D) 1,350,000
    (E) 1,500,000

37. Of the 26 miles Jessie ran for the marathon, her fastest mile took 5 minutes and her slowest mile took 10 minutes. The number of hours it took Jessie to finish the marathon must have been between

   (A) 2 and 5
   (B) 3 and 5
   (C) 4 and 6
   (D) 5 and 6
   (E) 5 and 7

38. On average, it takes Brian 1 hour and 45 minutes to finish each of his subjects for homework. If Brian starts his homework at 4 p.m. and has math, reading, social studies, and science to do, what time will it be when Brian is done with his homework?

   (A) 9:20 p.m.
   (B) 10:00 p.m.
   (C) 10:40 p.m.
   (D) 11:00 p.m.
   (E) 11:20 p.m.

39. Another way of writing $\dfrac{9,000}{25} + \dfrac{500}{25} + \dfrac{40}{25}$ is

   (A) $24.6\overline{)9,544}$
   (B) $24.6\overline{)9,540.4}$
   (C) $25\overline{)9,504}$
   (D) $25\overline{)9,540}$
   (E) $25\overline{)9,550}$

40. An elephant weighed 98 pounds at birth. After seven days, the elephant's weight had increased by 12%. Which of the following is closest to the elephant's weight at the end of the seventh day?

   (A) 93 pounds
   (B) 103 pounds
   (C) 104 pounds
   (D) 110 pounds
   (E) 111 pounds

41. Mrs. Kanter just won $750,000 in the lottery. She had to pay 40% in taxes. How much did she pay in taxes?

    (A) $25,250
    (B) $30,000
    (C) $250,250
    (D) $300,000
    (E) $325,500

42. Each of the 60 students in Mr. Collins's computer class owns a computer. If 37 own a Macintosh while 55 own an IBM, how many students own both a Macintosh and an IBM?

    (A) 23
    (B) 32
    (C) 37
    (D) 57
    (E) 92

43. 15 people in the office are planning to contribute $10 each to the boss's retirement party. Three of these people later decide not to contribute. How much more will each of the remaining people have to contribute so the office spends the same amount on the boss's retirement party?

    (A) $3.50
    (B) $3.25
    (C) $3.00
    (D) $2.75
    (E) $2.50

44. Louise was 4 feet $5\frac{1}{2}$ inches tall six years ago. She has grown $\frac{1}{4}$ of an inch per year since then. How tall is she now?

    (A) 4 feet and $5\frac{1}{4}$ inches

    (B) 4 feet and $5\frac{3}{4}$ inches

    (C) 4 feet and 6 inches

    (D) 4 feet and $6\frac{1}{2}$ inches

    (E) 4 feet and 7 inches

45. If the average of two numbers is 20, which of the following statements must be true?

 I.   If one of the two numbers is 11, the other number is less than 30.
 II. If a third number is added and the average jumps to 25, the third number is greater than 30.
 III. If each of the two numbers is reduced by 2, the average is reduced by 4.

 (A) I only
 (B) II only
 (C) III only
 (D) I and II only
 (E) I,II, and III

46. With $10, Leroy used to buy 10 tacos and still have $1.00 left over. But the price of tacos has gone up 10 cents per taco. With the price increase, how many tacos can Leroy afford to buy with $10 and still have $1.00 left over?

 (A) 7
 (B) 8
 (C) 9
 (D) 10
 (E) 12

SUMMIT
EDUCATIONAL
GROUP

Algebra

- ❑ Algebraic Expressions
- ❑ Algebraic Equations
- ❑ Translating
- ❑ Word Problems
- ❑ SSAT Functions
- ❑ Inequalities

Algebra

❑ Algebra is a form of math that uses numbers, symbols and letters to solve problems.

❑ In this chapter, you will:

- learn how to solve algebraic equations.

- learn to translate and solve word problems.

- learn how to attack "SSAT function" problems.

- learn how to solve inequalities.

Vocabulary

❑ **Terms** are the parts of an expression and are separated by + and − signs.

❑ **Variables** are letters (and sometimes symbols) used to represent numbers in algebraic expressions and equations.

❑ A **constant** is a fixed number. Constants are terms that do not contain variables.

❑ An **algebraic expression** is a phrase that contains one or more terms and does not contain an equal sign. An expression can include constants, variables, and operating symbols (such as addition signs and exponents).

❑ An **equation** is a statement that two expressions are equal.

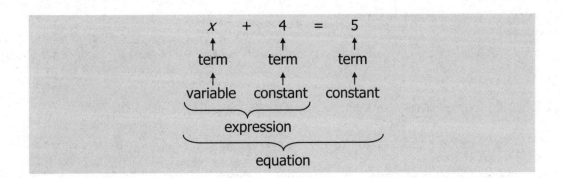

Algebraic Expressions

❑ **Simplifying** an algebraic expression is often the first step in solving an algebraic equation.

To simplify an algebraic expression, combine similar terms.

$$4 + x + 5 - 3x - 9 \implies (4 + 5 - 9) + (x - 3x) \implies 0 + (-2x) = -2x$$

❑ Use the **distributive property** to multiply a single term by an expression inside parentheses.

$$2(x + y) \implies 2(x + y) \implies (2x) + (2y) \implies 2x + 2y$$

Be careful when distributing a negative number. You must carry the negative sign through the entire distribution.

$$-6(2x - 4) \implies (-6 \times 2x) - (-6 \times 4) \implies (-12x) - (-24) \implies -12x + 24$$

❑ Algebraic expressions can be used to express situations in math terms.

Levi found 3 more bottle caps for his collection. $\implies$ $C + 3$

The amount Vanessa paid for 2 shirts and 4 dresses. $\implies$ $2S + 4D$

The price of the tickets increased by 10%. $\implies$ $T + (10\% \cdot T)$

Whitney spent a fourth of her savings. $\implies$ $S - \left(\dfrac{S}{4}\right)$

TRY IT OUT

Simplify the following expressions:

1. $13 + 4 + x + 2x$

2. $4 - x + 8 + 2x$

3. $1 + 2x + 8 - x - 9 - 5x$

4. $x^2 + 4 + 2x^2 - 1$

5. $2x^2 - x + 7 - 5x^2 + 5 + 6x$

6. $(2x + 1) + (x + 9)$

7. $(7 + 4x) - (6 + 3x)$

8. $(x - 3) + (4 + 2x)$

9. $(4 - 8x) - (6x - 3)$

10. $2(x + 3)$

11. $4(2x + 7)$

12. $-1(3 + 4x)$

13. $-3(x + 6)$

14. $-7(6 - 5x)$

15. $x(x + 1)$

16. $2x(x - 6)$

17. $-5x(x + 4)$

18. $-2x(-9 - 4x)$

19. $2(x + 3) + 4(5x - 1)$

20. $5x(x - 1) - 7(x + 2)$

PUT IT TOGETHER

1. Which of the following gives the number of cents in x pennies, y dimes, and 2 dollars?

    (A) $200 + x + 10y$
    (B) $200 + 1 + 10$
    (C) $2 + x + 10y$
    (D) $2 + 1 + 10y$
    (E) $2 + 1 + 10$

2. Marion bought half a dozen muffins that cost $1.50 each. Which of the following is a way to find how much she spent in <u>dollars</u>?

    (A) $6 \times 1\dfrac{1}{2}$

    (B) 6×150

    (C) $6 \times \dfrac{1.50}{2}$

    (D) $6 \times \dfrac{150}{2}$

    (E) $\dfrac{1}{6} \times 150$

3. If N is a whole number, then which of the following numbers can be written as $5N + 3$?

    (A) 15
    (B) 35
    (C) 37
    (D) 48
    (E) 50

$$\frac{1}{2}x+4$$

4. If x is a whole number, the expression shown above could represent which of the following?

    I.   The number of hours William does homework in a day if he works for half an hour four times

    II. The number of miles it takes to drive halfway to a destination that is more than four miles away

    III. The number of people left in a club if half the members leave and then four more members join

    (A) I only
    (B) III only
    (C) I and II only
    (D) I and III only
    (E) I, II, and III

5. In the expression $\frac{x}{yz}$, if x, y, and z are each doubled, then the original expression is

    (A) multiplied by 2
    (B) multiplied by 4
    (C) divided by 2
    (D) divided by 4
    (E) left unchanged

Algebraic Equations

❑ An equation has two expressions that are set equal to each other. If there is a single variable in the equation, the variable usually has a certain value that will satisfy the equation by making both sides equal.

> If $n + 3 = 8$, then what does n equal?
>
> In this equation, n is the variable. If we put 5 in for n, we get $5 + 3 = 8$, which is a true statement. In other words, n represents the number 5. 5 is the only value of n that satisfies the equation.

❑ To solve an equation, get the variable by itself on one side of the equal sign.

As you work to get the variable by itself, keep the equation balanced. If you do something to one side, such as add a number or divide by a number, you must do the same to the other side.

> Solve for x: $5x + 10 = 30$
>
> We will try to get the x alone on the left side of the equal sign.
>
> Step 1: Subtract 10 from both sides of the equation.
>
> $$5x + 10 = 30$$
> $$-10\ -10$$
> $$5x = 20$$
>
> Step 2: Divide both sides by 5.
>
> $$\frac{5x}{5} = \frac{20}{5} \quad \Rightarrow \quad x = 4$$

❑ When multiplying or dividing by a negative number, pay close attention to positive and negative signs.

Remember: Negative × Negative = Positive, and Negative × Positive = Negative

$$-2x - 8 = 14 \quad \Rightarrow \quad \begin{array}{c} -2x - 8 = 14 \\ \div -2 \quad \div -2 \end{array} \quad \Rightarrow \quad x + 4 = -7 \quad \Rightarrow \quad x = -11$$

❑ After you have solved an equation, check your answer by plugging your answer back into the original equation.

good 11/22/2018 age 11

TRY IT OUT

For each equation, find the value of the variable:

1. $R - 1 = 10$

    11

2. $n + 5 = 10$

    5

3. $(25,000) \times 0 = N$

    0

4. $x + 1 = 1,001$

    1000

5. $\Delta + 100 = 150$

    50

6. $100 \times N = 100$

    1

7. $4 + x + 4 = 28$

    20

8. $S - 20 = 105$

    125

9. $36 - T = 26$

    10

10. $2N = 26$

    13

11. $2N + N = 60$

    20

12. $\frac{1}{2} n = 50$

    100

13. 50% of y equals 30.

    60

14. $2x + 3 = 27$

    12

15. $4x - 2 = 14$

    4

16. $\frac{1}{3} n + 4 = 10$

    18

PUT IT TOGETHER

1. If $16 \times N = 16$, then $16 + N =$

    (A) 1
    (B) 15
    (C) 16
    (D) 17
    (E) 32

2. Which is true when $x = 9$?

    (A) $2x + 1 = 20$
    (B) $14 = 2x - 5$
    (C) $x + 2 \times 4 = 44$
    (D) $5(x - 4) = 25$
    (E) $44 = 5 + 3x$

3. If $x + 10 = y$, then $x + 17 =$

    (A) $y - 7$
    (B) $y - 3$
    (C) $y + 3$
    (D) $y + 7$
    (E) $y + 10$

4. If $2 + x + y = 18$, what is the value of $x + y$?

    (A) 7
    (B) 8
    (C) 9
    (D) 11
    (E) 16

5. If $m + 2n = 2m + n$, which of the following must be true?

    (A) $m = n$
    (B) $m = 2n$
    (C) $2m = n$
    (D) $3m = n$
    (E) $3 = mn$

---

6. If $2x - y = 7$ and $4 + 3y = 19$, then $x - y = ?$

    (A) -3
    (B) -2
    (C) 1
    (D) 3
    (E) 8

Translating

❑ Transforming words into mathematical equations is the first step in solving many SSAT problems. It is especially helpful in solving word problems.

❑ Learn the following common translations:

Words	Translation
of	×
product of	×
more than	+ or >
sum	+
increased by	+
less than	− or <
difference	−
decreased by	−
is, are, was	=
what	x
% or percent	÷100

❑ Translate math sentences word-by-word.

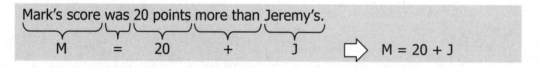

Mark's score was 20 points more than Jeremy's.

$$M \quad = \quad 20 \quad + \quad J \quad \Rightarrow \quad M = 20 + J$$

18 is three times the difference of 9 and a number. What is the number?

$$18 = \quad 3 \quad \times \quad (9-n) \quad \Rightarrow \quad 18 = 3(9-n) \Rightarrow$$

$$n = 3$$

TRY IT OUT

Change the following to mathematical equations, and solve for variables when possible:

1. 50% of 24 is x.

2. 6 fewer than y is 17.

3. 1/2 of 28 is what?

4. u more than 9 is a.

5. 1 increased by z equals what?

6. The sum of u, v, and w is 9.

7. The product of 7 and 4 is y.

8. -5 is the average of a, b, and c.

9. Sam is 2 years younger than Fred.

10. Twice N increased by 1 is 11.

PUT IT TOGETHER

1. Andy had N tokens more than twice as many tokens as Drew has. If Drew has 18 tokens, how many tokens does Andy have?

    (A) $18 + 2N$
    (B) $36 + 2N$
    (C) $36 - 2N$
    (D) $36 + N$
    (E) $36 - N$

2. Xavier has three times as many cards as Anna has. If Anna has N cards, which of the following expressions represents the total number of cards they have together?

    (A) $N + N$
    (B) $3N$
    (C) $3 + N$
    (D) $3N + N$
    (E) $3 \times (N + N)$

Word Problems

❑ Word problems are **very** common on the SSAT. Practice until you feel confident solving them.

❑ The text makes it difficult to determine what you are being given and what you are being asked to find. Here are four basic steps for solving word problems.

Step 1: Make certain you know what you are being asked.

After reading the question, state in your own words what the problem is asking you to find.

Step 2: Break the problem down into manageable parts.

In order to understand the bigger picture, you need to understand the smaller parts. Break the problem into its parts and make certain you understand each of them.

Step 3: Translate the parts into "math language."

Step 4: Use the math equations you have set up to get the answer.

A car dealer has twice as many Fords as Chryslers. He has 300 cars total. How many Fords does he have?

(A) 100
(B) 150
(C) 200
(D) 250
(E) 900

Step 1: How many Fords does he have? Let F = # of Fords.

Step 2: He has twice as many Fords as Chryslers. He has 300 cars total.

Step 3: $F = 2C$

$F + C = 300$

Step 4: $2C + C = 300$ (substitute)

$C = 100$

Since $F = 2C$, $F = 200$

TRY IT OUT

Try the following word problems:

1. Five less than seven times a certain number is 58. Find the number.

2. Tommy has six times as many apples as Bobby. Bobby has 7 more apples than Alice. If Alice has 2 apples, how many apples does Tommy have?

3. Suzy has 3 times as many marbles as Marty. Marty has 4 marbles less than Joey. If together they have 34 marbles, how many marbles does Joey have?

4. The length of a rectangle is 2 more than the width. If the perimeter of the rectangle is 48, what is the width of the rectangle?

5. The sum of 2 numbers is 18 and their difference is 8. What is the larger of the two numbers?

PUT IT TOGETHER

1. Ricky runs twice as fast as he jogs. If he can run a mile in 6 minutes, how many minutes will it take him to jog a mile?

    (A) 15
    (B) 12
    (C) 9
    (D) 3
    (E) 2

2. A trip on a ferry costs $15 for one person and $8 for each additional person. If seven people share the cost of a ferry trip equally, how much does each pay?

    (A) $9
    (B) $10
    (C) $11
    (D) $12
    (E) $13

3. A store sold $\frac{1}{2}$ of its T.V.s on Monday, and $\frac{1}{8}$ of its remaining T.V.s on Tuesday. If 7 T.V.s remained, how many T.V.s did the store start with on Monday morning?

    (A) 6
    (B) 12
    (C) 16
    (D) 24
    (E) 32

4. By accepting 40 more students, a school increased its total number of students by 25%. How many students did the school have after the increase?

    (A) 120
    (B) 160
    (C) 180
    (D) 200
    (E) 220

5. There are 22 students in a class and 14 of them are
    female. If 16 of the students have brown eyes, and if 3 of
    the male students do not have brown eyes, what is the
    total number of female students with brown eyes in the
    class?

    (A) 3
    (B) 9
    (C) 11
    (D) 13
    (E) 17

6. In the middle of a game, Team A was winning by 7
    points. In the end, Team B won by 4 points. If Team A
    scored 13 points in the second half of the game, how
    many points did Team B score in the second half of the
    game?

    (A) 2
    (B) 10
    (C) 11
    (D) 21
    (E) 24

7. A guitar and case sold for a regular price of $200 total.
    During a sale, the guitar was sold for half its regular price,
    and the total price for the guitar and case was $120. What
    was the price of the case?

    (A) $20
    (B) $40
    (C) $50
    (D) $60
    (E) $80

SSAT Functions

❑ On SSAT function problems, you will be asked to solve an equation using an unfamiliar symbol. The symbol represents the mathematical function to be carried out.

❑ Get comfortable with SSAT functions. The test writers have made up the symbols to confuse you. Don't panic when you encounter "@" or any other weird symbol. Just plug in the numbers or variables you're given, and simplify the expression.

SSAT function questions will give you an equation that shows how the function works. Use this like a formula or a set of directions to follow for whatever values are put into the function.

For all real numbers a and b, $a@b = \dfrac{a+b}{ab}$. What does $5@7$ equal?

In this question, $a = 5$, $b = 7$. Rewrite the expression, putting in a 5 for every a, and a 7 for every b:

$$5@7 \quad \Rightarrow \quad \frac{5+7}{5\times 7} \quad \Rightarrow \quad \frac{12}{35}$$

TRY IT OUT

The following definition applies to questions 1-3.

For all real numbers A, B, and C, $\langle A,B,C\rangle = \dfrac{A+B}{C}$

1. $\langle 2,4,1\rangle =$

    (A) 4
    (B) 5
    (C) 6
    (D) 12
    (E) 16

2. What is the value of x, if $\langle x,4,10\rangle = 1.4$?

    (A) 9
    (B) 10
    (C) 11
    (D) 12
    (E) 15

3. Which of the following must be true?

    I.   If $A = -B$, then $\langle A,B,C\rangle = 0$

    II. If $C = 0$, then $\langle A,B,C\rangle = 0$

    III. If $A = B = C$, then $\langle A,B,C\rangle = 2$

    (A) I only
    (B) II only
    (C) I and III only
    (D) II and III only
    (E) I, II, and III only

The following definition applies to questions 4 and 5.

For all real numbers S, R, and T,

$$\triangle \begin{smallmatrix} S \\ R\ T \end{smallmatrix} = (S\times 3R)+(S\times 5T).$$

4. $\triangle \begin{smallmatrix} 2 \\ 0\ 1 \end{smallmatrix} =$

    (A) 0
    (B) 8
    (C) 10
    (D) 40
    (E) 450

5. If $\triangle \begin{smallmatrix} 4 \\ n\ n \end{smallmatrix} = 160$, what is the value of n?

    (A) 5
    (B) 10
    (C) 20
    (D) 40
    (E) None of the above.

PUT IT TOGETHER

1. If $[\![n]\!] = 2n^2 - 2$, then $[\![5]\!] =$

   (A) 18
   (B) 38
   (C) 48
   (D) 88
   (E) 98

Questions 2-3 are based on the following definition.

$$\Uparrow x = x+2 \ \text{ when } \ x \le 4$$
$$\Uparrow x = x-3 \ \text{ when } \ x > 4$$

2. If $\Uparrow 3 = 5$ and $\Uparrow\Uparrow\Uparrow 3 = 2$, then $\Uparrow\Uparrow\Uparrow\Uparrow 4 =$

   (A) 2
   (B) 3
   (C) 4
   (D) 5
   (E) 6

3. Which of the following is equal to 6?

   (A) $\Uparrow\Uparrow\Uparrow 1$
   (B) $\Uparrow\Uparrow\Uparrow 2$
   (C) $\Uparrow\Uparrow\Uparrow 3$
   (D) $\Uparrow\Uparrow\Uparrow 4$
   (E) $\Uparrow\Uparrow\Uparrow 5$

Questions 4-6 refer to the table in Figure 1.

For any two positive numbers x and y, $\langle x|y \rangle = \dfrac{x-2}{y-3}$

Example: $\langle 4|8 \rangle = \dfrac{4-2}{8-3} = \dfrac{2}{5}$

Figure 1

4. If $\langle m|n \rangle = 0$, what is the value of m?

   (A) 1
   (B) 2
   (C) 3
   (D) 4
   (E) 5

5. If $j = k$ and $\langle j|k \rangle = 2$, what is the value of k?

   (A) 7
   (B) 6
   (C) 5
   (D) 4
   (E) 3

6. For integers s and t, $\langle s|t \rangle$ can result in which of the following?

   I.   a positive integer
   II. a positive fraction
   III. a negative integer
   IV. a negative fraction
   V.   zero

   (A) I, II, and V only
   (B) I and III only
   (C) II and IV only
   (D) III, IV, and V only
   (E) I, II, III, IV, and V

Inequalities

❑ An inequality contains one of the following symbols:

> greater than

< less than

≥ greater than or equal to

≤ less than or equal to

❑ The solution to an inequality can be a range of numbers.

> N is a number between 6 and 11. What are the possible values of N?
>
> $6 < N < 11$

> N is an odd number greater than 5 but less than 20. What are some possible values of N?
>
> In this case, the variable N can be one of several numbers: 7, 9, 11, 13, 15, 17, 19.

❑ Inequalities can be solved just like equations, with one important difference: if you multiply or divide both sides by a negative number, you must switch the direction of the inequality sign.

$$2x + 4 < 10 \implies \begin{matrix} 2x + 4 < 10 \\ -4 \quad -4 \end{matrix} \implies 2x < 6 \implies \begin{matrix} 2x < 6 \\ \div 2 \quad \div 2 \end{matrix} \implies x < 3$$

$$-2x + 4 < 10 \implies \begin{matrix} -2x + 4 < 10 \\ -4 \quad -4 \end{matrix} \implies -2x < 6 \implies \begin{matrix} -2x < 6 \\ \div 2 \quad \div 2 \end{matrix} \implies x > -3$$

TRY IT OUT

Write the set of numbers that expresses the possible values for each of the following variables.

1. N is a whole number between 2 and 5.

2. T is a positive odd number less than 9.

3. X is a negative integer greater than –3.

Write the inequality that expresses the range of possible values for each of the following variables.

4. $n + 2 > 6$

5. $x - 5 \leq 13$

6. $3x + 2 < 8$

7. $4s - 3 \geq 3$

8. $-x + 6 > 10$

9. $-2r + 1 < 7$

10. $-3m - 1 > -10$

PUT IT TOGETHER

1. If $5 < N < 10$, and N is a multiple of 4, then $N =$

    (A) -4
    (B) 0
    (C) 4
    (D) 8
    (E) 12

2. If half a certain number is greater than 21, then the number can be which of the following?

    (A) 10
    (B) 11
    (C) 22
    (D) 42
    (E) 84

3. If the value of $\frac{1}{3} + N < 1$, then N could be each of the

    following EXCEPT

    (A) $\frac{1}{3}$

    (B) $\frac{1}{2}$

    (C) $\frac{2}{3}$

    (D) $\frac{3}{5}$

    (E) $\frac{5}{8}$

4. If $x < 3$, then $4x + 11$ could be

   (A) 41
   (B) 27
   (C) 24
   (D) 23
   (E) 0

---

5. If $3(M + N) < 0$, then which of the following must be true?

   (A) $M > N$
   (B) $M < N$
   (C) $M - N > 0$
   (D) $M + N < 0$
   (E) $N - M < 0$

Chapter Review

❏ **Algebraic Expressions**

To simplify an algebraic expression, combine similar terms.

Be careful when distributing a negative number. You must carry the negative sign through the entire distribution.

❏ **Algebraic Equations**

To solve algebraic equations, isolate the variable on one side of the equal sign. Remember to keep the equation balanced.

Many SSAT algebraic equations can be solved by plugging in the answer choices.

❏ **Translating**

Know how to translate words into math symbols.

❏ **Word Problems**

There are 4 basic steps for solving word problems:

1. Make certain you know what you are being asked.

2. Break the problem down into manageable parts.

3. Translate the parts into "math language."

4. Use the math equations to solve the problem.

Use the answer choices and work backwards.

❑ SSAT Functions

Identify the relationship between the SSAT function and the math equation.

Plug in numbers for variables.

❑ **Inequalities**

The solution to an inequality can be a range of numbers.

Inequalities can be solved just like equations, with one important difference: if you multiply or divide both sides by a negative number, you must switch the direction of the inequality sign.

Algebra Practice

Algebraic Expressions

1. If x is a whole number, which of the following numbers can be written in the form $3x + 2$?

    (A) 54
    (B) 61
    (C) 72
    (D) 86
    (E) 93

2. Last year, Mark read t more books than Rob did. If Rob read 6 books last year, how many books did Mark read last year?

    (A) 6
    (B) $6 + t$
    (C) $6 - t$
    (D) $6 \times t$
    (E) It cannot be determined from the information given.

3. If a piece of gum costs x cents, then how many pieces of gum can you buy with $3.00?

    (A) $3 - x$
    (B) $x - 3$
    (C) $3x$
    (D) $3 \div x$
    (E) $300 \div x$

4. Rebecca is n years old. John is twice as old as Rebecca was 3 years ago. How old is John in terms of n?

    (A) $2n - 6$
    (B) $2n - 3$
    (C) $n + 8$
    (D) $2n + 2$
    (E) $2n + 5$

5. In one year, Bill will be three times as old as Monica. If Monica is M years old now, how old is Bill now?

(A) $3M+2$
(B) $3M-3$
(C) $3M-1$
(D) $3M+3$
(E) $\dfrac{M+1}{3}$

Algebraic Equations

6. If $2\times(M+N)=6$ and M is an integer, then N could NOT be

(A) -3
(B) 0
(C) 1
(D) 1.5
(E) 2

7. If $y = x + 1$, then which of the following is equal to $x - 3$?

(A) $y+4$
(B) $y+2$
(C) $y-2$
(D) $y-4$
(E) It cannot be determined from the information given.

8. If $3 \times 8 \times y = 0$, then $y =$

(A) -24
(B) -11
(C) 0
(D) $\dfrac{1}{24}$
(E) 1

9. If x and y are positive numbers and $\dfrac{(x-y)}{1}=1$,

which of the following must be true?

(A) y is greater than x
(B) $y=1$
(C) $x=y$
(D) $y=x+1$
(E) $x=y+1$

Translating

10. When 12 is divided by a number, the result is 6. When the same number is increased by 10, the result is

(A) 4
(B) 8
(C) 10
(D) 12
(E) 16

11. If 5 times N is 20, then 5 times $N+1$ is

(A) 15
(B) 25
(C) 30
(D) 60
(E) 105

Word Problems

12. It took Alice 45 minutes to complete her math homework. It took Diane t minutes to complete her science homework. What is the total amount of time that Alice and Diane spent on their homework?

(A) 45 minutes
(B) t minutes
(C) $45+t$ minutes
(D) $45\times t$ minutes
(E) $45-t$

13. At a peanut processing plant, 1/5 of all raw peanuts that arrive at the facility are not suitable to be processed and sold. If 1,000 pounds of peanuts need to be prepared for selling, how many pounds of raw peanuts should be received at the processing plant?

    (A) 1,100
    (B) 1,200
    (C) 1,250
    (D) 1,400
    (E) 1,500

14. For every hammer in a shop, there are between 6 and 8 screwdrivers. If there are y hammers in the shop, what is the largest number of hammers and screwdrivers that could be in the shop?

    (A) $8y+8$
    (B) $y+8$
    (C) $8y+6$
    (D) $9y$
    (E) $14y$

SSAT Functions

Questions 15 – 16 refer to the following definition.

For all real numbers r and s, $r \lozenge s = (r \times s) + (r - s)$

For example, $8 \lozenge 4 = (8 \times 4) + (8 - 4) = 32 + 4 = 36$

15. $5 \lozenge 2 =$

    (A) 3
    (B) 5
    (C) 10
    (D) 13
    (E) 17

16. If $N \lozenge 3 = 29$, then $N =$

    (A) 2
    (B) 8
    (C) 9
    (D) 26
    (E) 32

Inequalities

17. M is a whole number less than 11 and greater than 5.
Which of the following CANNOT be M?

(A) 10
(B) 9
(C) 8
(D) 7.5
(E) 6

18. If $x \leq 3$, then $x + 2$ must be less than or equal to

(A) 1
(B) 2
(C) 3
(D) 4
(E) 5

19. If $x + 2$ is greater than 5, then $3x$ could be which
of the following?

(A) 1
(B) 2
(C) 6
(D) 9
(E) 15

Algebra Practice
Middle Level

1. If $63,072 = 20,000 + 43,010 + N$, then $N =$

   (A) 9
   (B) 59
   (C) 62
   (D) 69
   (E) 72

---

2. If $3N = 24$, then $9N =$

   (A) 24
   (B) 27
   (C) 32
   (D) 48
   (E) 72

---

3. If $\dfrac{5}{6} = \dfrac{x}{24}$, then $x =$

   (A) 10
   (B) 15
   (C) 20
   (D) 24
   (E) 27

---

4. $7(1+10+100) = 420+57+\Phi$. What does Φ equal?

   (A) −6
   (B) 6
   (C) 300
   (D) 366
   (E) 400

5. If $40 \times x = 800,000$, what is x?

    (A) 2
    (B) 200
    (C) 2,000
    (D) 20,000
    (E) 200,000

6. If $\dfrac{100}{25} + \dfrac{70}{25} + \dfrac{A}{25} = 7$, what is A?

    (A) 0
    (B) 2
    (C) 5
    (D) 15
    (E) 25

7. When $x - 6 = 0$, what is the value of x?

    (A) –6
    (B) 6
    (C) x
    (D) 0
    (E) It cannot be determined from the information given.

8. If $18 \times w$ is an even integer, then w can be

    (A) 2
    (B) 3
    (C) 6
    (D) 7
    (E) all of the above

9. If $17 \times 11 = N$, $N =$

    (A) 17
    (B) 71
    (C) 78
    (D) 178
    (E) 187

10. If $100 + N = 110$, then $101 \times N =$

   (A) 10
   (B) 101
   (C) 202
   (D) 1,010
   (E) 4,001

---

11. If $200 \div q = 10$, what is q?

   (A) 2
   (B) 10
   (C) 20
   (D) 100
   (E) 200

---

12. If $419 \div 10 = 41$ with a remainder of R, what is R?

   (A) 2
   (B) 3
   (C) 5
   (D) 7
   (E) 9

---

13. How many months are there in M years?

   (A) M
   (B) $M \times 12$
   (C) $M \times 100$
   (D) $100 \div M$
   (E) 100

---

14. If $y = 47$, then 10% of $10y = $?

   (A) 4.7
   (B) 47
   (C) 50
   (D) 147
   (E) 470

15. The sum of 3 consecutive integers is 4 times the smallest number. What is the largest number?

    (A) 3
    (B) 4
    (C) 5
    (D) 6
    (E) 7

Let $\because N$ be defined as followed for all integers N:

$\because N = 2N$ if N is even.
$\because N = 3N$ if N is odd.

16. What is the value of $(\because 50) + (\because 1)$?

    (A) 51
    (B) 102
    (C) 103
    (D) 152
    (E) 153

---

17. If $2N + 5 = N + 30$, then $N =$

    (A) 10
    (B) 15
    (C) 20
    (D) 25
    (E) 30

---

18. If 20 is 60% of X, then 20 is 30% of what?

    (A) X
    (B) $2X$
    (C) $3X$
    (D) $4X$
    (E) $6X$

19. A is less than 1, but greater than 0. Which of the following must be true?

    (A) $3A < 1$

    (B) $\dfrac{1}{A} < 1$

    (C) $A > \dfrac{1}{A}$

    (D) $A > A^2$

    (E) $A + 1 < 1$

20. When N is divided by 4, the remainder is 2. What is the remainder when N is divided by 2?

    (A) 4
    (B) 3
    (C) 2
    (D) 1
    (E) 0

21. If 50% of X is 20, what is 25% of X?

    (A) 5
    (B) 10
    (C) 20
    (D) 40
    (E) 100

22. $12\square + 210 = \square\square\square$, where $\square$ is a digit. What digit does $\square$ represent?

    (A) 0
    (B) 1
    (C) 2
    (D) 3
    (E) 12

23. If $N \times N \times N = 1$, then $N =$

    (A) $\frac{1}{3}$

    (B) $\frac{1}{2}$

    (C) 1

    (D) $\frac{3}{2}$

    (E) 2

---

24. If $15 \times 13 = (100 \times 1) + (10 \times 9) + (1 \times \Omega)$, what is the value of Ω?

    (A) 1
    (B) 3
    (C) 4
    (D) 5
    (E) 6

---

25. Which of the following gives the best approximation for the number of days in w weeks, m months, and y years?

    (A) $\frac{w}{7} + \frac{m}{30} + \frac{y}{365}$

    (B) $\frac{7}{w} + \frac{30}{m} + \frac{365}{y}$

    (C) $365y + 30m + 7w$

    (D) $365y + 30m + w$

    (E) $y + m + w$

Algebra Practice

Upper Level

1. 3 less than 4 times a number is 17. What is the number?

    (A) 2
    (B) 5
    (C) 12
    (D) 20
    (E) 51

2. Which value of N does NOT satisfy $\dfrac{N}{4}+\dfrac{2}{3}>\dfrac{1}{6}$?

    (A) 2
    (B) 1
    (C) 0
    (D) -1
    (E) -2

3. If N is an integer, and $3(N+1)$ is even, which of the following CANNOT be true?

    (A) N is odd
    (B) N is even
    (C) $N+1$ is even
    (D) N is negative
    (E) $3N+3$ is even

4. If $y=8$, then $(y-1)^{2}=$

    (A) 81
    (B) 64
    (C) 49
    (D) 36
    (E) 25

5. *P* is a prime number less than 9. Which of the following
    CANNOT be *P*?

    (A) 2
    (B) 3
    (C) 4
    (D) 5
    (E) 7

6. If *M* > 2, then 2*M* + 2 CANNOT be

    (A) 14
    (B) 12
    (C) 10
    (D) 8
    (E) 6

7. If *m* + 5 = 10 and *n* − 6 = 3, then *m* × *n* =

    (A) 54
    (B) 45
    (C) 35
    (D) 14
    (E) 11

8. If $\dfrac{37}{A} = A \times 37$, what is the value of $A \times A$?

    (A) $\dfrac{1}{1,369}$

    (B) 1
    (C) 1,369

    (D) $\dfrac{1}{37}$

    (E) 37

9. Juan scored *N* − 5 points in the basketball game. Seth
    scored 2 more points than Juan. How many points did
    Seth score?

    (A) *N* − 7
    (B) *N* − 5
    (C) *N* − 3
    (D) *N*
    (E) *N* + 7

10. If $151 - A = 150$, then $150 \times A =$

    (A) 0

    (B) $\dfrac{1}{151}$

    (C) 1

    (D) 150

    (E) 151

---

11. What is $2N$ if $\dfrac{1}{2}N = 15$?

    (A) 5

    (B) 15

    (C) 30

    (D) 45

    (E) 60

---

12. If $50 - y = 50$, then $50y =$

    (A) −50

    (B) 0

    (C) $\dfrac{1}{50}$

    (D) 1

    (E) 10

---

13. Adding which of the following to $\dfrac{3}{7}$ will give a sum that is greater than 1?

    (A) $\dfrac{3}{7}$

    (B) $\dfrac{4}{7}$

    (C) $\dfrac{1}{2}$

    (D) $\dfrac{2}{5}$

    (E) $\dfrac{5}{8}$

14. If $(A+B) \div 6 > 2$, and A is equal to 7, B could be which of the following?

    (A) -3
    (B) 0
    (C) 4
    (D) $4\frac{1}{2}$
    (E) 6

15. If n is an even integer, which of the following must be an odd integer?

    (A) $n \div 2$
    (B) $3n$
    (C) $2n+1$
    (D) $n-2$
    (E) $2n$

$$R \rightarrow 1 = R$$
$$R \rightarrow 2 = 2R + R$$
$$R \rightarrow 3 = 3R + 2R + R$$

16. Following the pattern above, $R \rightarrow 4 =$

    (A) $5R$
    (B) $6R$
    (C) $7R$
    (D) $9R$
    (E) $10R$

17. X is equal to $\frac{2.8}{100}$. $10X$ is closest to which of the following?

    (A) 0.2
    (B) 0.3
    (C) 2.8
    (D) 28
    (E) 30

18. If $6y = 2x + 6$, then which of the following equals $3y$?

    (A) x
    (B) $6 - x$
    (C) $x + 3$
    (D) $x + 6$
    (E) $2x + 3$

19. If P is an integer, $4P - 1$ could be which of the following?

    (A) 10
    (B) 11
    (C) 12
    (D) 13
    (E) 14

20. If $245 = (2 \times A) + (4 \times B) + (5 \times C)$, which of the following could be true?

    (A) $A = 10$, $B = 1$, $C = 0$
    (B) $A = 10$, $B = 10$, $C = 10$
    (C) $A = 1$, $B = 1$, $C = 1$
    (D) $A = 100$, $B = 10$, $C = 1$
    (E) $A = 100$, $B = 10$, $C = 0$

21. If $2A$ is an odd integer, which of the following must be true?

    I. A is not an integer.
    II. $3A$ is also an odd integer.
    III. $3A + 1$ is also an odd integer.

    (A) I only
    (B) III only
    (C) I and III only
    (D) I and II only
    (E) I, II, and III

22. If L is a non-zero whole number, then $L \times (L+1)$ is always

 (A) odd
 (B) even
 (C) 0
 (D) negative
 (E) positive

___

23. 30% of $N =$

 (A) $3N$
 (B) $30N$
 (C) 15% of $2N$
 (D) $\dfrac{3}{100} \times N$
 (E) $\dfrac{1}{3}N$

___

24. If $3x < 9$, which of the following is a possible value of x?

 (A) 27
 (B) 9
 (C) 4.5
 (D) 3
 (E) 2

___

25. 500 books make up a collection. 125 books make up a bookshelf. 34 books make up a hobby. How many books are represented by c collections, b bookshelves, and 2 hobbies?

 (A) $\dfrac{c+b+2h}{500+125+34}$
 (B) $500c + 125b + 17h$
 (C) $\dfrac{a}{500} + \dfrac{b}{125} + \dfrac{2h}{34}$
 (D) $500c + 125b + 34h$
 (E) $500c + 125b + 68$

SUMMIT
EDUCATIONAL
GROUP

Geometry

- ❑ Angles
- ❑ Pairs of Angles
- ❑ Parallel Lines
- ❑ Triangles
- ❑ Area and Perimeter
- ❑ Circles
- ❑ Estimating Figures
- ❑ Volume
- ❑ Coordinate Plane
- ❑ Slope
- ❑ Graphing Lines

Geometry

❑ About one-fifth of SSAT math is geometry. In general, the geometric concepts you need to know deal with angle measurement, perimeter, and area.

❑ In this chapter, you will:

- study the basic geometric concepts of angles, perimeter, area, volume, and parallel lines.

- learn different strategies for attacking SSAT geometry problems.

Vocabulary

❑ To **bisect** means to divide into two equal parts.

❑ A **vertex** is a corner or a point where lines meet.

❑ **Perimeter** is the distance around the edge of a two-dimensional figure.

❑ **Area** is the measurement of the space inside a two-dimensional figure. Area is measured in square units.

❑ **Volume** is the amount of space occupied by a three-dimensional figure.

❑ **Coordinates** are the pairs of numbers which specify the position of points in a two-dimensional coordinate plane.

❑ It is important to understand common geometric symbols and notations.

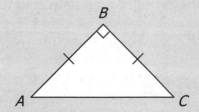

Triangles are denoted by the letter at their corners, or "vertices."
The triangle above is $\triangle ABC$.

Line segments are denoted by their endpoints.
The figure above contains line segments $\overline{AB}$, $\overline{BC}$, and $\overline{AC}$.

Tick marks are used to indicate line segments of equal length.
In the figure above, $AB = BC$.

90° angles are indicated by a small square at the vertex.
Angles are denoted by the vertex, or by three points with the vertex in the middle.
In the figure above, $\angle B = 90°$, or $\angle ABC = 90°$.

Angles

❑ When two lines cross, they form one or more angles. Angles are measured in degrees.

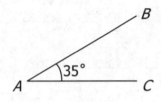

∠*BAC* has a measure of 35°.

A is the vertex.

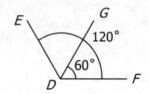

∠*EDF* has a measure of 120°.

Since $\overline{DG}$ splits ∠*EDF* into two equal angles, $\overline{DG}$ bisects ∠*EDF*.

❑ A **right angle** has a measure of 90°. This is indicated by a small square drawn at the vertex.

The lines that meet to form the right angle are said to be **perpendicular**.

The symbol for perpendicular is ⊥.

$\angle ABC = 90°$

$AB \perp BC$

❑ A **straight line** is a 180° angle.

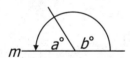

Line *m* has a measure of 180°.

Notice that $a + b = 180°$.

❑ There are 360° in a **circle**.

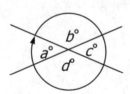

$a + b + c + d = 360°$

❑ Unless a problem says differently, all figures are drawn to scale. On figures that are drawn to scale, you can sometimes narrow down your answer choices by estimating angles.

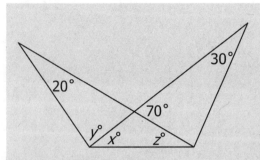

In the figure above, if $y = 2x$, $z =$

(A) 25
(B) 45
(C) 55
(D) 65
(E) 70

This problem is difficult, but because the figure is drawn to scale, estimation is a viable strategy.

z looks like it is less than half of a right angle, so it is likely less than 45°. (A) is the only answer choice less than 45, and it is the correct answer.

TRY IT OUT

1. Draw a 45° angle.

2. Draw a 60° angle.

3. Draw a 90° angle.

4. Draw a 120° angle.

Guess the measures of each of these four angles:

5.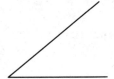

7.

6.

8.

9. What is the angle measure of each of the 4 corners of this page?

10. How many degrees are in a quarter of a circle?

11. If the hands of a watch read 3:00, what is the measure of the angle formed by the hands? What is the measure of the angle formed by the hands at 4:00?

12. Draw a line from the upper right corner of this page down to the lower left corner. Estimate the measures of the angles formed by this line and the edges of the page.

13. In the figure below, $x =$

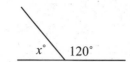

14. In the figure below, if $x = 35°$, what does y equal?

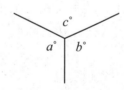

15. In the figure below, $y =$

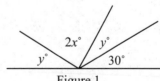

16. In the figure below, what is the sum of a, b and c?

PUT IT TOGETHER

1. If four lines meet as shown in Figure 1, what is the value of $x + y$?

    (A) 50
    (B) 60
    (C) 75
    (D) 150
    (E) It cannot be determined from the information given.

Figure 1

Pairs of Angles

❑ Two angles that are **congruent** have equal degree measures. Notice that it does not matter if the segments that form the angle are the same length.

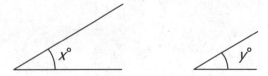

If the two angles above are congruent, then $x = y$.

❑ Two angles that share a common side are **adjacent**.

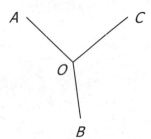

Since $\angle AOC$ and $\angle BOC$ share the common side $\overline{OC}$, they are adjacent angles.

❑ When two lines cross, four angles are formed. The angles opposite each other are called vertical angles. Vertical angles are equal.

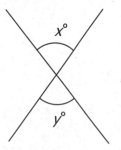

$x = y$

TRY IT OUT

Try the following:

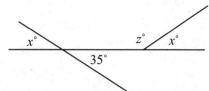

1. In the figure above, $z =$

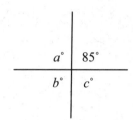

2. In the figure above, what are the values of a, b, and c?

PUT IT TOGETHER

1. In Figure 2, $x =$

    (A) 20
    (B) 40
    (C) 60
    (D) 180
    (E) 360

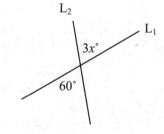

Figure 2

Parallel Lines

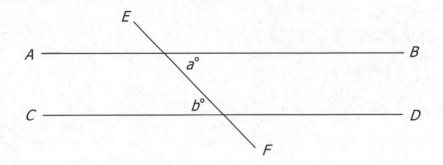

❑ Lines that would never cross if extended indefinitely are called **parallel lines**.

The opposite sides of a rectangle are parallel.

In the figure above, *AB* ∥ *CD*.

❑ A line that cuts across parallel lines is called a **transversal**.

In the figure above, *EF* is the transversal.

❑ The angles between the parallel lines that are on opposite sides of the transversal are called **alternate interior angles**.

Alternate interior angles are equal.

The marked angles in the figure above are alternate interior angles. *a* = *b*.

❑ A **parallelogram** is a four-sided shape with opposite sides parallel.

In a parallelogram, opposite sides are equal in length and opposite angles are equal in measure.

Squares and rectangles are parallelograms.

TRY IT OUT

Try the following:

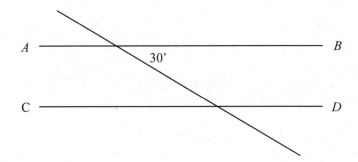

1. In the figure above, $AB \parallel CD$. Fill in the missing angles in the figure above.

PUT IT TOGETHER

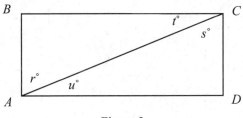

Figure 3

1. In the figure above, if $ABCD$ is a rectangle, which of the
    following must be true?

    (A) $r = t$
    (B) $r = u$
    (C) $r = 45°$
    (D) $t = u$
    (E) $u = s$

Triangles

❑ The sum of the three interior angles of a triangle is 180°.

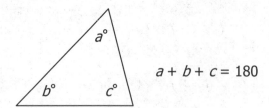

$a + b + c = 180$

❑ If you know two of the angles, you can figure out the third by adding the other two angles, and subtracting that sum from 180.

Solve for *a*.

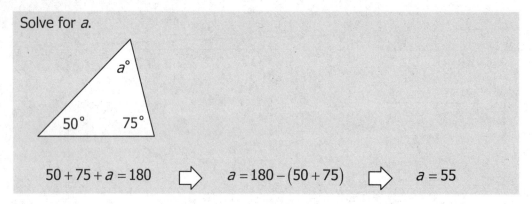

$50 + 75 + a = 180$ ⟹ $a = 180 - (50 + 75)$ ⟹ $a = 55$

Solve for *y* in terms of *x* and *z*.

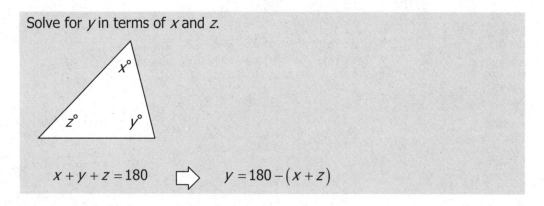

$x + y + z = 180$ ⟹ $y = 180 - (x + z)$

TRY IT OUT

Label the missing angle in each of the two triangles below:

1.

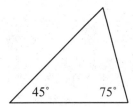

2.

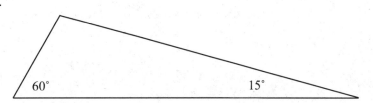

PUT IT TOGETHER

1. If two of the angles of a triangle are 56° and 42°, then the third angle is

   (A) 82°
   (B) 89°
   (C) 98°
   (D) 102°
   (E) 149°

---

2. If the angle measures of a triangle are represented by $2x°$, $3x°$, and $4x°$, what is the value of x?

   (A) 10
   (B) 20
   (C) 30
   (D) 40
   (E) It cannot be determined from the information given.

---

3. In Figure 4, the measures of three angles are shown. What is the value of $x + y + z$?

   (A) 180
   (B) 140
   (C) 120
   (D) 100
   (E) 60

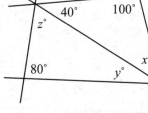

Figure 4

Isosceles and Equilateral Triangles

❑ An isosceles triangle is any triangle that has two equal sides. In addition, the angles opposite the congruent sides are equal.

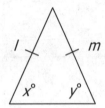

$l = m$ and $x = y$

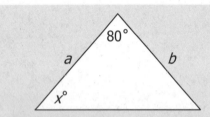

If $a = b$, what is the value of x?

Since sides a and b are equal, the triangle must be isosceles. Therefore, the angles opposite a and b must be equal. The angles of the triangle must be 80°, x°, and x°. Since the sum of the angles of a triangle is always 180°, we know that $80 + x + x = 180$.

$80 + 2x = 180$ ⟹ $2x = 100$ ⟹ $x = 50$

❑ An equilateral triangle is a triangle that has all three sides equal. In addition, all angles are 60°.

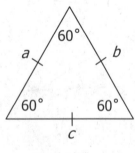

$a = b = c$

TRY IT OUT

Fill in the missing angles of the two triangles below:

1.

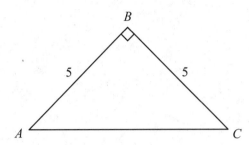

2.

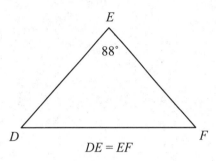

$DE = EF$

Fill in all the missing angles and sides in the triangle below:

3.

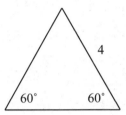

PUT IT TOGETHER

1. In Figure 5, what is the value of a?

    (A) 30
    (B) 45
    (C) 60
    (D) 90
    (E) It cannot be determined from the information given.

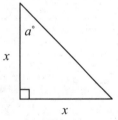

Figure 5

---

2. In Figure 6, if $z = 4x$, what is the value of y?

    (A) 30
    (B) 45
    (C) 60
    (D) 72
    (E) 90

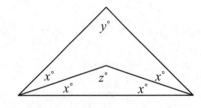

Figure 6
Note: Figure not drawn to scale.

Right Triangles

❑ A right triangle is any triangle that has a 90° angle as one of its angles.

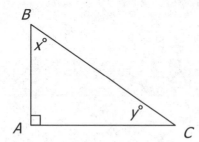

$\triangle ABC$ is a right triangle because $\angle BAC$ is a right angle.

Note: The sum of the two non-right angles in a right triangle is 90°. In the triangle above, $x + y = 90°$.

❑ The two sides that form the right angle are called the **legs**.

The third side is called the **hypotenuse**. The hypotenuse is opposite the right angle, and it is the longest side of a right triangle.

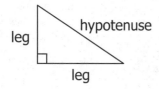

❑ The **Pythagorean Theorem** states that in any right triangle the square of the hypotenuse is equal to the sum of the squares of the other two sides.

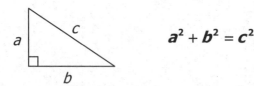

$$a^2 + b^2 = c^2$$

Find the value of x:

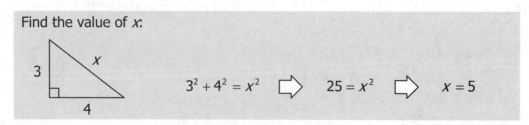

$3^2 + 4^2 = x^2$ ⟹ $25 = x^2$ ⟹ $x = 5$

TRY IT OUT

Try the following:

1. How do you know that the sum of the two non-right angles of a right triangle is 90°?

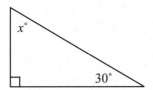

2. In the figure above, what is the value of x?

PUT IT TOGETHER

1. In a right isosceles triangle the three angles are

    (A) 45°, 45°, 90°
    (B) 30°, 60°, 90°
    (C) 40°, 40°, 100°
    (D) 60°, 60°, 60°
    (E) 50°, 50°, 100°

2. In Figure 7, if $z = 2x$, which of the following gives the value of y in terms of z?

    (A) $\dfrac{z}{2}$

    (B) $\dfrac{z}{3}$

    (C) $90 - \dfrac{z}{2}$

    (D) $180 - \dfrac{z}{2}$

    (E) $180 - z$

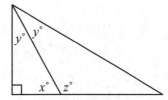

Figure 7

Area and Perimeter – Rectangle and Square

❑ **Perimeter** is the distance around the edge of a two-dimensional figure.

❑ **Area** is the measurement of the space inside a two-dimensional figure. Area is measured in square units.

❑ A **rectangle** is a 4-sided figure with 4 right angles. In a rectangle, opposite sides are equal.

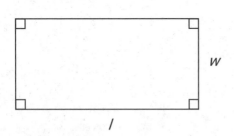

Perimeter   To find the perimeter of a rectangle, add the lengths of all of the sides.

$$Perimeter = l + l + w + w = (2 \times l) + (2 \times w)$$

Area   To find the area of a rectangle, multiply the length by the width.

$$Area = l \times w$$

❑ A **square** is a rectangle that has 4 equal sides.

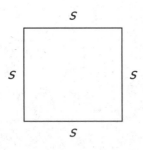

Perimeter   To find the perimeter of a square, add the lengths of all of the sides.

$$Perimeter = s + s + s + s = 4 \times s$$

Area   To find the area of a square, multiply one side by another side.

$$Area = s \times s$$

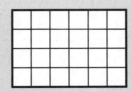

The rectangle above is divided into squares each 1 inch by 1 inch. What is the perimeter of the rectangle? What is the area?

To find the perimeter, we need the length and width. If we placed a ruler along the top edge of the rectangle and measured, we'd get 6 inches. (There are 6 squares along the top edge and each square has a length of 1 inch.) Similarly, for the width, we'd get 4 inches. Therefore, the perimeter of the rectangle is 6 + 6 + 4 + 4 = 20 inches.

The area is the space inside the rectangle measured in square units. One way to calculate the area is to count the squares. Each square is a square unit. Specifically, each square is one square inch. There are 24 squares (or square inches), so the area of the rectangle is 24 square inches.

A quicker way to calculate the area is to use the formula for area of a rectangle and multiply the length times the width. The length is 6 and the width is 4 so we get $6 \times 4 = 24$ square inches.

TRY IT OUT

Find the area and perimeter of the square and rectangle below:

1.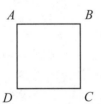

   ABCD is a square.

   $AB = 2$

   Perimeter of *ABCD* =

   Area of *ABCD* =

2.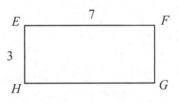

   Area of *EFGH* =

   Perimeter of *EFGH* =

PUT IT TOGETHER

1. Find the perimeter of the irregular shape in Figure 8.

    (A) 15 in.
    (B) 19 in.
    (C) 23 in.
    (D) 24 in.
    (E) 26 in.

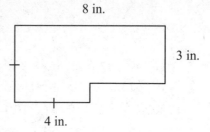

8 in.

3 in.

4 in.

Figure 8

2. In Figure 9, if *UVWX* is a square, the length of *VY* is 9, and the length of *VW* is 6, what is the area of rectangular region *YUXZ*?

    (A) 15
    (B) 18
    (C) 27
    (D) 36
    (E) 54

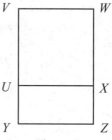

Figure 9

3. In Figure 10, *O* is the center of the circle that has a radius of 5 meters. What is the area, in square meters, of square *RSTU*?

    (A) 40
    (B) 80
    (C) 100
    (D) 160
    (E) 400

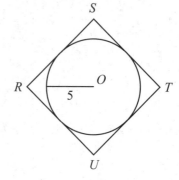

Figure 10

4. In Figure 11, *X* is a rectangular sheet of paper with a perimeter of 39 inches. *Y* shows the same sheet of paper after four squares, each with an area of 1 square inch, have been cut from the corners. What is the perimeter of the sheet of paper after it is cut?

    (A) 31 inches
    (B) 35 inches
    (C) 39 inches
    (D) 43 inches
    (E) 47 inches

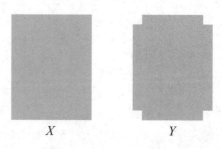

X   Y

Figure 11

5. In the figure below, rectangle *ABCD* has width 3 and
    length 5, and *AB* and *AD* bisect two squares, both with
    sides of length 2. What is the total area of the shaded
    regions?

    (A) 15
    (B) 16
    (C) 17
    (D) 18
    (E) 19

    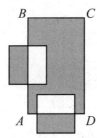

6. A rectangle is 2 centimeters longer than it is wide. If the
    perimeter is 28 centimeters, what is the area of the
    rectangle, in square centimeters?

    (A) 196
    (B) 192
    (C) 162
    (D) 56
    (E) 48

7. What is the greatest number of square blocks, 2 inches on
    each side, that can be placed into a storage box 13 inches
    long and 5 inches wide if no blocks can be stacked on top
    of each other?

    (A) 65
    (B) 48
    (C) 32
    (D) 16
    (E) 12

Area and Perimeter – Triangle

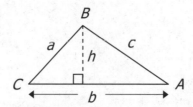

❑ To find the perimeter of a triangle, add the lengths of all of the sides.

   Perimeter of $\triangle ABC = a + b + c$

❑ To find the area of a triangle, use the following formula:

   $A = \frac{1}{2}bh$, where A = area, b = base, and h = height.

Note: The height of a triangle is not always the length of one of its sides. The height must be perpendicular from the base of the triangle.

TRY IT OUT

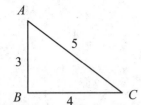

1. What is the perimeter of △*ABC* above?

2. What is the perimeter of an equilateral triangle that has one side of length 2?

3. The perimeter of an equilateral triangle is 18. What are the lengths of the sides of the triangle?

Find the area of each triangle below.

4.

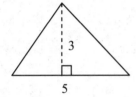

Area =

5.

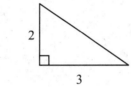

Area =

PUT IT TOGETHER

1. In Figure 12, if *WXYZ* is a square, what is the area of the shaded region?

    (A) 30
    (B) 24
    (C) 18
    (D) 16
    (E) 12

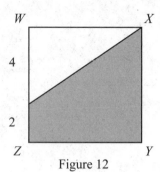

Figure 12

2. In Figure 13, shape *A* was made from shapes *B* and *C*. What is the perimeter of shape *A*?

    (A) 36
    (B) 32
    (C) 28
    (D) 16
    (E) 14

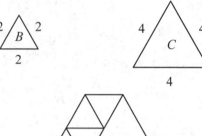

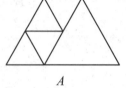

Figure 13

12

3. In Figure 14, W, X, Y, and Z are the midpoints of the line segments on which they lie. If A is the area of rectangular region $STUV$, what is the area of the shaded region, in terms of A?

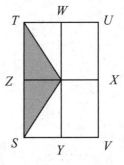

Figure 14

(A) $\dfrac{A}{2}$

(B) $\dfrac{A}{4}$

(C) $\dfrac{A}{6}$

(D) $\dfrac{A}{8}$

(E) $\dfrac{3}{4}A$

Circles

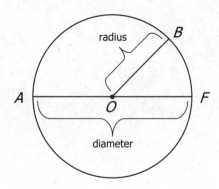

The **center** of the circle is located at *O*.

The **radius** of the circle ($\overline{OB}$) starts at the center and ends on the edge of the circle.

The **diameter** of the circle ($\overline{AF}$) cuts directly through the center of the circle and is twice the radius. All diameters have the same length.

❑ **Circumference** is the distance around the edge of the circle.

   Circumference $= 2 \times \pi \times r = \pi \times d$

❑ The **area** of a circle is found using the formula:

   Area $= \pi \times r^2$

❑ Pi (π), is the ratio of a circle's diameter to its circumference.

   The value of π is approximately 3.1416.

TRY IT OUT

Find the circumference of the circles below. Leave in terms of π.

1.

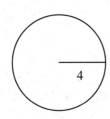

4

Radius = 4

Circumference =

2.

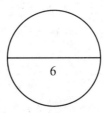

6

Diameter = 6

Circumference =

Find the area of each of the circles below:

3.

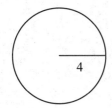

4

Radius = 4

Area =

4.

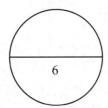

6

Diameter = 6

Area =

PUT IT TOGETHER

1. 24 coins are placed on the base of a rectangular display
    case as illustrated in Figure 15. The radius of each coin is
    half an inch. Which of the following is the area, in square
    inches, of the base of the display case?

    (A) 6
    (B) 12
    (C) 24
    (D) 36
    (E) 48

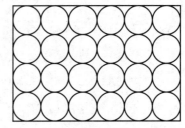

Figure 15

2. Circle A has a radius of 6. If Circle B has a radius half the
    length of the radius of Circle A, then the circumference of
    Circle B is

    (A) π
    (B) 3π
    (C) 6π
    (D) 9π
    (E) 12π

Estimating Figures

❑ Unless a problem says differently, all figures are drawn to scale. On figures that are drawn to scale, you can sometimes narrow down your answer choices by estimating lengths and areas.

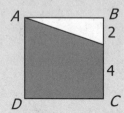

In the figure above, *ABCD* is a square. What is the area of the shaded region?

(A) 4
(B) 16
(C) 24
(D) 30
(E) 36

If you're not sure how to do this problem, estimating can help you get to the right answer.

Begin by finding the area of the square.

Since the side of the square is 6, the area of the square is 36.

The shaded area is definitely less than the 36, so eliminate (E).

It is more than half, so you can eliminate (A) and (B).

And it also looks like it is more than two-thirds of 36, so eliminate (C).

That leaves you with (D). (D) is the correct answer.

TRY IT OUT

Try the following by estimating:

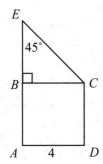

1. In the figure above, the length of a side of square *ABCD* is 4. What is the area of polygon *ABECD*?

    (A) 8
    (B) 16
    (C) 20
    (D) 24
    (E) 32

Volume

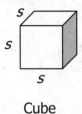

Cube

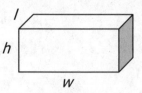

Rectangular Box

❑ **Volume** is the amount of space occupied by a three-dimensional figure.

❑ Volume of a cube: $V = s^3$

❑ Volume of a rectangular box: $V = l \times w \times h$

❑ To calculate the **weight** of a figure, you must first know the weight of a cubic unit. Multiply that weight by the figure's volume of cubic units.

❑ **Capacity** is the amount that something can hold. Calculating the capacity of a figure is usually the same as calculating volume. Solid figures are typically used for volume questions, whereas capacity questions typically involve hollow figures that are being filled with something.

TRY IT OUT

Find the volume of the cube and rectangular box below:

1.

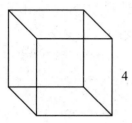

4

Volume =

2.

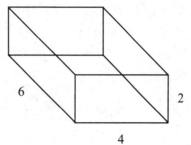

6

2

4

Volume =

PUT IT TOGETHER

1. Figure 16 shows a rectangular metal block. If the metal block were cut into two rectangular blocks of equal dimensions, which of the following could be the dimensions, in inches, of each of the smaller blocks?

    (A) $3 \times 6 \times 12$
    (B) $3 \times 6 \times 9$
    (C) $3 \times 12 \times 9$
    (D) $6 \times 3 \times 6$
    (E) $6 \times 6 \times 6$

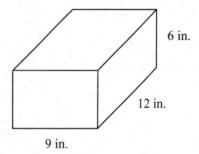

6 in.

12 in.

9 in.

Figure 16

Coordinate Plane

❑ The **coordinate plane** is a grid made up of two number lines – a horizontal number line called the **x-axis** and a vertical number line called the **y-axis**. These two lines meet at a point called the **origin**. This is the point where both number lines are labeled zero.

The x-axis is used to measure the value of x at any point on the plane. Points to the right of the origin have positive values of x, and points to the left of the origin have negative values of x.

The y-axis is used to measure the value of y at any point on the plane. Points above the origin have positive values of y, and points below the origin have negative values of y.

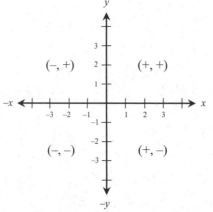

❑ We can describe the position of a point on the plane using a pair of numbers called an **ordered pair**. An ordered pair is also called the **coordinates** of the point.

The first number in the pair is the value of x at the point, called the **x-coordinate**.

The second number in the pair is the value of y at the point, called the **y-coordinate**.

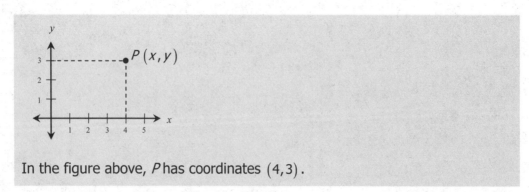

In the figure above, P has coordinates (4,3).

TRY IT OUT

1. Plot the following points on the graph below:

    A: (2, 2)   *B*: (–5, –1)   *C*: (4, –4)

    D: (–5, 3)   *E*: (–4, –3)   *F*: (–2, 4)

2. Find the coordinates of the following points:

    K:____   *L*:____   *M*:____

    N:____   *P*:____

    Q:____   *R*:____   *S*:____

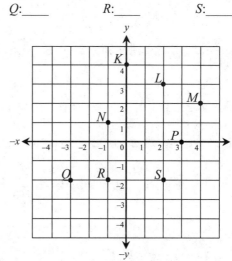

Slope

❑ The **slope** is the amount a line moves vertically for every unit the line moves horizontally. Lines that slant up to the right have positive slope. Lines that slant down to the right have negative slope.

❑ Use $\dfrac{\textbf{rise}}{\textbf{run}}$ to calculate slope. First, find two points on the line. The "rise" is how much the y value increases. The "run" is how much the x value increases between two points. The ratio of rise to run is the slope of the line through those points.

In other words, the slope of a line that passes through points (x_1, y_1) and (x_2, y_2)

is given by the formula: $\textbf{slope} = \dfrac{(\boldsymbol{y_2 - y_1})}{(\boldsymbol{x_2 - x_1})}$

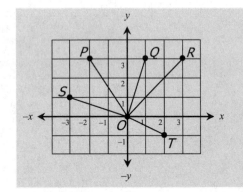

Find the slopes of the line segments:

$\overline{OP}$ _ −3/2 _

$\overline{OQ}$ _ 3 _

$\overline{OR}$ _____

$\overline{OS}$ _____

$\overline{OT}$ _____

❑ The slopes of **perpendicular lines** are negative reciprocals of each other.

For a line with slope $\dfrac{a}{b}$, a line that crosses it at a 90° angle would have slope $\dfrac{-b}{a}$.

❑ **Parallel lines** have equal slopes.

❑ **Vertical lines** have undefined slope, or infinite slope.

❑ **Horizontal lines** have slope = 0.

TRY IT OUT

Use the graph below to answer the following questions:

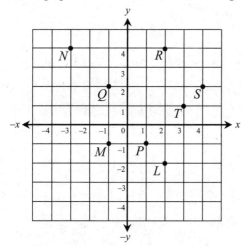

1. What is the slope of the line that passes through points T and S?

2. What is the slope of the line that passes through points L and T?

3. What is the slope of the line that passes through points R and T?

4. What is the slope of the line that passes through points Q and R?

5. What is the slope of the line that passes through points M and L?

6. The line between L and what other point has a slope of 2?

7. The line between N and what other point has a slope of $-\dfrac{1}{2}$?

Graphing Lines

❑ **Slope-intercept form**: $y = mx + b$.

In this equation, **m** is the slope of the line and **b** is the **y-intercept** (the point where the line crosses the y-axis and $x = 0$). Once you have converted a line to slope-intercept form, by setting the equation equal to y, you can easily identify the slope of the line and its y-intercept.

> If a line is given by the equation $6x - 2y = 7$, what are the slope and y-intercept of the line?
>
> 1. Put the equation in slope-intercept form by setting it equal to y.
>
> $$6x - 2y = 7 \implies -2y = -6x + 7 \implies y = 3x - \frac{7}{2}$$
>
> 2. For the equation $y = mx + b$, the slope is m and the y-intercept is b.
>
> $$\text{slope} = 3 \quad y\text{-intercept} = -\frac{7}{2}$$

❑ To graph the equation of a line in slope-intercept form, you can begin with the y-intercept and then draw a line with the equation's slope from that point.

You can also input values of x and find corresponding values of y, then plot the coordinates, and then connect the points to create a line.

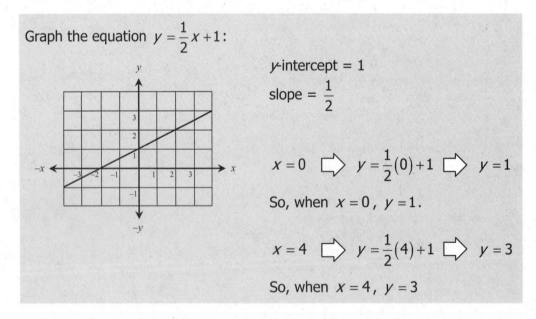

Graph the equation $y = \frac{1}{2}x + 1$:

y-intercept = 1

slope = $\frac{1}{2}$

$$x = 0 \implies y = \frac{1}{2}(0) + 1 \implies y = 1$$

So, when $x = 0$, $y = 1$.

$$x = 4 \implies y = \frac{1}{2}(4) + 1 \implies y = 3$$

So, when $x = 4$, $y = 3$

TRY IT OUT

1. Graph the following line equations:

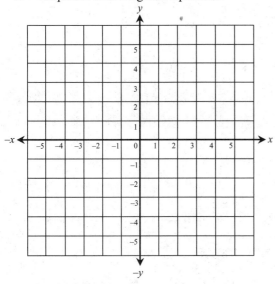

A. $y = x + 1$

B. $y = 2x - 2$

C. $y = \dfrac{2}{3}x + 2$

D. $y = -x + 1$

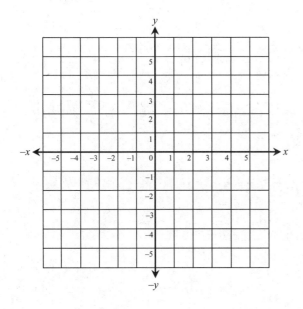

E. $y = -2x - 2$

F. $2y - x = 2$

G. $x = 3$

H. $y = -4$

2. Find the equations for the lines in the graph below:

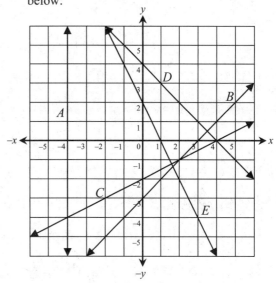

A. _____

B. _____

C. _____

D. _____

E. _____

3. Write the equation of a line with a slope of 1 that passes through the point $(-3, 1)$.

4. Write the equation of a line with a slope of -3 that passes through the point $(2, -4)$.

5. Write the equation of the line that passes through the points $(-3, 1)$ and $(6, -5)$.

Chapter Review

❑ Angles

A 90° angle is called a right angle.

The measure of a straight line is equal to 180°.

Guesstimate angles on figures that are drawn to scale.

❑ Pairs of Angles

Congruent angles are angles that have equal degree measures.

Two angles that share a common side are adjacent angles.

When two lines intersect, the angles opposite each other are called vertical angles. Vertical angles are equal.

❑ Parallel Lines

When two parallel lines are cut by a transversal, alternate interior angles are equal.

❑ Triangles

The sum of the interior angles of a triangle is 180°.

A triangle with a 90° angle in it is called a right triangle.

An isosceles triangle is any triangle that has two equal sides.

An equilateral triangle is a triangle that has all sides equal. All angles are 60°.

❑ Area and Perimeter

Perimeter is the distance around the edge of a two-dimensional figure.

Area is the amount of space inside a two-dimensional figure. Area is measured in square units.

Rectangle:

Perimeter $= (2\times l)+(2\times w)$

Area $= l \times w$

Square:

Perimeter $= 4\times s$

Area $= s\times s$

Triangle:

Perimeter $= s_1 + s_2 + s_3$

Area $= \dfrac{1}{2}\times b\times h$

Circle:

Circumference $= 2\times \pi \times r = \pi \times d$

Area $= \pi \times r^2$

Estimate areas and lengths on figures that are drawn to scale.

❑ Volume

Cube: Volume $= s^3$

Rectangle: Volume $= l\times w\times h$

❑ Coordinate Plane

In slope-intercept form ($y = mx + b$), m is slope and b is the y-intercept.

Geometry Practice

Angles

1. If *ABCD* is a square, what is the value of *x*?

   (A) 30
   (B) 45
   (C) 60
   (D) 90
   (E) It cannot be determined from the information given.

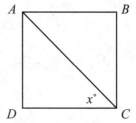

Figure 1

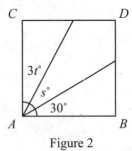

Figure 2

2. In Figure 2 above, *ABCD* is a square. What is the value of
   $2(3t + s)$?

   (A) 30°
   (B) 60°
   (C) 90°
   (D) 120°
   (E) It cannot be determined from the information given.

Triangles

3. Which of the following shapes can be made by putting
   two triangles together without overlapping?

   I.   Rectangle
   II. Square
   III. Triangle

   (A) I only
   (B) II only
   (C) I and II only
   (D) I, II, and III
   (E) None of the above

Area and Perimeter

4. If a rectangle has an area of 16, then what pair could NOT be the length and width of the rectangle?

    (A) 2, 8
    (B) 4, 4
    (C) 1, 7
    (D) 1, 16
    (E) $\frac{1}{2}$, 32

5. A rectangle has side lengths of x and $x + 3$. If the perimeter of the rectangle is 30, then what is the length of the longer side?

    (A) 3
    (B) 6
    (C) 9
    (D) 12
    (E) 27

6. In Figure 3, lines are spaced 1 unit apart. What is the area, in square units, of the shaded figure?

    (A) 16
    (B) 17
    (C) 8
    (D) 7
    (E) 6

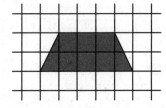

Figure 3

7. A square has a side length of 7. What is the difference between its area and its perimeter?

    (A) 7
    (B) 14
    (C) 21
    (D) 28
    (E) 49

Circles

8. How many circles of diameter 3' can be placed in a 12' × 7' rectangle, if none of the circles overlap each other?

   (A) 4
   (B) 6
   (C) 7
   (D) 8
   (E) 12

9. Find the area of the shaded region in Figure 4 in square units. Use the value 3.14 for π.

   (A) 4.48
   (B) 45.76
   (C) 70.88
   (D) 83.44
   (E) 89.72

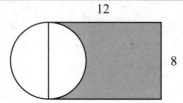

Figure 4

Volume

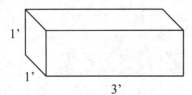

10. How many 1' × 1' × 1' blocks can be formed from the rectangular box above?

    (A) 9
    (B) 6
    (C) 5
    (D) 4
    (E) 3

Coordinate Plane

11. Which graph, if folded along the dotted line, would overlap exactly?

(A)

(B)

(C)

(D)

(E)

12. In the graph shown in Figure 5, which point has the coordinates (–2, 2)?

    (A) A
    (B) B
    (C) C
    (D) D
    (E) E

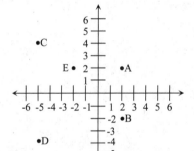

Figure 5

13. $\triangle ABC$ is formed by the points with the following coordinates: $A\,(-1, 4)$, $B\,(-1, -2)$, $C\,(2, 4)$. What is the area of $\triangle ABC$?

    (A) 3
    (B) 6
    (C) 9
    (D) 18
    (E) 27

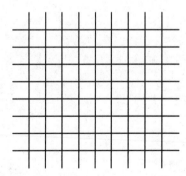

Slope

14. The slope of the line $3x - 2y = 12$ is

(A) -6

(B) $-\dfrac{2}{3}$

(C) $\dfrac{2}{3}$

(D) $\dfrac{3}{2}$

(E) 4

Geometry Practice

Middle Level

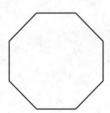

Figure 1

1. Figure 1 above shows a polygon with sides of equal
    length. If the perimeter of the polygon is 160, what is the
    length of each side?

    (A) 2
    (B) 10
    (C) 18
    (D) 20
    (E) 22

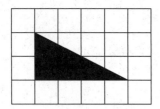

Figure 2

2. In Figure 2 above, what is the area of the shaded region if
    the area of each square is 1?

    (A) 4
    (B) 8
    (C) 16
    (D) 24
    (E) It cannot be determined from the information given.

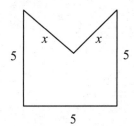

3. If the perimeter of the figure above is 21, the value of x is

    (A) 9
    (B) 4
    (C) 3
    (D) 2
    (E) 1

4. If a square is folded in half, which of the following could result?

    I.   A square
    II. A triangle
    III. A rectangle

    (A) None
    (B) III only
    (C) I and III only
    (D) II and III only
    (E) I, II, and III

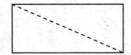

5. If the rectangle above is folded in half along the dotted line, which of the following figures could be the result?

(A)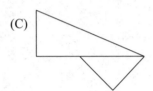

(B)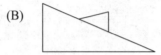

(C)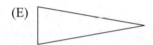

(D)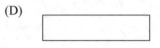

(E)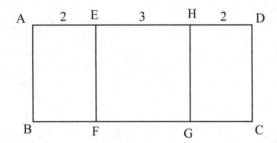

Figure 3

6. In Figure 3 shown above, what is the area of ABCD if EFGH is a square?

    (A) 14
    (B) 20
    (C) 21
    (D) 36
    (E) It cannot be determined from the information given.

7. Kenny uses 4 gallons of paint to paint a rectangular ceiling 20 feet wide by 50 feet long. How many gallons of paint does he use per square foot?

(A) .004
(B) .04
(C) .4
(D) 1
(E) 4

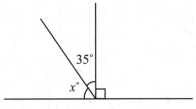

Figure 4

8. In Figure 4, what is the value of x?

(A) 45
(B) 55
(C) 65
(D) 145
(E) 155

9. What is the average length of a side of a quadrilateral that has a perimeter of 48?

(A) 6
(B) 8
(C) 12
(D) 208
(E) It cannot be determined from the information given.

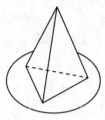

Note: Figure not drawn to scale.

10. A pyramid with four sides rests on a flat surface, as shown in the figure above. If the part of the pyramid touching the flat, circular surface was dipped in black ink before touching the surface, which of the following could be a representation of what the flat surface would look like if the pyramid were removed?

(A) ▼

(B) ■

(C) ●

(D) 🌰

(E) ▰

11. As shown in Figure 5, *ABCD* is a square. What path is the longest?

(A) *A* to *B* to *C* to *D*
(B) *A* to *D* to *B* to *C*
(C) *A* to *B* to *D* to *C*
(D) *A* to *C* to *B* to *D*
(E) *A* to *B* to *C* to *A*

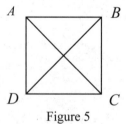

Figure 5

12. How many squares 2 inches on a side can be cut from a piece of paper 10 inches wide by 12 inches long?

    (A) 4
    (B) 20
    (C) 30
    (D) 60
    (E) 120

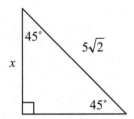

13. What does x equal in the figure above?

    (A) $\dfrac{\sqrt{2}}{5}$

    (B) 4

    (C) $4\sqrt{2}$

    (D) 5

    (E) It cannot be determined from the information given.

Geometry Practice

Upper Level

1. All of the sides of the shape shown in Figure 1 have a
    length of 6. What is the perimeter?

    (A) 1
    (B) 6
    (C) 12
    (D) 36
    (E) It cannot be determined from the information given.

Figure 1

2. A square has a perimeter of 16x. What is the length of a
    side of the square?

    (A) 2
    (B) 4
    (C) 8
    (D) 2x
    (E) 4x

3. Figure 2 shows a map of several streets which form two
    squares where they intersect (shaded). If the distance from
    A to B is 2 miles, which of the following routes from A to
    F is 6 miles long?

    (A) A to B to C to D to E to F
    (B) A to E to C to F
    (C) A to D to B to F
    (D) A to B to E to F
    (E) None of the above

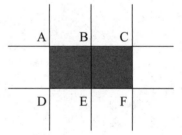

Figure 2

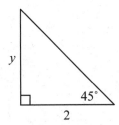

4. What is the value of *y* in the figure above?

    (A) 2
    (B) $2\sqrt{2}$
    (C) $2\sqrt{3}$
    (D) 4
    (E) It cannot be determined from the information given.

5. A prison is surrounded by 11 sides. If the perimeter of the prison is 220 yards, what is the average length in <u>feet</u> of one of the sides?

    (A) 20
    (B) 30
    (C) 60
    (D) 66
    (E) 204

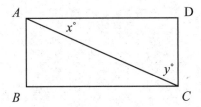

6. If *ABCD* is a rectangle, what is *y* in terms of *x*?

    (A) x
    (B) $90 - x$
    (C) $90 + x$
    (D) $180 - x$
    (E) $360 - x$

7. 24 feet of fence enclose Dan's rectangular back yard.
    What is the length of Dan's yard, if the width is $\frac{1}{3}$ of the
    length?

    (A) 3 feet
    (B) 6 feet
    (C) 9 feet
    (D) 18 feet
    (E) 64 feet

8. 20 squares, each measuring three inches on a side, can be
    cut from a piece of cloth with no cloth left over. What is
    the area of the cloth in square inches?

    (A) 9
    (B) 60
    (C) 180
    (D) 200
    (E) 1,800

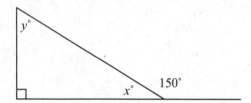

9. In the figure above, $y =$

    (A) 30
    (B) 40
    (C) 45
    (D) 50
    (E) 60

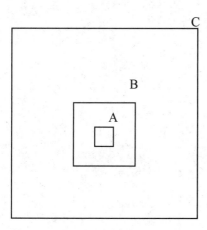

10. In the figure above, A, B, and C are squares. The area of
    C is 9 times that of B. The area of B is 9 times that of A.
    What is the ratio of the length of a side of A to the length
    of a side of C?

    (A) 1 to 3
    (B) 1 to 9
    (C) 9 to 1
    (D) 18 to 1
    (E) 1 to 27

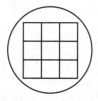

11. 9 four inch by four inch brownies are arranged on a
    circular tray as shown in the figure above. Which of the
    following could be the diameter of the tray?

    (A) 3 inches
    (B) 4 inches
    (C) 9 inches
    (D) 12 inches
    (E) 18 inches

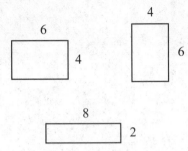

12. The rectangles shown in the figure above are repositioned without any overlapping so that the result is a square. Which of the following is the area of that square?

    (A) 16
    (B) 36
    (C) 64
    (D) 96
    (E) 144

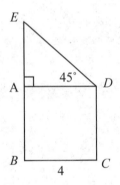

13. In the figure above, *ABCD* is a square with side of length 4. What is the area of polygon *ABCDE*?

    (A) 16
    (B) 24
    (C) 30
    (D) 36
    (E) 48

SUMMIT
EDUCATIONAL
GROUP

Synonyms

- ❑ General Information
- ❑ Anticipate the Answer
- ❑ Secondary Definitions
- ❑ Positive or Negative
- ❑ Attractors
- ❑ Roots
- ❑ Common Roots
- ❑ Word Groups

General Information

❑ Format/Directions

Synonym questions make up the first 30 of the 60 Verbal questions on the SSAT. The questions go from easy to difficult.

❑ Directions are as follows:

> Each of the following questions consists of one word followed by five words or phrases. You are to select the one word or phrase whose meaning is closest to the word in capital letters.
>
> Sample Question:
>
> FRAGILE:
>
> (A) delicate
> (B) useless
> (C) broken
> (D) moody
> (E) careless
>
>

SSAT Structure

Writing Sample – 25 minutes

Quantitative – 30 minutes

MATHEMATICS																								
1	2	3	4	5	6	7	8	9	10	11	12	13	14	15	16	17	18	19	20	21	22	23	24	25
EASY					→				MEDIUM					→				DIFFICULT						

Reading Comprehension – 40 minutes

READING PASSAGES																																							
1	2	3	4	5	6	7	8	9	10	11	12	13	14	15	16	17	18	19	20	21	22	23	24	25	26	27	28	29	30	31	32	33	34	35	36	37	38	39	40
NOT IN ORDER OF DIFFICULTY																																							

Verbal – 30 minutes

SYNONYMS																													
1	2	3	4	5	6	7	8	9	10	11	12	13	14	15	16	17	18	19	20	21	22	23	24	25	26	27	28	29	30
EASY					→				MEDIUM					→				DIFFICULT										

ANALOGIES																													
31	32	33	34	35	36	37	38	39	40	41	42	43	44	45	46	47	48	49	50	51	52	53	54	55	56	57	58	59	60
EASY					→				MEDIUM					→				DIFFICULT										

Quantitative – 30 minutes

MATHEMATICS																								
1	2	3	4	5	6	7	8	9	10	11	12	13	14	15	16	17	18	19	20	21	22	23	24	25
EASY					→				MEDIUM					→				DIFFICULT						

Anticipate the Answer

❑ If the stem word is familiar to you, try to come up with a definition of your own. Choose the answer that most closely resembles your definition.

> OBNOXIOUS:
>
> (A) clear
> (B) slick
> (C) offensive
> (D) odorous
> (E) athletic
>
>
> Before looking at the answers, try to define *OBNOXIOUS* in your own words. For instance, you might say *OBNOXIOUS* means "rude."
>
> *Offensive* (C) is the choice that most closely matches "rude."

TRY IT OUT

On the following synonym exercises, write your own definition of the stem word in the space provided, and then pick the answer choice that most closely matches your definition:

1. RELIABLE: _____

    (A) stable
    (B) creative
    (C) useful
    (D) variable
    (E) truthful

2. LIBERATE: _____

    (A) generate
    (B) enslave
    (C) argue
    (D) release
    (E) support

3. OBEDIENCE: _____

    (A) obscenity
    (B) debacle
    (C) defiance
    (D) conformity
    (E) royalty

Secondary Definitions

❏   Sometimes, your definition of the stem word won't fit the answer choices because a *secondary definition* (a less common meaning for the word) is being tested.

Note: Knowing the stem word's part of speech will help you figure out what definition is called for. Since parts of speech will always be consistent between the stem word and the answer choices, you can look to the answers to help you figure out what part of speech is being used.

> Train
>> *Train* can mean a locomotive, a part of a dress, or to teach.
>
> Minute
>> *Minute* can be used as a unit of time or as an adjective to mean very small or tiny.

TRY IT OUT

Think of **at least** two meanings for each of the following words:

set _____

run _____

stand _____

trail _____

pen _____

champion _____

moral _____

spring _____

hamper _____

revolution _____

TRY IT OUT

In the space provided, write at least two definitions for the stem word. Then try to complete the exercise.

1. BRIDGE: _____

    (A) connect
    (B) suspend
    (C) elevate
    (D) fell
    (E) digest

2. PROMPT: _____

    (A) timely
    (B) expelled
    (C) lax
    (D) candid
    (E) improvised

3. UNIFORM: _____

    (A) authoritative
    (B) consistent
    (C) restrictive
    (D) unprepared
    (E) shapeless

uniform (n) something worn
uniform (adj) being equal and the same

Positive or Negative

❑ Even if you can't define a word, you may have a sense of whether it's a positive or negative word.

Determine whether each answer choice is positive or negative and eliminate the ones that don't match the stem word. Put a "+" or a "−" next to the words to keep track. You can then guess from the remaining choices.

Keep in mind that some words are not necessarily positive or negative.

> − DESPICABLE:
>
> − (A) disdainful ?
> + (B) admirable ✕
> + (C) responsible ✕
> ± (D) animated ?
> − (E) horrible —
>
> If you know that *DESPICABLE* is a negative word, you know that another negative word must be the answer. You can eliminate (B) and (C) because they are positive words. You can eliminate (D) because it is neither positive nor negative. You can then choose between (A) and (E).

❑ Remember, checking whether words are positive or negative should NOT be your first strategy for synonyms questions. This is a backup strategy, and it should be used as a last resort when you cannot use other strategies because you don't know the meanings of the words.

TRY IT OUT

Put a + (for positive) or a – (for negative) next to each of the following words:

1. crass

2. caustic

3. beneficial

4. malice

5. squalor

6. paltry

7. vivacious

8. harmonious

9. ghastly

10. bountiful

Put a + or a – by the stem word and then make your best guess on the following synonyms:

11. BENEFICENT:

   (A) angry
   (B) sneaky
   (C) generous
   (D) attractive
   (E) majestic

12. NOXIOUS:

   (A) magnificent
   (B) religious
   (C) healthful
   (D) sinful
   (E) harmful

13. BANAL:

   (A) prolific
   (B) generous
   (C) eternal
   (D) soothing
   (E) bland

Attractors

❑ Some synonyms, especially medium and difficult ones, will contain incorrect answer choices that are there to steer you away from the correct answer. We call these answer choices attractors because they "attract your attention."

> BAZAAR:
>
> (A) oddity
> (B) market
> (C) publication
> (D) repository
> (E) deviation
>
> (A) attracts your attention because *BAZAAR* looks and sounds like "bizarre," which means odd.
>
> In fact, a *BAZAAR* is a market or marketplace, so (B) is correct.

> RENAISSANCE:
>
> (A) history
> (B) rebirth
> (C) festival
> (D) exploration
> (E) age
>
> If you've studied the *RENAISSANCE* in history, or been to a *RENAISSANCE* fair, you might be tempted to pick (A), (C), or possibly (E).
>
> (B) is the correct answer.

TRY IT OUT

Try to spot the attractors in the following synonym exercises. Why are they attractors?

1. FORTUNATE:

    (A) rich
    (B) golden
    (C) futuristic
    (D) lucky
    (E) protected

2. EXHAUSTIVE:

    (A) tired
    (B) thorough
    (C) polluted
    (D) mechanical
    (E) peculiar

3. BOMBASTIC:

    (A) explosive
    (B) destructive
    (C) pretentious
    (D) disastrous
    (E) ballistic

Roots

❑ Sometimes, a stem word may look like a word you know; it may be a different form of the word, or a related word. Using your knowledge of word roots, you can sometimes figure out the meanings of unknown words.

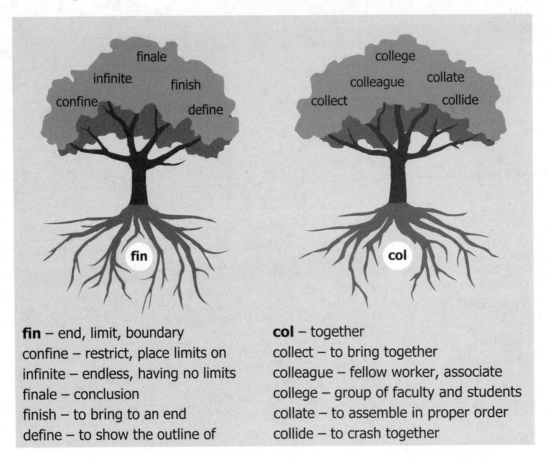

fin – end, limit, boundary
confine – restrict, place limits on
infinite – endless, having no limits
finale – conclusion
finish – to bring to an end
define – to show the outline of

col – together
collect – to bring together
colleague – fellow worker, associate
college – group of faculty and students
collate – to assemble in proper order
collide – to crash together

TRY IT OUT

For each of the following words, write a word of your own that seems related:

1. untimely   _____

2. alienate   _____

3. inexcusable   _____

4. vacuous   _____

5. malfunction   _____

6. detoxify   _____

7. inconsequential   _____

8. immovable   _____

9. beneficiary   _____

10. unobservant   _____

Now try to match the words to their definitions. Take your best guesses:

1) untimely		a)	unforgivable
2) alienate		b)	unimportant
3) inexcusable		c)	stationary
4) vacuous		d)	empty
5) malfunction		e)	inattentive
6) detoxify		f)	to remove poison
7) inconsequential		g)	failure
8) immovable		h)	to separate
9) beneficiary		i)	too early
10) unobservant		j)	person that receives profits or funds

TRY IT OUT

In the space provided, write a familiar word that looks similar to the stem word. Then try to complete the exercise.

1. EQUANIMITY: _____

    (A) nobility
    (B) level-headedness
    (C) sweetness
    (D) cowardice
    (E) imbalance

2. PREMATURE: _____

    (A) skillful
    (B) disorganized
    (C) hasty
    (D) backward
    (E) artificial

3. OPINIONATED: _____

    (A) clever
    (B) absurd
    (C) scarce
    (D) fierce
    (E) stubborn

4. POSTHUMOUS: _____

    (A) alongside
    (B) too late
    (C) appearing briefly
    (D) after death
    (E) with support

Common Roots

In the space provided, write any more words you know that use the root word:

ROOT	MEANING	EXAMPLES
animus	life, spirit	animal, animated, _____
annus, enn	year	annual, centennial, _____
arche, archi	chief, first	architect, archangel, _____
audire	to hear	audible, audit, _____
bios	life	biology, antibiotic, _____
capere	to take	capture, accept, _____
chronos	time	chronicle, chronometer, _____
credere	believe	credence, discredit, _____
dicere, dictum	to say, to speak	predict, dictate, _____
ducere, ductum	to lead	deduce, educate, _____
fluere	to flow	fluid, fluent, _____
greg	herd	gregarious, congregate, _____
gress	to go	digress, progress, _____
loqui	to speak	loquacious, eloquent, _____
lucere	to be lighted	lucid, translucent, _____
mittere, missum	to send	transmit, missile, _____
portare	to carry	deport, portable, _____
scribere, scriptum	to write	postscript, subscribe, _____
sentire, sensum	to feel	consent, sense, _____
specere, spectum	to look at	inspect, _____
tenere, tentum	to hold	tenure, intent, _____
trahere, tractum	to draw, to pull	attract, tractor, _____

Word Groups

Work through each word group in the following steps:

1. Look at the group title and think of similar or related words. Don't look at the SSAT words yet; cover them if necessary.

2. Once you've thought of words related to the group title, look at the SSAT words. See if there are any that you already thought of, then see if there are any other words that you already know in the group.

3. Circle any words that you have never seen before or that you don't know how to define. Look at their definitions, and see if they have the same definition as any other words you know.

Happy

complacent	smug, satisfied
ecstatic	delighted, in a state of great joy
elation	joy, happiness
euphoric	intensely happy, elated
jovial	joyful, cheerful
jubilant	joyful, triumphant

Sad / Miserable

despondent	dejected, hopeless
dismal	gloomy, hopeless
doleful	sad, mournful, sorrowful
dreary	depressing, causing sadness; or: dull, boring
forlorn	miserable, unhappy
mope	to be gloomy, to pout
morose	gloomy, having a sullen disposition
somber	gloomy, serious, depressing
woeful	unhappy, sorrowful

Hatred / Anger

abhor	to hate, to despise
animosity	hatred
disdain	contempt, intense dislike, scorn
indignant	offended, angry about unfair treatment
irate	very angry, furious
livid	very angry, furious
loathe	to hate, to feel disgust for something
malice	hatred, spite
outraged	angered, offended

Intelligent / Skilled

adept	skillful, proficient
adroit	skillful
aptitude	skill, ability
astute	wise, keen in judgment
competent	having sufficient skill, adequate, capable
deft	skillful, dexterous, smart
dexterous	skillful with the hands or body
erudite	scholarly, well-educated
ingenuity	cleverness, inventiveness
proficient	skillful
prodigy	person with extraordinary talent, highly skilled child
prowess	great skill or strength
sage	wise person
sagacious	wise, insightful
sapient	wise, insightful
shrewd	clever, keen, insightful
witty	clever, humorous

Unintelligent / Unskilled

ignorance	lack of knowledge
illiterate	unable to read or write
incompetent	unskilled, incapable, unqualified
inept	unskilled, clumsy
naïve	inexperienced, uninformed
novice	beginner, inexperienced learner
obtuse	slow to understand; or: insensitive

A Good Idea

feasible	capable of being done, practical, viable
meticulous	showing extreme care about details
novel	original, new
pragmatic	practical
prudent	careful, cautious, wise

A Bad Idea

futile	hopeless, useless
impetuous	acting without consideration, impulsive
implausible	unlikely, farfetched
inane	lacking sense, silly, mindless
tenuous	flimsy, weak, thin

Good Person

admirable	inspiring approval
compassionate	showing sympathy
empathy	understanding of the feelings of others
integrity	reliability; or: morality, honesty

Bad Person

abrasive	irritating, annoying; or: harsh, rough
cantankerous	argumentative, irritable, contentious
despicable	deserving contempt, hateful
hypocritical	claiming to have virtues one does not have
infamy	bad reputation, disgrace, opprobrium
notorious	unfavorably known, infamous, disreputable
pettiness	narrow-mindedness; or: stinginess
reprehensible	shameful, bad, deserving rebuke or censure
scoundrel	dishonorable person, villain

Honest / True

authentic	real, genuine
candid	honest, sincere
frank	honest, direct, blunt
legitimate	lawful, rightful
literal	explicit, exact, following the meaning of a word
objective	factual, without bias, not subjective
sincere	genuine, earnest, true, honest
valid	founded on facts

Fake / False

erroneous	incorrect, wrong
fallacious	incorrect, invalid; or: misleading, deceptive
feign	to pretend, to imitate
forgery	counterfeit, imitation, false reproduction
fraud	something false, impostor; or: deception, trickery
hoax	something intended to deceive
illusory	based on a false perception of reality, deceptive

Clear / Convincing

cogent	clear, convincing
coherent	clear, intelligible
lucid	clear, easy to understand

Unclear / Unknown

abstract	theoretical, not concrete, not easily grasped
ambiguous	having more than one possible meaning, uncertain
ambivalent	indecisive, of two minds about something
amorphous	shapeless
clandestine	secret, private, illicit, surreptitious
dubious	doubtful, unsure, not trustworthy
elusive	hard to catch, hard to understand or solve
enigma	puzzle, mystery
esoteric	understood only by a select few, mysterious
intangible	not capable of being touched, abstract
obscure	unclear, vague; or: hard to find

Support

advocate	to support, to speak in favor of, to recommend
buttress	to support, to encourage; or: reinforcement
champion	winner; or: to support
encourage	to inspire, to support
endorsement	support, sanction
nourish	to nurture, to sustain
promote	to encourage, to give a higher position

Praise

acclaim	praise, enthusiastic approval
extol	to praise
laud	to praise
revere	to respect
venerate	to respect

Criticism / Harsh Speech

chastise	to discipline, to criticize
chide	to express disapproval, to criticize
condescend	to talk down to, to act superior, to be patronizing
contradiction	assertion of the opposite, opposition, denial
denigrate	to criticize, to speak badly of, to defame, to belittle
diatribe	bitter speech or criticism, rant
rebuke	to express disapproval, to criticize
reprimand	formal criticism, disapproval
scold	to express disapproval, to criticize angrily
slander	strong criticism; or: false claims against a person
tirade	prolonged speech of abuse or condemnation

Make Better / To Calm

alleviate	to lighten, to relieve
ameliorate	to make better
appease	to calm, to make peace with
assuage	to calm, to ease
conciliate	to calm, to make peace, to reconcile,
mitigate	to make milder, to make less severe
mollify	to calm, to soften
placate	to calm
quench	to satisfy, to put out, to cool
soothe	to calm, to relieve, to comfort

Make Worse

aggravate	to make worse; or: to irritate
debilitating	weakening, incapacitating
deteriorate	to make worse, to disintegrate
detrimental	harmful, damaging
exacerbate	to make more severe or worse
impair	to make worse, to weaken or damage

Decrease / Reduce

abase	to humble, to reduce in rank
abate	to decrease, to weaken
abbreviate	to shorten, to reduce
abridge	to shorten, to reduce
atrophy	to waste away, to decline, to degenerate
diminish	to reduce, to make smaller, to lessen
dwindle	to become smaller, to shrink, to waste away
quell	to extinguish, to put an end to
recession	withdrawal, decline
retract	to withdraw, to take back
wane	to decrease, to decline
wither	to shrivel, to shrink, to decrease

Obstacle / To Hold Back

curtail	to cut short, to hold back
deterrent	something which prevents or discourages action
hamper	to impede, to get in the way, to fetter
hindrance	obstacle, something that impedes progress
impasse	dead end, situation in which progress is prevented
obstruct	to block, to hinder
prohibitive	discouraging, preventative, unaffordable
stymie	to block, to hinder

Stubborn

adamant	unyielding, inflexible
obdurate	stubborn
obstinate	stubborn, unbending
tenacious	stubborn, persistent

Agree

acquiesce	to go along with something, to consent, to agree
compliance	obedience, submissiveness
concur	to agree, to approve

Disagree

dissent	disagreement, difference of opinion, conflict
discord	disagreement, dispute

Join Together

amalgamation	combination, mixture
coalesce	to come together, to merge, to join
collaborate	to work jointly with others

Unchanging / Unmoving

dormant	inactive, hidden, resting
incessant	unceasing, continuous
stagnant	inactive, still
static	stationary, not moving
steadfast	loyal, constant

Changing

fluctuate	to shift back and forth, to change
capricious	unstable, whimsical, flighty
erratic	inconsistent, unpredictable
fickle	unpredictable, capricious, inconsistent, erratic
mercurial	rapidly changing, temperamental

Opinionated / Dedicated

biased	prejudiced, not neutral
bigot	intolerant or prejudiced person, dogmatist
dogmatic	stubbornly opinionated
zealot	fanatical partisan, passionate extremist

Unfeeling / Uncaring

apathetic	indifferent, uninterested
callous	insensitive, unfeeling
negligent	neglectful, careless, inattentive
stoic	unaffected by pleasure and pain, emotionless

Too Prideful

bombastic	proud, overstated
haughty	proud, arrogant
ostentatious	attempting to impress
pompous	arrogant, exaggeratedly self-important
pretentious	self-important, affected

Friendly

affable	friendly
amiable	friendly
congenial	friendly
gregarious	enjoying company, sociable

Disrespectful

flippant	not showing respect, lacking in seriousness
insolent	disrespectful, contemptuous, impudent
irreverent	disrespectful, impertinent

Starting Fights

antagonistic	acting in opposition, hostile
belligerent	warlike, aggressive
provoke	to cause to act, to rouse; or: to anger
pugnacious	inclined to fight
quarrelsome	inclined to argue
rancorous	vengeful, resentful

Attack / Damage / Destroy

assail	to assault
barrage	to attack, to bombard
debase	to demean, to degrade, to spoil
efface	to erase, to wipe out
eradicate	to destroy, to eliminate

Speech

articulate	expressed clearly
colloquial	conversational, characteristic of informal speech
decree	to command, to declare
eloquent	fluent in verbal expression
emphatic	strongly expressive, forceful
enunciate	to express clearly
gossip	idle talk, rumor
orator	public speaker
rhetoric	the art of speaking or writing effectively

Talkative

garrulous	excessively talkative, babbling
loquacious	talkative, garrulous
verbose	wordy, talkative

Brief

brevity	briefness, of short duration or length
concise	briefly and clearly stated, succinct
succinct	expressed in few words, laconic
terse	brief, pithy

Shy

introverted	shy, self-concerned
reticent	quiet, uncommunicative
taciturn	reserved, not talkative
timid	unconfident, shy

Get Started

coercion	use of force to compel an act or choice
compel	to force someone to do something
incentive	motivation, stimulus
incite	to cause to act, to provoke, to urge
initiate	to set in motion, to start
instigate	to stir up, to urge on
prompt	call to action, reminder

Give Up

abandon	to give up, to leave
abdicate	to give up a power or position
concede	to admit to be true; or: to forfeit
forsake	to give up, to leave, to quit
renounce	to give up
relinquish	to give up, to renounce
resign	to give up
surrender	to give up, to yield to another

Looking Forward

anticipation	prediction, expectation
forebode	to predict
imminent	happening soon, impending
inevitable	unavoidable, expected
ominous	threatening, warning of danger
portent	sign of something about to happen, omen
premonition	forewarning, intuition about the future
presumption	guess, assumption
prophesy	to predict, to foretell
unforeseen	unexpected

Looking Back

contrite	feeling guilt or regret, repentant
lament	to mourn, to feel regret
nostalgia	yearning for the past, homesickness
reminiscence	memory, recollection
remorse	guilt, shame
retrospect	reflection on the past, consideration of history

Boring / Common

banal	common, lacking originality, hackneyed
insipid	bland, boring, without zest
monotonous	without variety, tiresomely uniform
mundane	ordinary, dull, commonplace
pedestrian	common, dull, banal, unremarkable
tedious	boring, unpleasantly painstaking

Normal

conformity	matching in form, compliance with norm
conventional	matching accepted standards, ordinary
customary	according to custom, usual
uniformity	overall similarity, sameness

Odd / Weird

aberrant	abnormal, unusual, deviant
bizarre	unusual, weird
eccentric	deviating from the standard or norm
idiosyncratic	characteristic of a person, peculiar to an individual
peculiar	odd, strange, unusual

Differences

disparate	different, distinct
juxtapose	to place side by side for comparison
nuance	subtle difference

Rich

affluent	wealthy
opulent	wealthy, luxurious
prolific	productive, fertile, fecund
prosperous	successful, flourishing, wealthy, affluent

Poor

destitute	without food or shelter, deprived, needy
impoverish	to make poor, to deprive
indigent	without food or shelter, deprived, needy

Giving

altruism	unselfish interest in helping others
benevolent	good, kind-hearted
generous	liberal in giving or sharing, charitable

Wasteful

prodigal	extravagant, wasteful
squander	to spend extravagantly, to waste

Empty / Lacking

barren	not productive, infertile, depleted
desolate	deserted, inhospitable, bare
omission	something left out
scant	tiny amount, insufficient
scarce	not enough, insufficient
vacant	empty, void

Confusing / Challenging

arduous	requiring great effort, straining, difficult
bewilder	to confuse
confound	to confuse
perplex	to confuse
plight	difficult and unpleasant situation, struggle
predicament	difficult situation, dilemma
quandary	difficult situation, dilemma
strenuous	requiring great effort, straining, difficult

Tricky

beguile	to lure, to charm, to captivate
deceive	to cause someone to believe a lie, to mislead
guile	cunning, deceitfulness
wily	cunning, sly, crafty

Not A Problem

benign	harmless, beneficial, kind, gentle
frivolous	not serious, insignificant
indifferent	not concerned, not caring
latent	inactive, dormant; or: hidden
trivial	unimportant, insignificant

Calm

docile	easy to manage, obedient, submissive
placid	calm, serene
tranquil	calm, peaceful

Lazy / Tired

languid	slow, tired, drooping
lax	careless, slack, not strict
lethargic	lazy, lacking energy
listless	without energy or enthusiasm, uninterested
sluggish	lazy, slow to act
torpid	slow, inactive, hibernating

Chapter Review

❑ **Format/Directions**

"Each of the following questions consists of one word followed by five words or phrases. You are to select the one word or phrase whose meaning is closest to the word in capital letters."

❑ **Anticipate the answer.**

If the stem word is familiar to you, try to come up with a definition of your own. Choose the answer that most closely resembles your definition.

❑ **Consider secondary definitions of the stem word.**

Sometimes, your definition of the stem word won't fit the answer choices because a *secondary definition* (a less common meaning for the word) is being tested.

❑ **Determine whether the stem word is positive or negative.**

Even if you can't define a word, you may have a sense of whether it's a positive or negative word.

Keep in mind that some words are not necessarily positive or negative.

❑ **Watch out for attractors on medium and difficult synonyms.**

❑ **Look for familiar roots in unfamiliar words.**

Sometimes, a stem word may look like a word you know; it may be a different form of the word, or a related word. Using your knowledge of word roots, you can sometimes figure out the meanings of unknown words.

SUMMIT
EDUCATIONAL
GROUP

Synonyms Practice
Middle Level

1. AUDIBLE:

    (A) capable of being eaten
    (B) capable of being taught
    (C) capable of being heard
    (D) capable of being seen
    (E) capable of being touched

2. DURATION:

    (A) short
    (B) survive
    (C) sneak
    (D) stand
    (E) span

3. TIRESOME:

    (A) exciting
    (B) absurd
    (C) tedious
    (D) useless
    (E) unruly

4. DEVOTED:

    (A) distant
    (B) fearful
    (C) patient
    (D) faithful
    (E) insane

5. TYPICAL:

    (A) beautiful
    (B) normal
    (C) tardy
    (D) dense
    (E) secure

6. HUMILIATE:

    (A) crash
    (B) verify
    (C) praise
    (D) trust
    (E) shame

7. EXPERT:

    (A) comedian
    (B) director
    (C) authority
    (D) inventor
    (E) sculptor

8. BENEFICIAL:

    (A) wicked
    (B) boring
    (C) observant
    (D) helpful
    (E) sensitive

9. FRANTIC:

    (A) massive
    (B) dejected
    (C) tepid
    (D) isolated
    (E) agitated

10. IMMENSE:

    (A) minute
    (B) pensive
    (C) antique
    (D) fictitious
    (E) colossal

11. COZY:

 (A) cold
 (B) easy
 (C) snug
 (D) careful
 (E) shy

12. INTERIOR:

 (A) entrance
 (B) store
 (C) inside
 (D) terror
 (E) paint

13. FLATTER:

 (A) demolish
 (B) praise
 (C) mow
 (D) insult
 (E) desire

14. IDOLIZE:

 (A) mimic
 (B) adore
 (C) uphold
 (D) acquire
 (E) survey

15. INTRICATE:

 (A) harsh
 (B) polite
 (C) frustrating
 (D) complicated
 (E) perfect

16. MELODY:

 (A) instrument
 (B) spice
 (C) weapon
 (D) tune
 (E) story

17. AUTHENTIC

 (A) true
 (B) desirable
 (C) appropriate
 (D) helpful
 (E) copied

18. INCLEMENT:

 (A) severe
 (B) balmy
 (C) leafy
 (D) sadly
 (E) graceful

19. SURLY:

 (A) happy
 (B) positive
 (C) windy
 (D) unfriendly
 (E) soiled

20. NOVICE:

 (A) secret
 (B) ancient
 (C) beginner
 (D) thief
 (E) expert

21. CULPRIT:

 (A) vessel
 (B) savage
 (C) felon
 (D) star
 (E) patron

22. PLACID:

 (A) serene
 (B) arrange
 (C) uneasy
 (D) location
 (E) ideal

23. AMBLE:

   (A) stroll
   (B) wager
   (C) desire
   (D) risk
   (E) disturb

24. CELEBRITY:

   (A) precision
   (B) scandal
   (C) haste
   (D) purity
   (E) renown

25. WRATH:

   (A) cover
   (B) twist
   (C) quiet
   (D) fury
   (E) folder

26. ELUDE:

   (A) mimic
   (B) support
   (C) avoid
   (D) fling
   (E) pursue

27. MUNDANE:

   (A) foolish
   (B) ordinary
   (C) cheerful
   (D) irate
   (E) promising

28. CONCEIT:

   (A) secret
   (B) modesty
   (C) honesty
   (D) ability
   (E) arrogance

29. RATTLE:

   (A) unnerve
   (B) brace
   (C) fasten
   (D) magnify
   (E) deliver

30. EXHIBIT:

   (A) deplete
   (B) inspect
   (C) vacate
   (D) feature
   (E) restrain

31. CATASTROPHE:

   (A) series
   (B) land
   (C) fever
   (D) animal
   (E) disaster

32. PECULIAR:

   (A) similar
   (B) unusual
   (C) particular
   (D) ready
   (E) angry

33. PROPEL:

   (A) tie down
   (B) push forward
   (C) hold up
   (D) leave out
   (E) fly away

34. SAVOR:

   (A) subtract
   (B) relish
   (C) prefer
   (D) maintain
   (E) assist

35. INSOLENT:

   (A) bankrupt
   (B) disrespectful
   (C) intelligent
   (D) rowdy
   (E) careless

36. HAMPER:

   (A) inquire
   (B) obstruct
   (C) resolve
   (D) imitate
   (E) persist

37. MANACLES:

   (A) staples
   (B) immigrants
   (C) relatives
   (D) tractors
   (E) fetters

38. LACKLUSTER:

   (A) clean
   (B) interesting
   (C) acceptable
   (D) dull
   (E) difficult

Synonyms Practice

Upper Level

1. INGENUITY:

    (A) denseness
    (B) happiness
    (C) stupidity
    (D) creativity
    (E) luck

2. PUNY:

    (A) jarring
    (B) ample
    (C) feeble
    (D) robust
    (E) odorous

3. BARBARIAN:

    (A) hairdresser
    (B) stranger
    (C) savage
    (D) inhabitant
    (E) spike

4. SOLITARY:

    (A) insulated
    (B) circular
    (C) intimate
    (D) isolated
    (E) sterile

5. INHABIT:

    (A) motivate
    (B) occupy
    (C) vanish
    (D) repress
    (E) drift

6. BELATED:

    (A) prompt
    (B) contented
    (C) tardy
    (D) gloomy
    (E) departed

7. TRANQUIL:

    (A) calm
    (B) noisy
    (C) striking
    (D) painful
    (E) lucky

8. RESIDENCE:

    (A) frame
    (B) dwelling
    (C) assembly
    (D) company
    (E) substance

9. JOVIAL:

    (A) argumentative
    (B) heavy
    (C) amiable
    (D) serious
    (E) melancholy

10. IRATE:

    (A) inspired
    (B) incensed
    (C) incisive
    (D) infatuated
    (E) insipid

SUMMIT
EDUCATIONAL
GROUP

11. TEDIOUS:

   (A) enthralling
   (B) hateful
   (C) monotonous
   (D) inferior
   (E) profound

12. UNIQUE:

   (A) systematic
   (B) singular
   (C) simple
   (D) stale
   (E) syrupy

13. VIRTUOUS:

   (A) essential
   (B) indecent
   (C) lethal
   (D) energetic
   (E) scrupulous

14. PROPEL:

   (A) sustain
   (B) hinder
   (C) consume
   (D) launch
   (E) annoy

15. LIABLE:

   (A) exempt
   (B) variable
   (C) favorable
   (D) responsible
   (E) considerate

16. AGITATE:

   (A) fluster
   (B) stabilize
   (C) hasten
   (D) inscribe
   (E) pacify

17. ARID:

   (A) extra
   (B) frigid
   (C) dry
   (D) visible
   (E) cautious

18. INTACT:

   (A) impaired
   (B) polished
   (C) skillful
   (D) tricky
   (E) whole

19. DEBRIS:

   (A) waste
   (B) injury
   (C) clothes
   (D) name
   (E) storm

20. WILY:

   (A) crafty
   (B) silly
   (C) scary
   (D) careful
   (E) dangerous

21. BOISTEROUS:

   (A) unruly
   (B) masculine
   (C) contaminated
   (D) irritating
   (E) tame

22. LUCID:

   (A) cloudy
   (B) novel
   (C) real
   (D) clear
   (E) intense

23. STATURE:

(A) figure
(B) standing
(C) condition
(D) structure
(E) decree

24. CONTIGUOUS:

(A) adjacent
(B) proceed
(C) include
(D) regular
(E) collect

25. VOLATILE:

(A) disturb
(B) preference
(C) unstable
(D) massive
(E) steady

26. CHASM:

(A) acquaintance
(B) boundary
(C) actuary
(D) bough
(E) abyss

27. CRONY:

(A) witch
(B) dowager
(C) elevator
(D) associate
(E) traitor

28. RENOUNCE:

(A) disavow
(B) dispute
(C) disclose
(D) disappear
(E) distress

29. REPLICA:

(A) facsimile
(B) substitute
(C) response
(D) democracy
(E) original

30. ABHOR:

(A) detest
(B) cause
(C) assemble
(D) cherish
(E) desist

31. REFUSE:

(A) consent
(B) evidence
(C) beacon
(D) neglect
(E) debris

32. MOROSE:

(A) dejected
(B) detached
(C) dependable
(D) delighted
(E) defective

33. MAR:

(A) enhance
(B) transport
(C) orbit
(D) erase
(E) deface

34. PALATABLE:

(A) tasty
(B) polluted
(C) ruined
(D) insipid
(E) sanitary

35. ABODE:

    (A) buttress
    (B) volume
    (C) stanza
    (D) residence
    (E) reception

36. RAVENOUS:

    (A) gratified
    (B) murky
    (C) putrid
    (D) famished
    (E) authentic

37. POSTERITY:

    (A) permanence
    (B) descendants
    (C) rear
    (D) attitude
    (E) ancestry

38. EXTOL:

    (A) expire
    (B) acclaim
    (C) admonish
    (D) include
    (E) entertain

39. OBSTINATE:

    (A) malleable
    (B) dogged
    (C) moderate
    (D) hesitant
    (E) animated

SUMMIT
EDUCATIONAL
GROUP

Analogies

- ❏ General Information
- ❏ Defining the Relationship
- ❏ Applying the Relationship
- ❏ Refining the Relationship
- ❏ Common Analogy Relationships
- ❏ First and Third Analogies
- ❏ Attractors
- ❏ Being an Analogy Detective
- ❏ Solving Backwards

General Information

❏ Format/Directions

The verbal section of the SSAT has one set of 30 analogies. They appear after the 30 synonym questions. The questions go from easy to difficult.

Directions are as follows:

> The following questions ask you to find relationships between words. For each question, select the answer choice that best completes the meaning of the sentence.
>
> Sample Question:
>
> Cow is to bull as
>
> (A) rooster is to chicken
> (B) goose is to gander
> (C) pony is to horse
> (D) frog is to toad
> (E) dog is to cat.
>
>
>
> Choice (B) is the best answer because a bull is a male cow just as a gander is a male goose. Of all the answer choices, (B) states a relationship that is most like the relationship between <u>cow</u> and <u>bull</u>.

❏ Some analogies will give you the first three words of the analogy in the question and one word in each answer choice.

> Marigold is to flower as piranha is to
>
> (A) Venus Flytrap
> (B) tulip
> (C) shark
> (D) fish
> (E) ocean

SSAT Structure

Writing Sample – 25 minutes

Quantitative – 30 minutes

MATHEMATICS																								
1	2	3	4	5	6	7	8	9	10	11	12	13	14	15	16	17	18	19	20	21	22	23	24	25
EASY					→				MEDIUM					→			DIFFICULT							

Reading Comprehension – 40 minutes

READING PASSAGES																																							
1	2	3	4	5	6	7	8	9	10	11	12	13	14	15	16	17	18	19	20	21	22	23	24	25	26	27	28	29	30	31	32	33	34	35	36	37	38	39	40
NOT IN ORDER OF DIFFICULTY																																							

Verbal – 30 minutes

SYNONYMS																													
1	2	3	4	5	6	7	8	9	10	11	12	13	14	15	16	17	18	19	20	21	22	23	24	25	26	27	28	29	30
EASY					→				MEDIUM					→			DIFFICULT												

ANALOGIES																													
31	32	33	34	35	36	37	38	39	40	41	42	43	44	45	46	47	48	49	50	51	52	53	54	55	56	57	58	59	60
EASY					→				MEDIUM					→			DIFFICULT												

Quantitative – 30 minutes

MATHEMATICS																								
1	2	3	4	5	6	7	8	9	10	11	12	13	14	15	16	17	18	19	20	21	22	23	24	25
EASY					→				MEDIUM					→			DIFFICULT							

Defining the Relationship

❏ The key to solving an analogy is to determine what the relationship is between the paired words.

For most analogies, your relationship should be a short sentence that contains both of the stem words and defines one of the words in terms of the other.

❏ Clearly state the relationship.

Don't just look at the words and say "I know that these words are related." Express the relationship as a complete sentence. The more clearly you can state the relationship, the easier the analogy problem becomes.

> emerald is to gem
>
> An *emerald* is a type of *gem*.

❏ You can start the relationship with the first or second word. However, make sure you keep the same order when applying the stem relationship to the answers.

> degree is to temperature
>
> A *degree* is a unit of *temperature*.
>
> joy is to ecstasy
>
> *Ecstasy* means extreme *joy*.

TRY IT OUT

For each pair of words, state the relationship by defining one word in terms of the other. Make your relationships as clear and concise as possible.

1. Key is to padlock

    A key is used to open a padlock like

2. Pyramid is to triangle

    _____

3. Sculptor is to statue

    A sculptor can create a statue like

4. Playwright is to script

    A playwright is someone who creates a script like

5. Reign is to king

    A reign is what a king has like

6. Cumulus is to cloud

    Cumulus is a type of cloud

7. Melodious is to sound

    melodious describes a sound

8. Pancake is to batter

    A pancake is made with batter like

9. Sonnet is to poem

    Sonnet is a type of poem

10. Neurologist is to physician

    A neurologist is a type of physician like

Applying the Relationship

❑ Connect each pair of answer choices using the same relationship as you use to connect the stem words. Don't change the stem relationship to make it correspond to the relationship between a pair of answer choice words.

Helmet is to head	(A *helmet* is worn to protect the *head*)
(A) drug is to disease	(A *drug* is worn to protect a *disease*)
(B) lace is to shoe	(A *lace* is worn to protect a *shoe*)
(C) apron is to stain	(An *apron* is worn to protect a *stain*)
(D) field is to goal	(A *field* is worn to protect a *goal*)
(E) thimble is to finger	(A *thimble* is worn to protect a *finger*)

None of the choices make sense except for (E), the correct answer.

TRY IT OUT

State the relationship between the stem words and then apply that relationship to your answer choices:

1. Eye chart is to vision as _____

    (A) map is to island _____

    (B) drill is to cavity _____

    (C) stethoscope is to heartbeat _____

    (D) camera is to photograph _____

    (E) thermostat is to fuel _____

2. Poem is to stanzas as _____

    (A) novel is to contents _____

    (B) sentence is to punctuation _____

    (C) song is to verses _____

    (D) question is to answers _____

    (E) speech is to parts _____

3. Apple is to fruit as wheat is to _____

    (A) field _____

    (B) loaf _____

    (C) grain _____

    (D) rice _____

    (E) vine _____

Refining the Relationship

❑ If the relationship you make yields two or more correct answers, make the
relationship more specific.

Trunk is to automobile as

(A) limb is to tree
(B) closet is to bedroom
(C) page is to manual
(D) grass is to lawn
(E) toe is to body

First relationship: A *trunk* is part of an *automobile*.

If you apply this relationship, almost all of the answer choices work:

(A) a limb is part of a tree
(B) a closet is part of a bedroom
(C) a page is part of a manual
(E) a toe is part of a body

The relationship needs to be more specific.

More specific relationship: A *trunk* is the part of an *automobile* in which
one stores things.

Only one pair of words, choice (B), fits that relationship.

TRY IT OUT

State the relationship in the following analogies:

1. Judge is to courthouse as

    (A) cashier is to store
    (B) teacher is to school
    (C) secretary is to office
    (D) salesman is to car
    (E) captain is to ship

    Relationship: _____ The Judge is the head of the courthouse _____

2. Goggles are to welders as

    (A) chisels are to sculptors
    (B) armor is to knights
    (C) microscopes are to scientists
    (D) authors are to publishers
    (E) scripts are to actors

    Relationship: _____ Googles are a type of protection for welders _____

3. Rhinoceros is to horn as

    (A) weed is to root
    (B) vine is to leaf
    (C) tree is to bark
    (D) rose is to thorn
    (E) flower is to petal

    Relationship: _____ Rhinocer uses a horn for protection _____

SUMMIT
EDUCATIONAL
GROUP

Common Analogy Relationships

❑ Familiarize yourself with the following analogy relationship types.

Synonym

bold is to courageous	(bold means being courageous)
frenetic is to energetic	(frenetic means energetic)

Antonyms

offhand is to forethought	(offhand means without forethought)
impudent is to respectful	(impudent is the opposite of respectful)

Function or Use

bridge is to river	(a bridge is used for passage over a river)
aviary is to birds	(an aviary houses birds)

Person/Activity

spectator is to watch	(a spectator is someone who watches)
teacher is to instruct	(a teacher is someone who instructs)

Person/Tool

policeman is to handcuffs	(handcuffs are a tool of a policeman)
painter is to brush	(a brush is a tool of a painter)

Person/Creation

playwright is to script	(a playwright writes/creates scripts)
cobbler is to shoe	(a cobbler makes/creates shoes)

Action/Result

insult is to offended	(an insult will make someone offended)
assault is to injured	(an assault will make someone injured)

Characteristic

sphere is to round	(a sphere is round)
menace is to threatening	(a menace is threatening)

Type

fly is to insect	(a fly is a type of insect)

Part/Whole

flower is to bouquet	(a bouquet is an arrangement of flowers)
novel is to chapter	(a chapter is a part of a novel)

Degree of Intensity

hill is to mountain	(a mountain is a large hill)
cold is to frigid	(frigid means extremely cold)

TRY IT OUT

For each pair of stem words, identify the type of relationship (e.g., function, part/whole, etc.) and state the relationship between the words:

1. Carpenter is to hammer

   _____   _____
              type   relationship

2. Globe is to spherical

   _____   _____
           type   relationship

3. Sculptor is to statue

   _____   _____
           type   relationship

4. Atlas is to maps

   _____   _____
           type   relationship

5. Mask is to face

   _____   _____
           type   relationship

6. Stress is to agitated

   _____   _____
           type   relationship

7. Rodent is to mouse

   _____   _____
           type   relationship

8. Ripple is to tidal wave

   _____   _____
           type   relationship

9. Angry is to furious

   _____   _____
           type   relationship

10. Scalpel is to dissect

    _____   _____
            type   relationship

First and Third Analogies

❑ Occasionally, it will be the first and third words that are related, instead of the first two. We call these "First and Third" analogies.

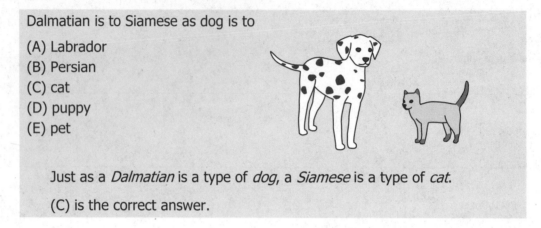

Dalmatian is to Siamese as dog is to

(A) Labrador
(B) Persian
(C) cat
(D) puppy
(E) pet

Just as a *Dalmatian* is a type of *dog*, a *Siamese* is a type of *cat*.

(C) is the correct answer.

❑ If you cannot determine a solid relationship between the first pair of words in an analogy, this is a good clue that it might be a "First and Third" analogy.

PUT IT TOGETHER

1. Hand is to foot as arm is to

    (A) knee
    (B) leg
    (C) wrist
    (D) body
    (E) hip

2. Brush is to chisel as painter is to

    (A) sculptor
    (B) palette
    (C) clay
    (D) art
    (E) gallery

3. Album is to atlas as pictures is to

    (A) journeys
    (B) states
    (C) maps
    (D) chapters
    (E) globes

Attractors

❑ Some analogies will contain answer choices that stand out because they contain words related to one or both of the stem words. Be careful not to choose these unless the answer choice has the same relationship as the stem.

Remember, you want to maintain the relationship between the two stem words.

> Shelter is to storm as
>
> (A) violation is to intrusion
> (B) downpour is to flood
> (C) inoculation is to disease
> (D) home is to protection
> (E) winter is to cold.
>
>
> Notice how the words in choices (B) and (D) attract your attention because they are related to the words in the stem pair.
> For example, *downpour* and *flood* in choice (B) relate to *storm*.
> Also, *home* and *protection* in choice (D) relate to *shelter*.
> These are attractors because they try to attract your attention and make you choose the wrong answer.
>
> The correct answer is (C) because the relationship in (C) is the same as the relationship in the stem.
> A *shelter* protects you from a *storm* just as an *inoculation* protects you from a *disease*.

TRY IT OUT

Circle the attractors in the following analogy and find the correct answer.

1.   Land is to acre as

     (A) farm is to soil
     (B) currency is to money
     (C) earth is to circumference
     (D) ground is to property
     (E) sound is to decibel ✓

Land is measured in acres

2.   Jungle is to tree as

     (A) swamp is to water
     (B) forest is to clearing
     (C) blade is to grass
     (D) swarm is to bee ✓
     (E) pack is to herd

A jungle is a large collection of trees

3.   Rifle is to trigger as

     (A) blade is to sheath
     (B) center is to target
     (C) car is to ignition ✓
     (D) bullet is to shell
     (E) lightning is to thunder

Rifle is started with a trigger

SUMMIT
EDUCATIONAL
GROUP

Being an Analogy Detective

❑ On analogy questions, you can often find the correct answer even when you don't know the meaning of a stem word.

❑ The correct answer to an SSAT analogy will almost always be a word pair that makes a concise and clear relationship, usually one where you can define one of the words in terms of the other in a short sentence.

Your first step when you are stumped by one of the stem words should be to look for the answer choice relationship(s) that are concise and clear. If you can't form a clear relationship, eliminate the answer choice.

deserted is to inhabitants

> *Deserted* means to have no *inhabitants* – a concise, clear relationship.

furniture is to wood

> *Furniture* can be made of *wood*, but it doesn't have to be, so this is not a strong relationship.

posture is to improve

> There is not a clear relationship between *posture* and *improve*. One's *posture* may or may not need to *improve*.

smile is to awe

> *Smile* is not related to *awe* at all.

oil is to lubricant

> *Oil*, by definition, is a type of *lubricant*.

TRY IT OUT

Determine if each pair of words is related. If the words relate, state the relationship in the space provided.

1. champion is to speed   _____

2. storm is to hurricane   _____

3. editor is to personality _____

4. success is to expect   _____

5. goggles is to eyes   _____

6. arrogant is to silly   _____

7. quartz is to rock   _____

8. ticket is to admission   _____

9. shoe is to leather   _____

10. nightmare is to dream   _____

11. radio is to television   _____

12. class is to practice   _____

13. common is to rare   _____

14. cage is to endangered   _____

15. wheat is to flour   _____

Assume you don't know the meaning of the stem words in each of the following analogies.
Circle the answer choices that form clear and concise relationships, and cross out those that don't.

16. ????? is to ????? as

    (A) lawyer is to document
    (B) architect is to office
    (C) potter is to clay
    (D) painter is to brush
    (E) gardener is to vine

17. ????? is to ????? as

    (A) extreme is to moderate
    (B) unanimous is to elected
    (C) superlative is to good
    (D) simultaneous is to timed
    (E) inconsiderate is to immoral

Solving Backwards

❑ Take each answer choice and define one word in terms of the other. Test the relationship on the stem. Pick the answer choice whose relationship seems to work best.

> ????? is to wealth as
>
> (A) bleached is to texture
> (B) energetic is to uncaring
> (C) friendly is to hostility
> (D) eager is to anxiety
> (E) melodious is to sound
>
> Assume that you don't know what the first stem word means, so use the answer choices to "solve backwards."
>
> (A) There is no relationship at all between these two words.
>
> (B) The relationship is shaky at best. Having energy has nothing to do with caring.
>
> (C) *Friendly* means lacking *hostility*. Concise and clear. A definite possibility.
>
> (D) There is no clear relationship. An *eager* person may have *anxiety*, but also may not.
>
> (E) *Melodious* means having a nice *sound*. Concise and clear. A definite possibility.
>
> You've now narrowed your choices down to (C) and (E).
>
> Now, solve backwards by applying the relationships you've come up with to the stem words.
>
> Could the first word mean lacking *wealth*, just as *friendly* means lacking *hostility*? It could, if it's a synonym for poor.
>
> Could it mean having a nice *wealth*? Probably not — you wouldn't say that someone has a "nice" *wealth*, or a "mean" one.
>
> Therefore, you pick (C) as your answer.

TRY IT OUT

Solve backwards to answer the following analogies:

1. Eardrum is to ????? as

    (A) air is to nostril
    (B) blood is to vein
    (C) retina is to eye
    (D) virus is to illness
    (E) scalp is to hair

2. ????? is to foresight as

    (A) talkative is to conversation
    (B) logical is to idea
    (C) cloudy is to sight
    (D) hopeful is to peace
    (E) perfect is to flaw

Chapter Review

❑ **Format/Directions**

"The following questions ask you to find relationships between words. For each question, select the answer choice that best completes the meaning of the sentence."

❑ **Making the Relationship**

The key to solving an analogy is to determine what the relationship is between the paired words.

For most analogies, your relationship should be a short sentence that contains both of the stem words and defines one of the words in terms of the other.

You can start your relationship with the first or second word.

Apply the stem relationship to your answer choices.

If the relationship you make yields two or more correct answers, make the relationship more specific.

Familiarize yourself with common analogy relationships.

Beware of attractors.

❑ **Being an Analogy Detective**

The correct answer to an SSAT analogy will almost always be a word pair that makes a concise and clear relationship, usually one where you can define one of the words in terms of the other in a short sentence.

Look for the answer choices with concise and clear relationships. Eliminate the rest.

Deal with the known answers first, then the unknown.

Analogies Practice

Middle Level

1. Hungry is to eat as

    (A) thirsty is to pour
    (B) tired is to sleep
    (C) happy is to cry
    (D) itchy is to bite
    (E) cold is to huddle

2. Car is to land as

    (A) train is to track
    (B) bicycle is to wheel
    (C) skate is to board
    (D) tire is to engine
    (E) boat is to water

3. Sick is to healthy as poor is to

    (A) lazy
    (B) destitute
    (C) wealthy
    (D) unfortunate
    (E) joyous

4. Cow is to calf as

    (A) ram is to lamb
    (B) duck is to duckling
    (C) colt is to pony
    (D) fox is to coyote
    (E) puppy is to kitten

5. Tooth is to dentist as

    (A) leg is to doctor
    (B) car is to mechanic
    (C) house is to architect
    (D) scalpel is to surgeon
    (E) trial is to lawyer

6. Water is to ice as

    (A) rain is to hail
    (B) blood is to vein
    (C) juice is to fruit
    (D) milk is to cream
    (E) cola is to soda

7. Airplane is to bird as submarine is to

    (A) boat
    (B) snorkel
    (C) animal
    (D) water
    (E) fish

8. Duck is to quack as

    (A) dog is to purr
    (B) bird is to beak
    (C) cow is to milk
    (D) cat is to meow
    (E) goose is to gander

9. Hammer is to wrench as carpenter is to

    (A) builder
    (B) architect
    (C) plumber
    (D) chauffeur
    (E) piper

10. Cotton is to plant as silk is to

    (A) worm
    (B) tree
    (C) cloth
    (D) factory
    (E) satin

11. Half-time is to game as

(A) inning is to baseball
(B) scene is to opera
(C) intermission is to play
(D) foul is to penalty
(E) pause is to video

12. Book is to film as publisher is to

(A) writer
(B) producer
(C) audience
(D) actor
(E) editor

13. Furious is to angry as ravenous is to

(A) flighty
(B) calm
(C) hungry
(D) tired
(E) shy

14. Opera is to music as

(A) vegetable is to fruit
(B) heart is to body
(C) song is to singer
(D) flower is to petal
(E) dog is to animal

15. Inch is to centimeter as yard is to

(A) meter
(B) kilogram
(C) foot
(D) mile
(E) quart

16. Fish is to school as

(A) cow is to ranch
(B) sock is to dresser
(C) soldier is to battle
(D) pupil is to bus
(E) bird is to flock

17. Guitar is to strum as flute is to

(A) listen
(B) press
(C) blow
(D) beat
(E) buzz

18. Teacher is to school as surgeon is to

(A) college
(B) stadium
(C) study
(D) courtroom
(E) hospital

19. Book is to chapter as

(A) play is to act
(B) word is to line
(C) magazine is to journal
(D) poem is to anthology
(E) scene is to stage

20. Ruler is to thermometer as length is to

(A) depth
(B) strength
(C) season
(D) temperature
(E) wind

21. Start is to begin as

(A) finish is to launch
(B) stop is to cease
(C) end is to repeat
(D) lead is to follow
(E) move is to dance

22. Hut is to house as

(A) flower is to stem
(B) roof is to floor
(C) grass is to skirt
(D) raft is to boat
(E) wall is to building

23. Telephone is to talking as letter is to

   (A) writing
   (B) recording
   (C) hearing
   (D) sending
   (E) seeing

24. Medicine is to pharmacist as meat is to

   (A) farmer
   (B) vendor
   (C) butcher
   (D) baker
   (E) grocer

25. Arm is to body as

   (A) husk is to corn
   (B) fur is to bear
   (C) wheel is to car
   (D) branch is to tree
   (E) pearl is to oyster

26. Drum is to percussion as

   (A) clarinet is to music
   (B) oboe is to woodwind
   (C) violin is to bow
   (D) cymbals is to crash
   (E) trumpet is to trombone

27. Orange is to rind as

   (A) slice is to loaf
   (B) milk is to butter
   (C) egg is to yolk
   (D) walnut is to shell
   (E) cherry is to stem

28. Painter is to brush as

   (A) cook is to egg
   (B) conductor is to violin
   (C) writer is to newspaper
   (D) sculptor is to chisel
   (E) teacher is to student

29. Circle is to sphere as

   (A) line is to point
   (B) triangle is to pyramid
   (C) hexagon is to cone
   (D) square is to rectangle
   (E) trapezoid is to cylinder

30. Visible is to seeing as

   (A) edible is to hearing
   (B) optical is to sensing
   (C) audible is to smelling
   (D) amiable is to speaking
   (E) tangible is to touching

31. Pipe is to plumber as acrylics are to

   (A) tailor
   (B) painter
   (C) carpenter
   (D) mechanic
   (E) critic

32. Doorbell is to chime as

   (A) telephone is to ring
   (B) sound is to sight
   (C) drum is to cymbal
   (D) book is to announcement
   (E) lamp is to light

33. Boundary is to border as

   (A) center is to nucleus
   (B) edge is to middle
   (C) library is to book
   (D) side is to front
   (E) fence is to neighbor

34. Greenhouse is to plants as incubator is to

   (A) animals
   (B) eggs
   (C) tomatoes
   (D) sunshine
   (E) weeds

35. Sculptor is to clay as

    (A) author is to board
    (B) gambler is to challenge
    (C) printer is to plastic
    (D) weaver is to yarn
    (E) manager is to desk

36. Cradle is to baby as

    (A) nest is to hatchling
    (B) toy is to child
    (C) rattle is to infant
    (D) bed is to rocker
    (E) lily pad is to frog

37. Adept is to unable as

    (A) predicted is to rainy
    (B) preferred is to choosy
    (C) precise is to careless
    (D) previewed is to ugly
    (E) prepared is to arranged

38. Leopard is to spots as

    (A) camel is to desert
    (B) robin is to speck
    (C) butterfly is to moth
    (D) cricket is to music
    (E) zebra is to stripes

39. Fly is to airplane as operate is to

    (A) surgeon
    (B) machinery
    (C) exploration
    (D) land
    (E) opening

40. Blue is to sadness as

    (A) yellow is to sky
    (B) purple is to tears
    (C) red is to paper
    (D) orange is to banana
    (E) green is to envy

41. Ewe is to lamb as

    (A) buck is to deer
    (B) puppy is to dog
    (C) goose is to gander
    (D) cow is to bull
    (E) doe is to fawn

42. Step is to staircase as rung is to

    (A) hallway
    (B) telephone
    (C) ladder
    (D) rooftop
    (E) railing

43. Milk is to cow as egg is to

    (A) rooster
    (B) pig
    (C) horse
    (D) hen
    (E) sheep

44. Soda is to beverage as

    (A) cereal is to sugar
    (B) milk is to water
    (C) rye is to bread
    (D) juice is to fruit
    (E) candy is to chocolate

45. Waiter is to waitress as

    (A) calf is to cow
    (B) cat is to lioness
    (C) sheep is to ewe
    (D) chicken is to egg
    (E) duck is to duckling

46. Flute is to woodwind as

    (A) violin is to music
    (B) sound is to instrument
    (C) trumpet is to brass
    (D) stick is to drum
    (E) percussion is to viola

47. Kilometer is to mile as

    (A) foot is to inch
    (B) gram is to pound
    (C) millimeter is to centimeter
    (D) speed is to distance
    (E) one thousand is to one hundred

48. Paragraph is to prose as

    (A) letter is to salutation
    (B) essay is to writing
    (C) story is to sentence
    (D) song is to chorus
    (E) stanza is to poetry

49. Drama is to tragedy as

    (A) book is to reading
    (B) poem is to anthology
    (C) performance is to stage
    (D) poem is to sonnet
    (E) biography is to nonfiction

50. Affable is to friendly as

    (A) amiable is to perfect
    (B) sullen is to dirty
    (C) irritable is to easygoing
    (D) insolent is to rude
    (E) tasteful is to fancy

Analogies Practice

Upper Level

1. Poverty is to money as

    (A) happiness is to whistle
    (B) pride is to danger
    (C) relief is to laughter
    (D) confidence is to faith
    (E) ignorance is to education ✓

2. Ream is to paper as

    (A) page is to book
    — (B) deck is to cards
    (C) column is to magazine
    (D) package is to gift
    (E) jar is to honey

3. Aquarium is to fish as

    (A) terrarium is to plants ✓
    (B) library is to lawn
    (C) garage is to sale
    (D) planetarium is to Martians
    (E) museum is to history

4. Picnic is to ants as   *picnic can be ruined by ants* ✓

    (A) swim is to jellyfish ✓
    (B) hunt is to deer
    (C) hike is to trail
    (D) badminton is to tennis
    (E) lunch is to eat

5. Altitude is to mountain as

    (A) width is to candle
    (B) temperature is to valley
    (C) depth is to ocean ✓
    (D) weight is to river
    (E) length is to paper

6. Wealthy is to impoverished as vigorous is to

    (A) growing
    (B) worried
    (C) loud
    (D) poor
    ✓ (E) lethargic

7. Dime is to nickel as

    (A) change is to silver
    (B) penny is to dollar
    ✓ (C) whole is to half
    (D) money is to wallet
    (E) part is to quarter

8. Pride is to lions as

    (A) honor is to person
    ✓ (B) gaggle is to geese
    (C) herd is to music
    (D) hump is to camel
    (E) bull is to frog

9. Valiant is to cowardly as

    (A) victorious is to glorious
    (B) frank is to dishonest ✓
    (C) fearful is to miserable
    (D) cautious is to careful
    (E) controllable is to manageable

10. Cross is to grumpy as cheerful is to

    (A) sad
    (B) buoyant ✓
    (C) manic
    (D) religious
    (E) clairvoyant

11. Glacier is to ice as

   (A) river is to ocean
   (B) jungle is to sand
   (C) sun is to frost
   (D) reef is to coral
   (E) grass is to lawn

12. Dwell is to domain as

   (A) walk is to library
   (B) dine is to bistro
   (C) stroll is to bazaar
   (D) read is to spectacles
   (E) print is to gallery

13. Fertilizer is to nourish is as

   (A) poison is to destroy
   (B) weed is to garden
   (C) insect is to burrow
   (D) wall is to border
   (E) blanket is to knit

14. Hot is to tepid as

   (A) spicy is to zesty
   (B) freezing is to cool
   (C) strong is to forceful
   (D) sweet is to tasty
   (E) loving is to childish

15. Century is to years as

   (A) book is to pages
   (B) poem is to verses
   (C) dollar is to pennies
   (D) hour is to minutes
   (E) year is to days

what is the best answer

16. Bed is to cot as

   (A) couch is to chair
   (B) room is to house
   (C) house is to mansion
   (D) lake is to fish
   (E) sleep is to dream

17. Abhor is to detest as

   (A) love is to hate
   (B) mope is to merriment
   (C) admire is to disgust
   (D) adore is to revere
   (E) attack is to exalt

18. Goose is to geese as

   (A) abode is to adobe
   (B) mouse is to mice
   (C) choose is to piece
   (D) moose is to antler
   (E) spouse is to spice

19. Permit is to allow as

   (A) forbid is to prohibit
   (B) license is to drive
   (C) ventilate is to irritate
   (D) repair is to realize
   (E) divert is to recognize

20. Battery is to power as

   (A) acid is to base
   (B) jigsaw is to piece
   (C) carburetor is to car
   (D) fuel is to energy
   (E) string is to kite

21. Hurdle is to jump as

   (A) obstacle is to course
   (B) wing is to fly
   (C) blender is to mix
   (D) vehicle is to stall
   (E) discus is to throw

22. Poet is to words as

   (A) choreographer is to movement
   (B) cinematographer is to editing
   (C) calligrapher is to pictures
   (D) graphic designer is to public relations
   (E) singer is to accompanist

23. Cage is to bird as hutch is to

(A) dog
(B) pigeon
(C) chicken
(D) rabbit
(E) cow

24. Counselor is to guidance as

(A) master is to deliberation
(B) teacher is to verification
(C) minister is to obligation
(D) decorator is to ramification
(E) overseer is to supervision

25. Sentry is to fortress as

(A) warden is to prison
(B) goalie is to soccer
(C) chief is to engine
(D) witch is to mirror
(E) inmate is to asylum

26. Bluebird is to happiness as

(A) pigeon is to nuisance
(B) swallow is to consumption
(C) dove is to peace
(D) robin is to tint
(E) turkey is to celebration

27. Ignite is to fire as incite is to

(A) riot
(B) notation
(C) perception
(D) flames
(E) job

28. Sunset is to daybreak as

(A) region is to vicinity
(B) dusk is to dawn
(C) morning is to sunrise
(D) crisis is to conclusion
(E) afternoon is to recess

29. Crocus is to spring as

(A) rain is to summer
(B) frog is to pond
(C) frost is to winter
(D) summer is to autumn
(E) garden is to harvest

30. Joy is to agony as

(A) hope is to happiness
(B) delight is to detail
(C) sad is to heartache
(D) nasty is to nervous
(E) pleasure is to pain

31. Rectangle is to box as

(A) triangle is to staple
(B) square is to pyramid
(C) ellipse is to circle
(D) circle is to tube
(E) hexagon is to traffic

32. Doe is to buck as

(A) cow is to bull
(B) puppy is to kitten
(C) frog is to tadpole
(D) minnow is to bait
(E) caterpillar is to cricket

33. Prevail is to defeat as

(A) persuade is to convince
(B) detain is to gloat
(C) salvage is to isolate
(D) saunter is to soothe
(E) protect is to incarcerate

34. Seasoned is to unskilled as mature is to

(A) old
(B) impractical
(C) green
(D) unable
(E) senior

35. Sweet is to sugar as aromatic is to

    (A) mechanical
    (B) dynamic
    (C) passion
    (D) sound
    (E) fragrance

36. Lofty is to humble as

    (A) fancy is to ornate
    (B) flowery is to plain
    (C) simple is to poor
    (D) windy is to breezy
    (E) hard is to tough

37. Pick is to bow as

    (A) flute is to piccolo
    (B) guitar is to violin
    (C) banjo is to cymbal
    (D) tuba is to trombone
    (E) piano is to cello

38. Virtuoso is to neophyte as

    (A) sophisticated is to naive
    (B) virulent is to lucid
    (C) sanguine is to inebriated
    (D) palatable is to delectable
    (E) realistic is to nihilistic

39. Pristine is to spotless as

    (A) unkempt is to sloppy
    (B) sterile is to miserable
    (C) serene is to distraught
    (D) affluent is to effective
    (E) chaste is to promiscuous

40. Prudent is to careless as stingy is to

    (A) careful
    (B) generous
    (C) mean
    (D) playful
    (E) jealous

41. Indifferent is to emotion as

    (A) immediate is to feedback
    (B) impassive is to reaction
    (C) insincere is to lie
    (D) immature is to behavior
    (E) insecure is to worry

42. Chaos is to order as

    (A) disorder is to disaster
    (B) peace is to harmony
    (C) disarray is to organization
    (D) confusion is to corruption
    (E) neatness is to cleanliness

43. Visibility is to seeing as mobility is to

    (A) moving
    (B) looking
    (C) writing
    (D) listening
    (E) acting

44. Land is to sound as acre is to

    (A) speedometer
    (B) decibel
    (C) money
    (D) scale
    (E) calendar

45. Eloquent is to writing as

    (A) expensive is to money
    (B) graceful is to movement
    (C) wealthy is to demeanor
    (D) fanciful is to whimsy
    (E) acceptable is to risk

46. Avaricious is to greed as

    (A) entitled is to ignorance
    (B) stable is to equality
    (C) deceptive is to honor
    (D) disgruntled is to faith
    (E) altruistic is to generosity

47. Anonymous is to name as

    (A) incognito is to identity
    (B) recognizable is to face
    (C) clandestine is to affair
    (D) enormous is to pressure
    (E) curious is to knowledge

48. Proud is to arrogant as talkative is to

    (A) specious
    (B) meticulous
    (C) mutinous
    (D) garrulous
    (E) ponderous

49. Clean is to immaculate as thrifty is to

    (A) obdurate
    (B) meticulous
    (C) parsimonious
    (D) intrepid
    (E) illustrious

SUMMIT
EDUCATIONAL
GROUP

Reading Comprehension

- ❏ General Information
- ❏ Active Reading
- ❏ Mapping the Passage
- ❏ Anticipate the Answer
- ❏ Process of Elimination
- ❏ Passage Types
- ❏ Answering the Questions
- ❏ Main Idea Questions
- ❏ Detail / Supporting Idea Questions
- ❏ Vocabulary Questions
- ❏ Tone / Attitude Questions
- ❏ Inference Questions
- ❏ Application Questions
- ❏ Except / Least / Not Questions
- ❏ Roman Numeral Questions

General Information

❑ Format/Directions

The SSAT contains one Reading Comprehension section. This section is 40 minutes and has 40 questions.

❑ Directions are as follows:

> Read each passage carefully and then answer the questions about it. For each question, decide on the basis of the passage which one of the choices best answers the question.

❑ There are four basic types of passages on the SSAT.

In **fact** passages, the author describes something using details and objective information. Examples might include a description of the way a volcano erupts, an explanation of the digestive system, or a biography of Florence Nightingale.

In **opinion** passages, the author offers and explains his or her opinion on a topic. Examples might include an argument that drinking water should contain fluoride or that economic factors, not slavery, caused the Civil War.

In **prose** passages, the author tells a story. This can be a story from the author's own experiences or a fictional story. Examples might include a musician's memories of how she learned to play an instrument, a father describing his child's first steps, or a story of a fight between a girl and her best friend.

In **poetry** passages, the author tells a story or describes an imagined scene. Examples might include a poem about the ocean, the emotion of love, or a woman's life.

❑ The passages are taken out of context, and may have been edited to fit the questions and the length required for the test. As a result, you may find that the passages are boring or confusing, especially if they are on unfamiliar topics. Don't worry; this is normal.

SSAT Structure

Writing Sample – 25 minutes

Quantitative – 30 minutes

MATHEMATICS																								
1	2	3	4	5	6	7	8	9	10	11	12	13	14	15	16	17	18	19	20	21	22	23	24	25
EASY					→			MEDIUM			→			DIFFICULT										

Reading Comprehension – 40 minutes

READING PASSAGES																																							
1	2	3	4	5	6	7	8	9	10	11	12	13	14	15	16	17	18	19	20	21	22	23	24	25	26	27	28	29	30	31	32	33	34	35	36	37	38	39	40
NOT IN ORDER OF DIFFICULTY																																							

Verbal – 30 minutes

SYNONYMS																													
1	2	3	4	5	6	7	8	9	10	11	12	13	14	15	16	17	18	19	20	21	22	23	24	25	26	27	28	29	30
EASY					→			MEDIUM			→			DIFFICULT															

ANALOGIES																													
31	32	33	34	35	36	37	38	39	40	41	42	43	44	45	46	47	48	49	50	51	52	53	54	55	56	57	58	59	60
EASY					→			MEDIUM			→			DIFFICULT															

Quantitative – 30 minutes

MATHEMATICS																								
1	2	3	4	5	6	7	8	9	10	11	12	13	14	15	16	17	18	19	20	21	22	23	24	25
EASY					→			MEDIUM			→			DIFFICULT										

Active Reading

❑ Because there are many passages on the test, you may feel tempted to rush through them. However, if you read too quickly, you may miss important information in the passage. The key to reading comprehension is to read swiftly but carefully.

❑ We do **not** recommend reading the questions first. It is difficult enough to understand a passage without having to keep so many questions in your head as well.

❑ Be an active reader.

Never expect a passage to interest or entertain you. You have to get into it, on your own. Reading is not a passive experience. It's something you do **actively**. Don't wait to see what a passage says; go get it!

❑ Summarize and make connections.

Restate phrases, sentences, and paragraphs in your own words. This will help you understand and remember what you have read.

Pay attention to how different parts of a passage are related. Information and details might be used to explain, support, contrast, describe, etc.

❑ As you read, analyze the passage and ask questions:

What topic is the author writing about?

What type of passage is it?

What is the author's purpose?

What is the main idea of each paragraph?

What will come next?

❑ Underline or write down the main ideas of each paragraph.

Marking the passage will force you to search actively for the important points, and it will also help keep your mind from wandering as you read.

TRY IT OUT

Read the following passage actively and be prepared to answer the "active reading" questions that follow:

The Hopi people of northeastern Arizona are known for the Kachina dolls. The Kachinas are known to be divine spirits who represent natural forces, elements, animals, or ancestors. People in the tribe carve figures of the Kachinas from cottonwood. These figures are given as gifts and symbolize different types of Kachina. Early Kachina dolls were carved from single pieces of cottonwood root and were painted with basic pigments. Over the last century, the dolls have become more intricate, with exquisite details, multiple pieces, and high-quality paints. The creation of these dolls has evolved from a traditional practice to a profitable art, with individual dolls selling for thousands of dollars.

The Kachina dolls are an important part of Hopi culture, which the Hopi have struggled to protect throughout the last several centuries. When the first European settlers came to America, many tribesmen gave up their traditional Hopi culture in exchange for European beliefs and customs. Today, the Hopi are surrounded by different cultures. Due to the Dawes Allotment Act of 1887, the Hopi have retained only a small patch of their land in the Arizona desert, and this territory is in the middle of the much larger Navajo Reservation. Because the U.S. government granted them so little land, the Hopi were not able to maintain the type of farming that had been so important to their culture and prosperity. The Hopi have had to find other resources in order to survive. For the modern Hopi tribe, Kachina dolls are not only a cherished tradition but also a necessary form of income for many Hopi artists.

1. What do Kachina dolls represent for the Hopi?

2. How have Kachina dolls changed over time?

3. What two reasons does the author give for the importance of Kachina dolls?

TRY IT OUT

Read the following passage actively and be prepared to answer the "active reading" questions that follow:

The photography bug bit me when I was young. The first time I rode a bike, and when I learned to juggle, and on my earliest birthdays: my mother was always there with her Polaroid. Within seconds of her snapping a shot, a picture came crawling out from the slot on the front of the camera. The image would be black at first, but within a few minutes, the photo would materialize, as if a dark fog was clearing. It is hard to describe the joy I felt as I watched the images form in these Polaroid photographs. There was an *inexplicable* excitement in waiting to see what would develop in the little square frame of the picture. It was a feeling like nothing else, and it is linked to many of my favorite memories of growing up. That anticipation is why I am a photographer today.

In modern photography, film is being replaced by digital technologies. Pictures no longer develop; they appear instantly on digital displays and are stored as data. Despite these advancements, I stubbornly continue to use my old cameras. Whenever I can, I use actual film in creating my photos because I don't want immediate, predictable results. For me, the joy of photography lies in a childlike sense of wonder and excited expectation.

4. What does the author mean by "The photography bug bit me"?

5. Do you know the meaning of the word "inexplicable"? What do you think it means?

6. Why did the author decide to become a photographer?

7. What is the author comparing in the second paragraph?

8. How does the author feel about digital photography? How does this relate to his passion for photography?

PUT IT TOGETHER

Astray: A Tale of a Country Town, is a very serious volume. It has taken four people to write it, and even to read it requires assistance. Its dullness is premeditated and deliberate and comes from a laudable desire to rescue fiction from flippancy. It is, in fact, tedious from the noblest motives and wearisome through its good intentions. Yet the story itself is not an uninteresting one. Quite the contrary. It deals with the attempt of a young doctor to build up a noble manhood on the ruins of a wasted youth. Burton King, while little more than a reckless lad, forges the name of a dying man, is arrested and sent to penal servitude for seven years. On his discharge he comes to live with his sisters in a little country town and finds that his real punishment begins when he is free, for prison has made him a pariah. Still, through the nobility and self-sacrifice of his life, he gradually wins himself a position, and ultimately marries the prettiest girl in the book. His character is, on the whole, well drawn, and the authors have almost succeeded in making him good without making him priggish. The method, however, by which the story is told is extremely tiresome. It consists of an interminable series of long letters by different people and of extracts from various diaries. The book consequently is piecemeal and unsatisfactory. It fails in producing any unity of effect. It contains the rough material for a story, but is not a completed work of art. It is, in fact, more of a notebook than a novel. We fear that too many collaborators are like too many cooks and spoil the dinner. Still, in this tale of a country town there are certain solid qualities, and it is a book that one can with perfect safety recommend to other people.

1. The primary purpose of this passage is to

   (A) consider the use of letters and diaries in the telling of a story
   (B) judge the strengths and weaknesses of a particular book
   (C) summarize the events of a story
   (D) argue against the opinions of a group of authors
   (E) demonstrate the effectiveness of collaborating in writing

2. The author implies that *Astray: A Tale of a Country Town* is a novel that

   (A) is entirely composed of literary essays
   (B) does not effectively describe its characters
   (C) narrates a series of difficulties and hardships
   (D) is based on traditional folk tales
   (E) succeeds in creating a cohesive, exciting story

3. According to the passage, *Astray: A Tale of a Country Town* is organized in a form that resembles

   (A) an archive of personal writings
   (B) a newspaper
   (C) a popular magazine
   (D) a comedic play
   (E) an encyclopedia article

4. The author criticizes *Astray: A Tale of a Country Town* by commenting that the novel

   (A) does not have an interesting story
   (B) is too fragmented, due to its many authors
   (C) tells a story that is too simple and obvious
   (D) is not believable
   (E) is too short for such an ambitious story

Mapping the Passage

❑ Don't try to retain every detail in the passage. Instead, try to develop a mental "picture" of the passage, so you'll know where to look to answer specific questions.

❑ Break the passage down into its parts.

As you read, try to follow the path of the passage as it shifts from point to point. Pay attention to the first and last sentence in each paragraph as they will often announce the transition from one point to the next. Mark with a check in the margin where each shift takes place.

Sometimes a shift can take place mid-paragraph. Be on the lookout for words like: *but, nevertheless, however, despite, on the other hand.*

❑ After you finish a paragraph or supporting point, ask yourself how it fits into the overall main idea, and then underline the main point or make a brief note in the margin summarizing the point.

❑ Don't waste time on a difficult sentence or word. There probably won't be a question on it. If you do get a question about the sentence or word, you can go back and figure it out then.

TRY IT OUT

Read the following passage actively and be prepared to answer the "active reading" questions that follow:

Slash-and-burn agriculture was practiced for thousands of years in the tropical rain forests of South America with little effect on the environment. It is a primitive agricultural system in which sections of forest are repeatedly cleared, cultivated, and allowed to regrow over a period of many years. Small groups practicing slash-and-burn agriculture generally clear one or two new plots a year, working a few areas at various stages of cultivation at a time. As the nutrients are used up and the land produces less, a plot cleared for slash-and-burn agriculture is rarely abandoned; species such as fruit trees are still cultivated as the forest begins to reclaim the open spaces.

Although it is relatively harmless when practiced on a small scale, this system of agriculture can cause considerable destruction when practiced by too many people. The pressures exerted by a rapidly growing population in South America have made slash-and-burn agriculture much more harmful. As the population grows, more and more peasants do not own their own land; they have been forced to move into the forests, where they support themselves by practicing slash-and-burn agriculture. More of these forests are being destroyed and some species have already been forced into extinction. If we fail to respond to this crisis in time, the loss of these forests will have permanently damaged the planet for us and for future generations.

1. What topic is the passage about?

2. What type of passage is it?

3. What is the main idea of paragraph 1?

4. What is the main idea of paragraph 2?

5. What is the author's main idea?

6. Why did the author write the passage?

Anticipate the Answer

❑ Before looking at the answer choices, try to think of the answer in your head. Try not to look at the answer choices until you know what the answer should be. Then find the answer that most closely matches your anticipated one.

❑ On many SSAT reading questions, there are multiple answer choices that **could be** correct, but there is only one **best** answer. If you try to test if you can prove the answer choices correct, you might get stuck with several answers that seem right. Instead, focus on finding your own best answer first.

> Surprisingly, the history of flea circuses begins with watchmaking. In a display of their incredibly precise metal-working skills, watchmakers created tiny props for fleas. This led to the first flea circuses. Fleas were used as the performers because of their strength and availability. At the time, before effective pest control, fleas were a common part of everyday life.
>
> According to the passage, flea circuses were created in order to
>
> (A) pass the time while watchmakers were not busy working
> (B) promote the need for pest control to eliminate fleas
> (C) test the capabilities of different metals and metal-working tools
> (D) demonstrate the talents of watchmakers
> (E) exhibit the incredible skill of fleas
>
> This might be a challenging question, because several answer choices could be correct.
>
> (A) could be right, because making flea circuses could have been a hobby to pass the time.
>
> (C) could be right, because the watchmakers could test new materials and methods by creating the tiny props.
>
> (E) could be right, because the circuses would show the strength of fleas.
>
> If you ignore the answer choices and just consider the question, it is clear from the information in the passage that flea circuses were made to display watchmakers' skills. (D) is the answer that best matches this idea.

❑ Anticipating the answer will save you time on the Reading Comprehension section because it allows you to find the answer by solving the question once.

TRY IT OUT

Many organisms have developed incredible adaptations for the environments in which they live. The most impressive examples are classified as "extremophiles," which are organisms that can thrive in conditions that are too harsh for most forms of life. One of the most well-known and unique extremophiles is the tardigrade, also known as the "water bear" or "moss piglet." This microscopic animal looks like a cross between a grub and a gummy bear.
5   Tardigrades can survive in environments that would be lethal to any other animal. They can live in termperatures colder than -400 degrees and hotter than 300 degrees Fahrenheit. They can also survive without water for nearly a decade. This is necessary because tardigrades commonly live in puddles and moss, which often dry out. They can reduce their metabolism to less than one-thousandth of their normal rate, and will return from this dormant state when they have a supply of water. Tardigrades have been found in many of the harshest environments on earth, such
10   as boiling hotsprings and arctic ice. They can even survive the vacuum of space! These amazing creatures show the surprising resilience of life. Research on extremophiles has led to new discoveries that allow scientists to work in conditions that would be too severe for our own bodies.

1. The author mentions "boiling hotsprings" (line 10) as an example of

    _____

    _____

    _____

2. As used in line 8, "state" means which of the following?

    _____

    _____

    _____

3. It can be inferred from the passage that the tardigrade can survive dehydration by

    _____

    _____

    _____

4. This passage is primarily about

    _____

    _____

    _____

SUMMIT
EDUCATIONAL
GROUP

PUT IT TOGETHER

Many organisms have developed incredible adaptations for the environments in which they live. The most impressive examples are classified as "extremophiles," which are organisms that can thrive in conditions that are too harsh for most forms of life. One of the most well-known and unique extremophiles is the tardigrade, also known as the "water bear" or "moss piglet." This microscopic animal looks like a cross between a grub and a gummy bear.
5   Tardigrades can survive in environments that would be lethal to any other animal. They can live in temperatures colder than -400 degrees and hotter than 300 degrees Fahrenheit. They can also survive without water for nearly a decade. This is necessary because tardigrades commonly live in puddles and moss, which often dry out. They can reduce their metabolism to less than one-thousandth of their normal rate, and will return from this dormant state when they have a supply of water. Tardigrades have been found in many of the harshest environments on earth, such
10   as boiling hotsprings and arctic ice. They can even survive the vacuum of space! These amazing creatures show the surprising resilience of life. Research on extremophiles has led to new discoveries that allow scientists to work in conditions that would be too severe for our own bodies.

1.   The author mentions "boiling hotsprings" (line 10) as an example of

(A) new scientific discoveries
(B) a source of water for dehydrated tardigrades
(C) the most common habitat for extremophiles
(D) how organisms affect their environment
(E) an extreme environment in which most organisms cannot survive

2.   As used in line 8, "state" means which of the following?

(A) area
(B) declare
(C) condition
(D) public
(E) structure

3.   It can be inferred from the passage that the tardigrade can survive dehydration by

(A) shrinking its size
(B) slowing its bodily processes
(C) living on moss
(D) burrowing underground
(E) melting ice

4.   This passage is primarily about

(A) the hardiness and adaptability of organisms
(B) why tardigrades do not need water
(C) the world's smallest living animal
(D) the tardigrade's ability to survive in extreme temperatures
(E) the benefits of biological research

Process of Elimination

❏ Eliminate answers which are too broad, too narrow, or simply incorrect.

As you read through the possible answers, eliminate answer choices that:

- cover more than the passage does.
- talk only about a portion of the passage.
- have nothing to do with the discussed topic.

❏ Process of elimination is extremely effective on Reading Comprehension since you will usually have at least some understanding of the passage. Eliminate wrong answers and then make an educated guess.

> What better way to show the values of a society than through its folklore? America is known for its rugged individuality, work ethic, and national pride. In its frontier legends, with heroes such as Paul Bunyan, Davy Crockett, and Pecos Bill, this American spirit shines brightly.
>
> The passage is primarily concerned with
>
> (A) describing American traditions
> (B) evaluating the connection between myth and reality
> (C) explaining how folklore is a source for symbols of cultural values
> (D) summarizing the author's favorite stories
> (E) examining how national pride is represented in stories
>
> > With this question, it might be hard to anticipate the answer before looking at the answer choices, so it is best to use Process of Elimination.
> >
> > (A) is not correct, because the passage is focused on folklore, not all American traditions: **too broad**.
> >
> > (B) is not correct, because the passage is concerned with folklore and social values. "Myth and reality" is **too broad**.
> >
> > (D) is not correct, because there is no mention of "favorite stories": **incorrect**.
> >
> > (E) is not correct, because the passage is concerned with all social values, not only "national pride." This answer is **too narrow**.
> >
> > Through the Process of Elimination, we can reason that (C) is the best answer.

❏ For an answer choice to be correct, it must be **entirely** correct. Do not get stuck on answer choices that are only partly right.

TRY IT OUT

Give reasons for eliminating answer choices (e.g. too broad, too narrow, incorrect) and find the correct answers.

When groups of people live together, massive amounts of waste are produced. Some of the waste, such as paper, food scraps, and other natural materials, is biodegradable. Biodegradable materials can break down in a short time, degrading into useful nutrients and resources. However, some waste materials, like plastics, are not biodegradable. These can remain in their original form in the environment for hundreds of years. Scientists are working to replace many of the non-biodegradable materials with biodegradable ones, such as plastics made from potato starch. Also, scientists have discovered a fungus from the Amazon that is capable of breaking down and consuming plastic. This research could dramatically reduce the amount of non-biodegradable waste. However, this will not entirely solve the problem of waste, and the amount of available space where waste can be deposited is diminishing rapidly. Earth may soon become little more than a garbage dump, unless even more imaginative methods of dealing with waste materials are developed in the near future.

1. The purpose of the passage is to

    (A) persuade readers to invest in research on plastics.

    (B) show the connection between the environment and human civilization.

    (C) describe the processes of biodegradation of different materials.

    (D) demonstrate that even the most troubling problems can have simple solutions.

    (E) present the problem of waste disposal and describe potential scientific solutions.

    (A) _____

    (B) _____

    (C) _____

    (D) _____

    (E) _____

2. Which of the following questions is fully answered by the passage?

    (A) What type of waste is the most biodegradable?

    (B) What are the consequences and effects of modern human society?

    (C) Why is plastic less biodegradable than other materials?

    (D) What are some solutions to the problem of non-biodegradable waste?

    (E) How much waste is biodegradable?

    (A) _____

    (B) _____

    (C) _____

    (D) _____

    (E) _____

TRY IT OUT

The widespread popularity of TV dinners began in the 1950s, with the Swanson company. After Thanksgiving one year, Swanson had a large surplus of turkeys. Trying to figure out what to do with the leftover holiday turkey is a common concern for many families, but Swanson was faced with over 200 tons of extra turkey! Fortunately, one of the company's executives had an idea. While on an airplane trip, he noticed that the flight service offered meals that had been pre-cooked and packaged. The flight attendants only had to reheat the meals, and they were quickly ready to serve. The executive imagined that meals at home could be prepared in a similar fashion, which would be a convenience for busy families as well as a solution to Swanson's surplus turkey problem.

Although they are convenient, TV dinners are usually less healthy than freshly prepared meals: the freezing process degrades the taste of the food, and so extra fat and salt are often added. Because of this, TV dinners are not as popular today as they were decades ago. Even so, the TV dinner remains in the iconic image of the 1950s American family, pioneers of convenience, gathered around their television set and dining from dinner trays.

3. On the airplane, the Swanson executive realized

   (A) many families value the convenience of
         modern technologies.

   (B) families often gather around their television
         set to enjoy meals together.

   (C) the company needed a way to sell their large
         amount of extra turkey.

   (D) the company could sell prepared meals in
         order to utilize its extra turkey.

   (E) frozen meals are often not as healthy as
         fresh foods.

4. It can be inferred from the passage that modern
     American families are

   (A) more concerned with the health of meals
         than earlier generations were.

   (B) less interested in watching television
         together than earlier generations were.

   (C) unaware of the traditions of earlier
         generations.

   (D) more capable of utilizing leftover foods than
         earlier generations were.

   (E) often enjoying meals on airplanes.

SUMMIT
EDUCATIONAL
GROUP

Passage Types

❏ Learn to recognize passage types.

Different types of passages may require different approaches.

❏ Adapt the focus of your reading depending on the type of passage.

In **fact** passages, pay attention to details and information. Look for explanations and reasons why things occurred.

In **opinion** passages, understand the author's argument and the logic that supports it. Look for information that the author uses to support the argument. Try to distinguish between what is fact and what is opinion.

In **prose** passages, understand the major events of the story and the emotions of the characters. Read dialogue carefully, because characters may use metaphors or mean more than the literal words they say.

In **poetry** passages, pay careful attention to descriptions and metaphors. Most poems have a deeper meaning, so try to determine if the poem is referring to something more than its literal meaning. Note strong words, because these may be used to create a certain tone.

Answering the Questions

❑ Learn to recognize question types.

Unlike the rest of the test, Reading Comprehension questions do not progress from easy to difficult. It may help to skip around, but try to complete all of the questions relating to a passage before you move on to the next passage.

Both easy and hard questions are worth one point, so learn to spot the easy questions and do them first. In general, questions break down as follows:

Easier: Detail, Main Idea, Vocabulary

Harder: Tone, Inference, Application

There are more inference questions on the Upper Level SSAT than there are on the Middle Level SSAT.

❑ Do one question at a time.

You may feel pressed for time during the reading. Relax! Rushing or jumping from one question to the next will only lessen your effectiveness. Work methodically.

❑ Use process of elimination.

Main Idea Questions

❑ Main idea questions ask you to identify the "primary purpose" or "focus" of the passage. In order to answer these questions correctly, you must be able to identify the main point of the passage and those ideas that support this point.

❑ Common main idea questions:

- Which of the following most accurately states the main idea of the passage?

- The primary purpose of the passage is to...

- The passage is primarily concerned with which of the following?

- The author of this passage is primarily concerned with...

- The main point made by the passage is that...

Main Idea questions will often contain these words: *main, primary, overall, purpose*

❑ The main idea of a passage is not simply the topic that the passage is about. Instead, the main idea is an idea, opinion, or feeling about the passage's topic.

❑ As you read, ask "What is the author's purpose?"

For *fact passages* ask: What is the author trying to explain to me?

For *opinion passages* ask: What is the author trying to convince me of?

For *prose passages* ask: What is the author sharing with me? What does the story show about the characters?

For *poetry passages* ask: What is the author trying to evoke? What thoughts or feelings is the author trying to share?

TRY IT OUT

In African cultures, as elsewhere, art has served both religious and practical purposes. A bronze figure of a king is a symbol of the ruler's divine nature. It is also a decorative work. Beautifully carved masks also have a dual purpose. A dancer wears a mask to represent a spirit in a religious ceremony. According to traditional beliefs, the mask gives the dancer the powers of that spirit.

African artists are probably best known for their fine sculpture. In forested areas, artists carved green wood into human figures, masks, and everyday objects. Other African sculptors created excellent works in bronze. Ancient craftsmen from the African nation of Benin are renowned for their many incredible casts of bronze heads and wall plaques that showed important events in history. These bronze figures can be appreciated for both their aesthetic and their instructive value.

1. The main idea of the passage is that

    _____

    _____

2. The passage is mostly about the

    (A) cost of different types of art
    (B) evolution of artistic styles in Africa
    (C) reasons why art gains popularity
    (D) materials used in African art
    (E) different ways in which African art
        functions

3. According to the passage, African sculptors are

    (A) wealthy nobles
    (B) incredibly talented
    (C) underappreciated
    (D) highly religious
    (E) researchers of history

4. The most appropriate title of the passage would be

    (A) Africa: The Land of Bronze
    (B) Africa: A King's Wealth
    (C) The Multiple Roles of African Art
    (D) The Great Expense of African Sculpture
    (E) The History of Great Art

5. The author's main purpose in the passage is to

    (A) describe the skill of African artists and the
        different purposes of their art
    (B) point out the differences between African
        and European art
    (C) amuse and entertain the reader by ridiculing
        the absurd price of sculpture materials
    (D) discredit the inefficiency of certain sculpting
        methods
    (E) illustrate the cultural influences on African
        artistic styles

Detail / Supporting Idea Questions

❑ Detail questions ask for specific facts from the passage.

Most of the questions that fit into this category could be called "find the fact" as they rely on your ability to find a specific piece of information, often contained in two or three sentences. Unlike main idea questions, which are more broad, these questions refer to a specific idea.

❑ Common detail / supporting idea questions:

- According to the passage, which of the following is true of _____?

- According to the passage, if _____ occurs then...

- The passage states that _____ occurs because...

- The author believes...

- On line 10, the author compares pollution to...

Detail questions will often contain these words: *states*, *mentions*, *specific*, *example*

❑ The answers to detail questions can be found in specific parts of the passage. For most detail questions, you won't remember the answer from the first reading. However, if you map the passage, you may remember where the detail appears in the passage. Go to the appropriate place in the passage and search for the answer.

❑ You should be able to support your answer with material in the passage. Practice defending your answer choices.

❑ Read above and below any line-numbers cited in the question to get the full context of the sentence. Line numbers point you to the general area where the answer is found. You will usually need the context around those lines to get the right answer.

TRY IT OUT

Plato, it seems, was the first person to define the characteristics of the soul. Plato considered the soul to be divided into three distinct energies that are at the core of all human behavior. His reason for this view was based on the conflicting desires people often have; people are often attracted to and averse to something at the same time, such as when someone both wants to commit a crime and is reluctant to do it. Plato believe there must be multiple
5   parts of the soul that control these contradictory motivations. According to Plato, the soul consists of three parts: Reason, Emotion, and Appetite. Plato compared these, metaphorically, to the brain, the heart, and the stomach. He believed that each of these parts of the soul was essential and that they must work in balance in order to live in peace. He gave Reason the greatest value, arguing that a person who is virtuous and wise will use reason to control their passions and desires and that this is the only way to achieve true happiness. He believed so strongly in this idea
10   of the soul that he designed social systems based on it, believing that the harmony of the soul could serve as a model for harmony in the operation of an entire civilization.

1. According to the passage, Plato based his social design on his concept of the soul because

    _____

    _____

2. According to the passage, Plato believed that the most influential part of the soul should be

    (A) the heart
    (B) the stomach
    (C) Emotion
    (D) Reason
    (E) Appetite

3. The author mentions parts of the body (line 6) as an example of

    (A) Plato's knowledge of anatomy
    (B) the different energies of the soul as theorized by Plato
    (C) factors that contribute to criminal behavior
    (D) opposing theories of the characteristics of the soul
    (E) the modern understanding of biology

Vocabulary Questions

❑ Vocabulary questions ask you to define a word in the context in which it is used. The word may be unfamiliar to you, or the word may normally be used in another context.

❑ Common vocabulary questions:

- In line 6, the word "appreciate" most nearly means...

- Which of the following best captures the meaning of the word "compensate" in line 2?

Vocabulary questions will often contain these words: *the word, meaning, definition, in context*

❑ Anticipate the answer on vocabulary questions.

Pretend the word in question is a blank. Without looking at the choices, try to fill in the blank with your own word(s). Look for the answer choice that most nearly matches your anticipated answer.

❑ Watch for attractor answers.

Often, vocabulary questions ask you to define words that have more than one meaning. Usually, the most common definition of the word is not the right answer. Be sure to look back at the sentence in which the word appears. The right answer should make sense when you plug it into the sentence.

TRY IT OUT

The geography of Southeast Asia has contributed to ethnic and cultural diversity. The mountains cut groups of people off from one another. In many countries, a majority ethnic group controls the rich river valleys as well as the government. For example, Laos is the home to Lao, Tai, Hmong, Mon, and Khmer peoples, as well as to many Chinese and Vietnamese. The Lao make up 48% of the population and occupy the valleys of the Mekong River and
5   its tributaries. They control the government, determine the official language, and set education policies.

Ethnic minorities often live in the rugged highlands of the main land. Since the poor soil can support only a sparse population, highlanders tend to live in smaller groups. Cut off from other people, these minorities have preserved their own languages and customs. Many feel little kinship to the lowlanders or loyalty to the central government.

1. What is the meaning of "kinship" as used in line 8?

   _____

   _____

2. As used in line 2, "rich" means which of the following?

   (A) fertile
   (B) heavy
   (C) wealthy
   (D) settled
   (E) lowland

3. When the author mentions "tributaries" in line 5, he is referring to

   (A) donations
   (B) testimonials
   (C) small rivers
   (D) highlands
   (E) wishes

4. Which of the following can best be substituted for the phrase "Cut off" (line 7) without changing the author's meaning?

   (A) Disfigured
   (B) Attacked
   (C) Separated
   (D) Plucked
   (E) Ruined

Tone / Attitude Questions

❑ Tone questions ask you to identify the author's tone, or the mood of the passage. Look for words to clue you in to the author's opinions or feeling about the topic of the passage.

❑ Common tone / attitude questions:

- The author's tone can best be described as...

- Which of the following best describes the author's attitude?

Tone questions will often contain these words: *tone*, *attitude*, *mood*, *feel*, *opinion*

❑ When determining the tone of a passage, look for words that convey emotion or judgment.

> Dark house, by which once more I stand
> Here in the long unlovely street,
> Doors, where my heart was used to beat
> So quickly, waiting for a hand,
>
> A hand that can be clasped no more--
> Behold me, for I cannot sleep,
> And like a guilty thing I creep
> At earliest morning to the door.
>
> He is not here; but far away
> The noise of life begins again,
> And ghastly through the drizzling rain
> On the bald street breaks the blank day.
>
>
> The tone of this poem is gloomy and sad. The somber mood is clearly seen in words such as "dark," "guilty," and "ghastly." A sense of loss is felt in the images of a heart that "used to beat so quickly" and "a hand that can be clasped no more."
> Even if you struggle to understand what the poem is about, it is easy to see that it is not a happy subject.

TRY IT OUT

One of the greatest testaments to the ingenuity and perseverance of modern man is the success of the desert cities of the American Southwest. In the middle of a vast, harsh land, great cities have grown and thrived. The success of our desert cities is especially remarkable because of the many challenges presented by the desert environment. With most rain falling in the hills and mountains of California, very little moisture comes as far as
5   Utah, Arizona, or New Mexico. With no access to oceans and few rivers, these areas rely on man-made canals and reservoirs for their necessary water. The city of Phoenix receives only a few inches of rain per year; however, the average inhabitant uses 150 gallons of water per day. In order to bring water to the city, an impressive 300-mile system of pumps, pipes, and aqueducts was built to bring water from Lake Havasu across the desert to the residents of Arizona's largest city. 20 years in the making, this project is an amazing achievement of engineering and
10   determination. This is a sign of the great abundance and productiveness of the whole United States. These desert cities show that we can succeed in even the harshest and most unproductive land because of our hard work and many resources.

There are some critics who would argue that the cities of the American Southwest are a drain on our country and that there is no compelling reason for so many people to live in such a remote, unproductive area. However,
15   while it is true that the modern cities of the Southwest are dependent on the resources they can bring from other areas, these desert cities also provide valuable resources to other regions. The Southwest is a major source of American copper, gold, silver, and uranium. While these deserts may be harsh, they contain a wealth of resources.

1. The tone of this passage is best described as

    (A) delighted
    (B) skeptical
    (C) critical
    (D) admiring
    (E) mocking

2. The style of this passage is most like what would
    be found in

    (A) an author's diary
    (B) a geography textbook
    (C) a dramatic novel
    (D) a short story
    (E) a letter sent to a friend

3. The attitude expressed by "some critics" (line
    13) can best be described as

    (A) sarcastic
    (B) humorous
    (C) negative
    (D) sympathetic
    (E) curious

Inference Questions

❑ Inference questions ask you to draw logical conclusions based on what is written.

❑ Common inference questions:

- The author talks about _____ primarily to illustrate...

- The author's conclusion is supported most directly by...

- The author assumes all of the following except...

- It can be inferred from the passage that

- The passage suggests which of the following about _____?

Inference questions will often contain these words: *assumes, illustrates, infers, implies, suggests*

❑ Answers to inference questions are never directly stated in the passage.

Inference questions ask you to interpret the information in the passage, or to apply the ideas from the passage to something new.

TRY IT OUT

The contestants stand side by side, shuffling tentatively on a crumpling asphalt track. All around them are weeds that climb the chain-link fence and muscle up through cracks in the soft, hot asphalt. You get so used to seeing weeds in this neighborhood, you don't even notice them after a while. They are just there, like the drugs and the tragedy, blending into the wounded landscape. On the other side of the playground is deserted Condon Middle School, gloomy and massive, vulnerable to thieves who circle the building in trucks, then move in and peck away like buzzards. Before they gathered at the starting line, there was talk about a guy named Johnson. His street name was Bang, and he considered himself pretty fast. He had planned on being there for the event. But Bang was gunned down the night before. He was twenty-five.

1. What sport are the contestants probably doing? How do you know?

2. Is the neighborhood in a city, the country, or the suburbs? How do you know?

3. About how old are the contestants? How do you know?

4. What sort of mood is the author trying to create? How do you know?

5. Why does the author point out the growing weeds?

TRY IT OUT

9 July 1825

Dear Mama,

   Tomorrow will be the most important day of my 11 years. The lawyers will read Miss Margaret's will at the court house. I know that I was her favorite, and all my friends think that she will set me free. Freedom! The word tastes like Christmas when I say it out loud. Like a juicy orange or a cup of sweetened milk.

   Grandma has always been a hopeful person like you, Mama. But she says she cannot let hope in the door. You're worth too much money, she tells me. She recalls that Mark was worth one hundred dollars when he was only a boy of twelve, and now he's a grown man of 25.

   I am not afraid to hope. I know Miss Margaret has remembered you, her childhood friend, and the promise she made the night you died. Besides, she taught me these words: Love thy neighbor as thyself.

   Tomorrow I will taste freedom.

You loving daughter,

–Harriet Ann.

6.   How old is the author? How do you know?

7.   What does she hope for? How do you know?

8.   Who is Miss Margaret? How do you know?

9.   What does the author mean when she says "the word tastes like Christmas. . . a juicy orange or a cup of sweetened milk"?

PUT IT TOGETHER

At the age of six, Amos Alcott already recognized the risk of his ambitions. As a young boy, he witnessed a total solar eclipse and, bewildered by the phenomenon, he and his friends threw stones up toward the moon. Amos was too excited and not careful enough; he fell and dislocated his shoulder. Over sixty years later, he judged that this boyhood accident represented much of the rest of his life, because he often pursued grand ideals that led to trouble and failure.

As an adult, Alcott was plagued with disappointments. His books were ridiculed for being too dense and abstract. His Fruitlands experiment, an attempt to create a perfect agricultural community, failed disastrously. His progressive educational ideas were underappreciated and misunderstood. He often had to borrow money, because his ethics were more important than his income. Amos Alcott was perhaps too ambitious and idealistic, but despite his criticisms and failures he has left a positive legacy. His thoughts on education have been particularly influential in promoting the interaction, self-expression, and critical thinking seen in modern classrooms. Thanks to the ideas of Alcott, school instruction has shifted away from repetition and memorization and toward discussion, reflection, and problem-solving. He is remembered for his determination, his innovation, and his bold defense of equality and creativity, which pioneered many changes seen in modern education.

1. It can be inferred from the passage that Amos Alcott would agree with which of the following statements?

   (A) The most effective education is achieved by memorizing a large number of facts.
   (B) Students learn the most when they are allowed to think and express themselves creatively.
   (C) More classes should focus on research on astronomical phenomena.
   (D) The easiest plans are always the best.
   (E) All accidents are the result of poor planning.

2. The author suggests that Amos Alcott

   (A) never recognized that he failed in so many of his endeavors
   (B) would have been more successful if he had pursued grander goals
   (C) was given more praise than he deserved
   (D) was a profoundly different person as an adult than he was as a child
   (E) was ultimately successful

3. The passage implies that Alcott was very concerned about

   (A) avoiding risk and disappointment
   (B) making his ideas easy to understand
   (C) earning as much money as possible
   (D) putting grand ideas into action
   (E) correcting the mistakes he made as a child

Application Questions

❑ Application questions ask you to take information and conclusions in the passage and connect them to similar situations or ideas. The key to this question type is the ability to identify the core of an argument or idea in the passage.

❑ Common application questions:

- The author of the passage would be most likely to agree with which of the following?

- Which of the following statements would provide the most logical continuation of the final paragraph?

Application questions will often contain these words: *most likely, probably*

TRY IT OUT

The birth of modern computer development is often considered to be around the year 1890. To prepare for the population census of the United States that year, Herman Hollerith developed a machine that used electromagnetism to "read" information encoded in cards punched with holes. The holes in the cards allowed small electrical currents to pass through, which activated counters. By employing this system, Hollerith completed the 1890 census in one quarter of the time it had taken for the 1880 census! The invention of the punch card system symbolizes the dawn of the computer age.

In 1946, the United States military developed the first general purpose computer. Dubbed ENIAC, or the Electronic Numerical Integrator and Calculator, the massive computer consisted of thousands of vacuum tubes and filled an entire warehouse. It broke down often, costing millions of dollars to repair. In addition, ENIAC used enormous amounts of energy, generated great amounts of heat, and was costly to maintain. Compared to computers today, ENIAC was ploddingly slow, completing only about 6,000 calculations per second.

Computers became available to the public through advances in technology and reduction in size and cost, which were driven by increased demand. Interest in computer technology encouraged research and development of faster, cheaper, and smaller transistors and the invention of integrated circuits. These advances made computers more efficient, more useful, and more affordable, bringing computers within the reach of small businesses and home users.

Intense research and development in computer technology has led to great progress since the development of the ENIAC. Integrated circuits called microprocessors have been developed to provide processing capability in tiny chips. Also, large groups of computers have been connected to form supercomputers to provide huge amounts of processing. Whether smaller and more efficient or interconnected and more powerful, computer technology continues to advance far beyond the punch cards Herman Hollerith created.

1. Which of the following is the author most likely to discuss next?

    _____

    _____

2. From the information in the passage, how would one expect modern computer technology to continue advancing?

    _____

    _____

3. Which of the following would the author probably believe best represents the advancement of computer technology since the earliest computers?

    (A) increased reliability and decreased cost
    (B) increased size and decreased energy usage
    (C) increased speed and decreased efficiency
    (D) increased cost and decreased reliability
    (E) increased efficiency and decreased speed

4. As described by the author, when the ENIAC was first created it was most like

    (A) a sports car used for recreational driving
    (B) an enormous, costly vehicle used to haul large amounts of material
    (C) an old train that is still used because a newer model would be too expensive
    (D) an appliance that is used for something other than its intended function
    (E) a modern laptop computer used for creative projects

Except/Least/Not Questions

❑ Except/least/not questions twist questions around by asking you to identify an answer choice that is not supported by the passage.

These questions may take longer to solve, because you cannot anticipate the answer; instead, you have to carefully test each answer choice.

❑ Common except/least/not questions:

- The author would probably agree with all of the following EXCEPT. . .

- Which is the LEAST likely to be. . .

- Which of the following is NOT a characteristic of _____. . .

❑ Find which answer choice doesn't fit with the others.

You can use process of elimination by crossing out the four answers that are supported by the passage, leaving the correct answer.

Roman Numeral Questions

❑ Roman numeral questions present multiple true/false options. These questions also take longer to solve, because each option must be tested.

❑ Common Roman numeral questions:

- It can be inferred that the author would agree with which of the following?

- The _____ includes which of the following?

TRY IT OUT

Most people can appreciate the pleasing effects of music. When your head is bobbing, your feet are tapping, or when you feel a sense of calmness or invigoration, music clearly has a unique and distinctive power. So it is no surprise that therapists are able to use music to great advantage in many forms of treatment.

For millennia, music has been used as a method of healing. Hippocrates, the "Father of Medicine," used music as a treatment for mental illness. Aristotle also described the importance of music, writing, "Music is able to produce a certain effect on the character of the soul." Many therapists today recognize the deep effects that music can have and continue to use it to manage emotional and behavioral disorders. Music therapy comes in many forms: playing instruments, listening, composing, and following rhythms are all activities used in modern treatment.

What makes music so therapeutic? For some people, music is a way to express ideas and emotions. Another benefit is that, in its very nature, music harmonizes. By attuning oneself to the rhythms of a musical composition, one's mind and body can find a sense of regularity. According to studies, this bond with music begins in the womb, where the fetus experiences the mother's heartbeat. Our relationships with music are universal and widespread. The effects of music can be felt by everyone, and in this way it serves to unify us and can help ease troubled minds.

Most people have their own particular songs, musicians, and composers that bring them joy. Also, most people have particular pieces of music that help them through sad or stressful times, as well as music that calms or excites them. In these ways, we use our favorite music as a form of self-treatment, because we recognize the force it has on us.

1. The author mentions all of the following as an effect of music EXCEPT

    (A) calming
    (B) pleasing
    (C) exciting
    (D) stressing
    (E) energizing

2. According to the passage, which of the following is NOT a reason why music can be therapeutic?

    (A) It allows people to bond.
    (B) It promotes stability and consistency.
    (C) It can influence emotions.
    (D) It is used in one standardized form.
    (E) It allows people to express themselves.

3. According to the passage, music therapy involves which of the following practices?

    I.   creating new musical compositions
    II. reading books about music history
    III. listening to favorite pieces of music

    (A) I only
    (B) I and II only
    (C) I and III only
    (D) II and III only
    (E) I, II, and III

Chapter Review

❑ **Format/Directions**

"Read each passage carefully and then answer the questions about it. For each question, decide on the basis of the passage which one of the choices best answers the question."

There are four basic types of passages: fact, opinion, prose, and poetry.

Determining what type of passage you're reading can help you determine what to focus on as you read.

❑ **Reading the Passage**

Don't read the questions first.

Be an active reader. Ask questions as you read. Search for the main idea of each paragraph.

Summarize and make connections.

Break the passage down into its parts.

After you finish a paragraph or supporting point, ask yourself how it fits into the overall main idea, and then underline the main point or make a brief note in the margin summarizing the point.

Make a map of the passage so you'll know where to look to answer specific questions.

❑ **Using Your Time Wisely**

Reading carefully will allow you to work through the questions more quickly.

Don't get bogged down in difficult words or details.

❏ Anticipate the Answer

Before looking at the answer choices, try to think of the answer in your head. Try not to look at the answer choices until you know what the answer should be. Then find the answer that most closely matches your anticipated one.

On many SSAT reading questions, there are multiple answer choices that could be correct, but there is only one best answer.

❏ Answering the Questions

Learn to recognize question types.

Do one question at a time. Look at each answer choice one at a time.

Use process of elimination. Eliminate answers which are too broad, too narrow, or simply wrong.

Main idea questions ask for the main idea or author's opinion. Anticipate the answer to main idea questions. Eliminate answers that are too broad, too narrow, or simply wrong.

Vocabulary questions ask you to define a word as it is used in context.

Defend your answer to detail questions with information from the passage.

Inference questions ask you to draw conclusions based on what is written. Do not expect the answer to be explicitly stated in the passage.

On except/least/not questions, find which answer choice doesn't fit with the others.

Use process of elimination to solve Roman numeral questions.

Reading Practice

Middle Level

During the Viking period (about 800 AD to 1050 AD), Scandinavian navigational practices may have been the most skillful in Europe. True, the Viking sailor may have been no better than others while traveling coastal waters. Knowing the location of sandbars and other hazards and the tendencies of tides, coastal winds, and currents was part of any sailor's stock-in-trade since at least the time of the ancient Greeks. What distinguished the Viking as a

5   navigator were his methods of crossing wide and open seas during the traditional sailing season from April to October.

As is often the case with the history of early navigation, direct contemporary evidence for Viking navigation is lacking; the Viking navigator passed along only orally what he learned for himself and what he had learned from previous generations. We are forced to gather what we can about his practices from mostly casual references in

10   sagas and other accounts of his time that were written considerably afterward, usually by men who themselves were inexperienced at sea. Inadequate as it is, this evidence reveals at least the Viking's most important navigational methods.

Faced with the dangers of sudden shifts of wind or lack of it altogether, blanketing fog, and other perils of the harsh North Atlantic, the Viking who crossed the vast ocean was always an intrepid adventurer. That the mishaps he

15   had, as recounted in sagas and other sources, are the exception rather than the rule owes much to his navigational skill.

1. The primary purpose(s) of this passage is (are) to

   (A) criticize today's sailors for failing to learn from the Vikings
   (B) give a historical overview of Viking culture and describe its influence on America
   (C) familiarize readers with weather patterns in the North Atlantic
   (D) describe the skill of Viking navigators and explain how we came to learn about it
   (E) depict the dangers of sailing in the Atlantic

2. According to the passage, Viking sailors differed from other sailors mainly through their

   (A) advanced methods of ship construction
   (B) skill in reading the compass
   (C) method of sailing in the open seas
   (D) willingness to sail in cold weather
   (E) ability to recognize hazards

3. Which of the following best describes the author's attitude toward Viking navigators?

   (A) Angry
   (B) Admiring
   (C) Envious
   (D) Indifferent
   (E) Encouraging

4. The author suggests that our knowledge of Viking navigation methods comes from what source?

   (A) Written accounts by later authors
   (B) Written accounts by the Vikings themselves
   (C) Careful study of Viking ships
   (D) Ancient Greek written accounts
   (E) Logical assumptions by modern sailors

5. The author implies that our knowledge of Viking navigation methods is

   (A) incomplete
   (B) comprehensive
   (C) likely to improve in the near future
   (D) fundamentally wrong
   (E) unfortunately biased

6. The last paragraph suggests that

   (A) the Vikings are the discoverers of America
   (B) sailing the North Atlantic posed no problems to the Vikings
   (C) the Vikings occasionally encountered problems, despite their skill
   (D) the author questions the courage of certain Viking sailors
   (E) only the Vikings could sail in the Atlantic

To see the earth as it truly is, small and blue and beautiful in that eternal silence where it floats, is to see ourselves as riders on the earth together, brothers on that bright loveliness in the eternal cold – brothers who know now they are truly brothers.

We are astronauts – all of us. We ride a spaceship called Earth on its endless journey around the sun. This ship
5 of ours is blessed with life-support systems so ingenious that they are self-renewing, so massive that they can supply the needs of billions.

But for centuries we have taken them for granted, considering their capacity limitless. At last we have begun to monitor the systems, and the findings are deeply disturbing.

Scientists and government officials of the United States and other countries agree that we are in trouble. Unless
10 we stop abusing our vital life-support systems, they will fail. We must maintain them, or pay the penalty. The penalty is death.

7. The main purpose of this passage is to

   (A) persuade
   (B) entertain
   (C) relive
   (D) discriminate
   (E) dictate

8. In the 2nd paragraph, the author uses the word "astronauts" as

   (A) a satirical commentary
   (B) an alliteration
   (C) a truism
   (D) an analogy
   (E) a criticism

9. With which of the following statements would the author most likely agree?

   (A) It is impossible to get a clear understanding of the way the planet survives.
   (B) Natural resources are unlimited.
   (C) Earth is dying and there is nothing people can do about it.
   (D) Unless humanity takes better care of the planet, there will be dire consequences.
   (E) Ecology and conservation are only to be understood by scientists.

10. The author compares the earth to a spaceship in order to

   (A) explain his interest in science fiction
   (B) illustrate the interdependent structure of systems on earth
   (C) explain the rotation of the planets
   (D) give a reason for government officials to perform studies
   (E) describe unexplained occurrences

Martin Gray, a survivor of the Warsaw Ghetto and the Holocaust, writes of his life in a book called *For Those I Loved*. He tells how, after the hardships of the Holocaust, he rebuilt his life, became successful, married, and raised a family. Life seemed good after the horrors of the concentration camp. Then one day, his wife and children were killed when a forest fire ravaged their home in the South of France. Gray was distraught, pushed almost to the
5 breaking point by this added tragedy. People urged him to demand an inquiry into what caused the fire, but instead he chose to put his resources into a movement to protect nature from future fires. He explained that an inquiry, an investigation, would focus only on the past, on issues of pain and sorrow and blame. He wanted to focus on the future instead. An inquiry would set him against other people – "Was someone negligent? Whose fault was it?" – and being against other people, setting out to find a villain, accusing other people of being responsible for your
10 misery, only makes a lonely person lonelier. Life, he concluded, has to be lived for something, not just against something.

11. The word "distraught" in line 4 means

   (A) peaceful
   (B) troubled
   (C) accusatory
   (D) alert
   (E) shattered

12. Martin Gray is most likely

   (A) an example of how to handle suffering
   (B) a fictional character
   (C) not very inquisitive
   (D) an infamous writer
   (E) shy and passive

13. The author would likely agree that

   (A) people always get what they deserve
   (B) success leads to loneliness
   (C) tragedy ruins people's lives forever
   (D) a positive attitude helps people to cope with troubles
   (E) mysteries are meant to be solved

14. What does the author mean when he says that "life… has to be lived for something, not just against something?"

   (A) People should never question circumstances.
   (B) It is better to do something positive than to concentrate on negative things.
   (C) Dreams don't always come true.
   (D) Happiness is fleeting.
   (E) The best way to understand something is to recognize its opposite.

In a society impregnated with racism, even the most secure and respectable black home cannot shelter a child from the ugly realities which daily ravage his or her life and those of millions. Martin got his first lesson in "race relations" when he was six. Among his playmates from the time he was very little were two white boys, the neighborhood grocer's sons. When Martin entered first grade, they were not among his classmates – they attended

5   another school for whites only. Martin attached little importance to this at first, but whenever he ran across the street to see them, their mother found some excuse to send him away. Finally she told Martin what she had already told her sons: "We're white and you're colored, and you can't play together anymore."

Bewildered and hurt, Martin burst into tears and ran home to his mother. As best she could, she told the boy how their ancestors had been abducted and enslaved, brought to America generations ago and used like animals,

10   sometimes kindly, often brutally, but always under the control of the white man. Negroes deserved to be free, they supposedly had been for over seventy years. But white people remained afraid, and so there was a whole system of Jim Crow laws and practices and attitudes. But for every question Mrs. King could answer, there arose others which the child would carry with him into adolescence and adulthood. "So I'm colored," the boy thought. "Why is that? What does it really mean? Why should things be the way they are?" His mother could not satisfactorily deal with

15   such questions. So she brought him back to his rejection by the grocer's wife. "Don't let this thing impress you," she said. "Don't let it make you feel you are not as good as white people. You are just as good as anyone else, and don't you forget it."

15. "Impregnated" in line 1 most closely means

(A) untouched by
(B) filled with
(C) immune to
(D) ashamed of
(E) free from

16. Which of the following would be the best title for the passage?

(A) The History Of Slavery
(B) The Cruelty Of Children
(C) A Lesson In Injustice
(D) Believe In Yourself
(E) Friends for Life

17. How would the author describe the young Martin?

(A) emotionally unstable
(B) unpopular
(C) inquisitive
(D) hot-tempered
(E) jealous

18. The author suggests that Martin's mother was

(A) insensitive and unable to answer simple questions
(B) uneducated and illiterate
(C) loving and overprotective
(D) wise and nurturing
(E) strong and harsh

19. The author suggests all of the following reasons for poor "race relations" EXCEPT

(A) white people's fear
(B) the biological difference between colored people and whites
(C) the legacy of slavery
(D) Jim Crow laws
(E) an ongoing culture of racist behavior

The Federal judicial system of the United States is made by the Constitution independent both of the Legislature and of the Executive. It consists of the Supreme Court, the circuit courts, and the district courts.

The Supreme Court is created and authorized by the Constitution, and consists of nine judges, who are nominated by the President and confirmed by the Senate. They hold office during "good behavior," that is, they are
5   removable only by impeachment, thus having a tenure more secure than that of English judges. The court sits in Washington from October to July in every year. A rule requiring the presence of six judges to pronounce a decision prevents the division of the court into two or more benches; and while this secures a thorough consideration of every case, it also slows down the dispatch of business.

The jurisdiction of the Federal courts extends only to those cases in which the Constitution makes Federal law
10   applicable. All other cases are left to the state courts, unless where some specific point arises which is affected by the Federal Constitution or a Federal law.

20. The Supreme Court gets its authority from

(A) the President
(B) the House of Representatives
(C) the Senate
(D) the Constitution
(E) the circuit courts

21. The passage implies that once appointed, Supreme Court justices can remain in office

(A) for life
(B) as long as the President says
(C) from October to July
(D) four years
(E) until they are voted out of office

22. To which of the following are the Supreme Court Justices compared in the passage?

(A) Circuit court judges
(B) District court judges
(C) The President
(D) Senators
(E) English judges

23. It can be inferred that the author would be most critical of

(A) the size of the Supreme Court
(B) the circuit courts
(C) the speed of the Supreme Court
(D) the rules of impeachment
(E) English judges

24. Which of the following is NOT true of the Federal Supreme Court?

(A) It has authority to decide questions of Federal law.
(B) It meets every year.
(C) Six or more judges are needed to pronounce a decision.
(D) Its justices cannot be removed.
(E) It has authority only in matters of Federal law or the Federal Constitution.

I was six when my mother taught me the art of invisible strength. It was a strategy for winning arguments, respect from others, and eventually, though neither of us knew it at the time, chess games.

"Bite back your tongue," scolded my mother when I cried loudly, yanking her hand toward the store that sold bags of salted plums. At home, she said, "Wise man, he not go against wind. In Chinese we say, Come from South,
5   blow with wind – poom! – North will follow. Strongest wind cannot be seen."

The next week I bit back my tongue as we entered the store with the forbidden candies. When my mother finished her shopping, she quietly plucked a small bag of plums from the rack and put it on the counter with the rest of the items.

25. The narrator's mother would most likely agree with which of the following statements?

    (A) The strongest people are those who fight for what they want.
    (B) Self-control can be a powerful source of strength.
    (C) Strong people do not talk.
    (D) Chinese people are naturally stronger than other people.
    (E) Eating salted plums keeps you from being strong.

31. "Strategy" (line 1) most nearly means

    (A) game
    (B) battle
    (C) conspiracy
    (D) level
    (E) technique

32. According to the passage, the narrator's mother

    (A) did not want her daughter to eat salted plums
    (B) bought her daughter whatever she wanted
    (C) wanted her daughter to express herself more openly
    (D) used the plums to teach her daughter a lesson
    (E) only bought the things she absolutely needed

33. The passage implies that the mother bought the plums at the end because

    (A) she was convinced by her daughter's arguments
    (B) she wanted some for herself
    (C) they were on sale
    (D) she wanted to reward her daughter for controlling herself
    (E) she accidentally mixed them in with her other groceries

It wasn't until the twentieth century that the intimate life of the duckbill platypus came to be known. It is an aquatic animal, living in Australian fresh water at a wide variety of temperatures – from tropical streams at sea level to cold lakes at an elevation of a mile.

The duckbill is well adapted to aquatic life, with its dense fur, its flat tail, and its webbed feet. Its bill has
5   nothing really in common with that of the duck, however. The nostrils are differently located and the platypus bill is different in structure, rubbery rather than duckishly horny. It serves the same function as the duck's bill, however, so it has been shaped similarly by the pressures of natural selection.

The water in which the duckbill lives is invariably muddy at the bottom and it is in this mud that the duckbill roots for its food supply. The duckbill's large bill, ridged with horny plates, is used as a sieve, dredging about
10   sensitively in the deep mud, filtering out the shrimps, earthworms, tadpoles and other small creatures that serve as its food.

34. It can be inferred from the passage that in the nineteenth century

(A) scientists did not fully understand the duckbill's lifestyle
(B) duckbills were considered strange and dangerous
(C) duckbills did not yet exist
(D) platypuses were too common to arouse much interest
(E) science had a better understanding of duckbills than we do today

35. According to the passage, the duckbill is equipped for aquatic life in all of the following ways EXCEPT:

(A) thick fur
(B) ability to adapt to large range of water temperatures
(C) webbed feet
(D) fish-like gills
(E) flat tail

36. As used in line 9, "roots" means

(A) anchors itself
(B) supports
(C) fights
(D) travels
(E) rummages

37. The passage states that the duckbill platypus's bill differs from the duck's in which of the following ways?

(A) It serves a different function.
(B) It has no nostrils.
(C) Natural selection has shaped it differently.
(D) It has a different structure.
(E) It is not used for finding food.

38. This passage is primarily about

(A) the history of the duckbill platypus
(B) the duckbill platypus's aquatic lifestyle
(C) twentieth-century zoological discoveries
(D) the difficulties of classifying aquatic animals
(E) the uses of a platypus's bill

Reading Practice

Upper Level

It was Joe Dillon who introduced the Wild West to us. He had a little library made up of old numbers of *The Union Jack*, *Pluck* and *The Halfpenny Marvel*. Every evening after school we met in his back garden and arranged Indian battles. He and his fat young brother, Leo, held the loft of the stable while we tried to carry it by storm; or we fought a pitched battle on the grass. But, however well we fought, we never won siege or battle and all our bouts
5   ended with Joe Dillon's war dance of victory. His parents went to eight-o'clock mass every morning in Gardiner Street and the peaceful odor of Mrs. Dillon was prevalent in the hall of the house. But he played too fiercely for us who were younger and more timid. He looked like some kind of an Indian when he capered round the garden, an old tea-cosy on his head, beating a tin with his fist and yelling: "Ya! yaka, yaka, yaka!"

No one could believe it when it was reported that he had entered the priesthood. Nevertheless it was true.
10   We banded ourselves together, some boldly, some in jest and some almost in fear: and of the number of these latter, the reluctant Indians who were afraid to seem studious or lacking in robustness, I was one. The adventures related in the literature of the Wild West were remote from my nature but, at least, they opened doors of escape.

1. The narrator of the story is probably

    (A) a young boy
    (B) a grown man
    (C) an American Indian
    (D) still friends with Joe Dillon
    (E) a cowboy

2. The author mentions Mrs. Dillon's "peaceful odor" in order to

    (A) ridicule her lack of cleanliness
    (B) contrast with the odor of his own house
    (C) contrast with Joe Dillon's fierceness
    (D) impress the reader with his sense of smell
    (E) all of the above

3. Why could no one believe that Joe Dillon entered the priesthood?

    (A) He had never attended church.
    (B) He did not believe in God.
    (C) Everyone thought that he would move to the Wild West and fight Indians.
    (D) He seemed too violent to become a priest.
    (E) All of the above.

4. Why did the narrator join in the Indian battle games?

    (A) He was of American Indian ancestry.
    (B) He was afraid his friends would make fun of him if he did not.
    (C) He was basically a violent person.
    (D) He hated Joe Dillon.
    (E) He also hoped to join the priesthood.

On October 1, 1949, the People's Republic of China was formally established, with its national capital at Beijing. "The Chinese people have stood up!" declared Chairman Mao as he announced the creation of a "people's democratic dictatorship." The people were defined as a coalition of four social classes: the workers, the peasants, the middle class, and the capitalists. The four classes were to be led by the Chinese Communist Party (CCP). At that
5 time the CCP claimed a membership of 4.5 million, of which members of peasant origin accounted for nearly 90 percent. The party was under Mao's chairmanship, and the government was headed by Zhou Enlai (1898-1976) as premier of the State Administrative Council (the predecessor of the State Council).

For the first time in decades a Chinese government was met with peace, instead of massive military opposition, within its territory. The new leadership was highly disciplined and, having a decade of wartime administrative
10 experience to draw on, was able to embark on a program of national integration and reform. In the first year of Communist administration, moderate social and economic policies were implemented with skill and effectiveness. The leadership realized that the overwhelming and multitudinous task of economic reconstruction and achievement of political and social stability required the goodwill and cooperation of all classes of people. Results were impressive by any standard, and popular support was widespread.

5. The main purpose of the passage is

   (A) to persuade the reader to adopt a point of view
   (B) to inform the reader about a subject
   (C) to frighten the reader into taking action
   (D) to condemn the reader for his/her ignorance of a subject
   (E) to distract the reader from the real issues

6. By saying "The Chinese people have stood up!" Mao seems to mean that

   (A) they are cheering him for his leadership
   (B) many of them had been engaged in "sit-down" strikes against the government
   (C) he will have difficulty acting as their leader
   (D) the people have taken power into their own hands
   (E) the people oppose economic reconstruction

7. It can be assumed that "multitudinous" (line 12) means

   (A) having more than one color
   (B) unimportant
   (C) many-sided
   (D) one-dimensional
   (E) life-threatening

8. The author states that the Chinese Communists' first tasks were

   (A) creating national unity and economic reform
   (B) killing their enemies and imprisoning their families
   (C) defeating military opposition and building the army
   (D) recruiting Party members and spreading propaganda
   (E) electing a leader and state council

9. The author would likely agree with which of the following statements?

   (A) Mao was better suited to leadership than Zhou Enlai.
   (B) The Chinese Communists had no right to run the country.
   (C) The Chinese Communists were unfair to the peasants.
   (D) The Chinese Communists met with success at first.
   (E) The Chinese economy was worse under Mao than it had been before.

SUMMIT
EDUCATIONAL
GROUP

The picture of Robin Hood that is widely held today contrasts in many respects with that of the outlaw of medieval legend. While the modern image was created by dramatists and writers during the sixteenth and seventeenth centuries, the medieval Robin Hood, who was probably the creation of wandering minstrels, is a more elusive figure who lives principally in early ballads and a handful of historical sources.

5   From the very start, there appear to have been contradictory elements in the character of the legend of Robin Hood. To the 15th century writer Wyntoun, Robin Hood was an outlaw; to Walter Bower, who wrote at the same time, he was an assassin whose name could be used as a term of abuse and whose deeds were celebrated only by foolish people; yet to John Major, writing in 1520, Robin Hood was the kindliest of robbers.

In an endeavor to date the origin of the Robin Hood tales, many historical Robin Hoods have been searched for. 10   The "outlaw hero" has rarely if ever been purely a fictional creation; and the activities of the leader of some group of outlaws may lie behind the legends of Robin Hood. It was in this way that legends grew up around modern outlaws like Jesse James and Sam Bass, and such may be the case with the original of Robin Hood. Nonetheless, attempts to identify a historical Robin Hood have on the whole been unsuccessful.

10. According to the passage, when was the "modern" image of Robin Hood created?

(A) during this century
(B) in medieval times
(C) in the sixteenth and seventeenth centuries
(D) around the year 1000 AD
(E) in the year 1520

11. The author implies that the real Robin Hood

(A) definitely never existed
(B) was well known to the writer Wyntoun
(C) was probably a wandering minstrel
(D) has not been positively identified
(E) was an assassin

12. The author mentions the writers Wyntoun, Bower, and Major in order to

(A) prove that Robin Hood is completely fictional
(B) show the contradictory views of Robin Hood
(C) support his argument that Robin Hood was an evil character
(D) counter arguments that 16th century writers knew Robin Hood's real identity
(E) deny any personal knowledge of Robin Hood's crimes

13. Which of the following, if true, would contradict the author?

(A) A manuscript discovered in the 1930s establishing Robin Hood's real identity.
(B) Jesse James was never convicted of any crime.
(C) Walter Bower had no personal knowledge of Robin Hood.
(D) Robin Hood only robbed from the rich.
(E) Robin Hood came from a family of noblemen.

14. The word "elusive," as used in line 4, most nearly means

(A) hard to capture
(B) flexible
(C) extremely fast moving
(D) very old
(E) illegal

Who does not love the *Titanic?*
If they sold passage tomorrow for that same crossing,
Who would not buy?

To go down…We all go down, mostly
5   alone. But with crowds of people, friends, servants,
well fed, with music, with lights! Ah!

And the world, shocked, mourns, as it ought to do
and almost never does. There will be the books and movies
to remind our grandchildren who we were
10   and how we died, and give them a good cry.

Not so bad, after all. The cold
water is so anesthetic and very quick.
The cries on all sides must be a comfort.

We all go: only a few, first-class.

15. What is the tone of this poem?

    (A) Solemn
    (B) Mournful
    (C) Terrified
    (D) Sentimental
    (E) Ironic

16. This poem suggests that

    (A) life is short, and luxury makes life worth
        living
    (B) people should not remember the Titanic
        because it will only make them sad.
    (C) love is the only thing that lasts, it is stronger
        than death.
    (D) dying for a good cause is better than life.
    (E) cruise ships are better than airplanes.

17. "To go down… We all go down, mostly alone"
    is a reference to

    (A) the depths of the ocean
    (B) depression
    (C) solitude
    (D) death
    (E) the nature of love

18. The writer of this poem is most likely

    (A) an actual passenger of the Titanic
    (B) a fan of the blockbuster movie
    (C) a person living at the same time as the
        sinking of the ship
    (D) a person looking back on an historical event
    (E) a deep sea diver

Some 2,300 years ago the Greek philosophers Democritus and Leucippus proposed that if you cut an object, such as a loaf of bread, in half, and then in half again until you could do it no longer, you would reach the ultimate building block. They called it an atom.

The atom is infinitesimal. Your every breath holds a trillion atoms. And because atoms in the everyday world
5 we inhabit are virtually indestructible, the air you suck into your lungs may include an atom or two gasped out by Democritus with his dying breath.

To grasp the scale of the atom and the world within, look at a letter "i" on this page. Magnify its dot a million times with an electron microscope, and you should see an array of a million ink molecules. This is the domain of the chemist. Look closely at one ink molecule and you would see a fuzzy image of the largest atoms that compose it.
10 Whether by eye, camera, or microscope, no one has ever seen the internal structure of an atom: Minute as atoms are, they consist of still smaller subatomic particles. Protons, carrying a positive electric charge, and electrically neutral particles called neutrons cluster within the atom's central region, or nucleus – one hundred-thousandth the diameter of the atom. Nuclear physicists work at this level of matter.

19. According to the passage, the internal structure of an atom is

(A) a 20th century concept
(B) found primarily in bread and ink
(C) infinite and immense
(D) studied by nuclear physicists
(E) easily seen

20. The passage implies that chemists

(A) have a job that is less important than physicists
(B) study subatomic particles
(C) study molecules
(D) make great discoveries
(E) understand Greek philosophy

21. The word "infinitesimal" in line 4 most closely means

(A) minuscule
(B) eternal
(C) numerical
(D) containing oxygen
(E) multitudinous

22. The tone of the passage is most like that found in

(A) a highly technical scientific journal
(B) a Greek textbook
(C) a magazine article on popular science
(D) a press release
(E) laboratory report

23. According to the passage no one

(A) has ever written about this topic before
(B) believed Democritus until his dying breath
(C) wants to study molecules anymore
(D) grasps the importance of scientific inquiry
(E) can see the subatomic structure of an atom

(The following passage was written by the composer Ludwig van Beethoven.)

Oh you men who think or say that I am malevolent or stubborn, how greatly do you wrong me. You do not know the secret cause which makes me seem that way to you. From childhood on, my heart and soul have been full of the tender feeling of goodwill, and I was ever inclined to accomplish great things. But, think that for six years now I have been hopelessly afflicted, made worse by senseless physicians, from year to year deceived with hopes of

5   improvement, finally compelled to face the prospect of a lasting sickness (whose cure will take years or, perhaps, be impossible). Though born with a fiery, active temperament, even receptive to the diversions of society, I was soon compelled to withdraw myself, to live life alone. If at times I tried to forget all this, oh how harshly I was I flung back by the doubly sad experience of my bad hearing. Yet it was impossible for me to say to people, "Speak louder, shout, for I am deaf."

10   Ah, how could I possibly admit an imperfection in the one sense which ought to be more perfect in me than others, a sense which I once possessed in the highest perfection, a perfection such as few in my profession enjoy or ever have enjoyed. Oh I cannot do it; therefore forgive me when you see me draw back when I would have gladly mingled with you. Oh fellow men, when at some point you read this, consider then that you have done me an injustice; someone who has had misfortune can console himself to find a similar case to his, who despite all the

15   limitations of Nature nevertheless did everything within his powers to become accepted among worthy artists and men.

24. In the 3rd sentence, the word "inclined" most nearly means

(A) tilted
(B) discouraged
(C) eager
(D) opposed
(E) prejudiced

25. The main purpose of the passage is to

(A) allow Beethoven to explain himself
(B) accuse others of unkindness
(C) show Beethoven's hatred of humanity
(D) explain Beethoven's musical decline
(E) prove that deaf people can play music

26. According to Beethoven, if not for his deafness

(A) he would have written more music
(B) he would have been a better person
(C) he would have sought out the company of others more
(D) he would never have written music
(E) he would have lived in the country

27. A fitting title for this selection would be

(A) The Power of Music
(B) Deafness: Its Causes and Cure
(C) The Sounds of Silence
(D) A Hater of Humanity
(E) A Plea for Understanding

28. The tone of the passage is

(A) sarcastic
(B) congratulating
(C) grateful
(D) threatening
(E) pleading

There were very few schools in the United States 150 years ago. If a child's parents were rich, they hired a tutor to teach the child reading, writing, spelling, and simple arithmetic. Often several children met at the teacher's house to be taught together. Because most of the teachers had also gone to inadequate schools, they knew little more than their pupils. Other children met in church and were taught by the minister. Their only school book was the Bible.

5   But if a child's parents were poor, he might never go to school at all. Instead, he had to work very hard. Some boys and girls worked on their families' farms, while others worked in mills and factories. They had little time to play. In fact, many children were forced to work such long hours that child labor laws were passed to set a limit on how long a boy or girl could work. In 1842, a law was passed in Massachusetts which said that children under 12 could work only 10 hours a day.

10   Some common schools did exist, and like our public schools of today, they were open to anyone. But conditions in American schools were very bad. They were cramped and uncomfortable. There were no maps, charts, or blackboards. In one Boston school of 400 students, there were about 65 whippings a day. Most of the school's windowpanes were broken and the floors were covered with mud.

29. The passage mentions all of the following schools EXCEPT

   (A) schools taught by the minister in the church
   (B) private tutors for children of rich parents
   (C) boarding schools to prepare students for college
   (D) common schools that were open to anyone
   (E) several children meeting at a teacher's house

30. It can be inferred from the passage that before 1842

   (A) children under 12 were not allowed to work
   (B) all children spent 5 hours a day in school
   (C) rich children worked more than poor children
   (D) children were only allowed to work 10 hours a day
   (E) some children under 12 were working more than 10 hours a day

31. As used in line 3, the word "inadequate" means

   (A) subtracted
   (B) lacking
   (C) not helpful
   (D) nearby
   (E) gifted

32. This passage is primarily about

   (A) religious education in Massachusetts
   (B) the hard lives of poor children
   (C) the creation of child labor laws in the United States
   (D) how Boston teachers punished bad students
   (E) American schools in the 1800s

33. The author mentions the 65 whippings a day (lines 12) in order to

   (A) show how effective school discipline was
   (B) call for stricter child abuse laws
   (C) convince readers that schools are a bad idea
   (D) demonstrate the harsh conditions in the school
   (E) persuade people to move to Boston

34. Which of the following best describes the tone of this passage?

   (A) playful
   (B) nostalgic
   (C) informative
   (D) sarcastic
   (E) bored

Every human language has been shaped by, and changes to meet, the needs of its speakers. In this limited sense, all human languages can be said to be both equal and perfect. Some Inuit languages, for example, have many different words for different types of snow: wet snow, powdery snow, blowing snow, and so forth. This extensive vocabulary obviously results from the importance of snow in the Inuit environment and the need to be able to talk
5   about it in detailed ways. In Chicago, where snow is just an occasional annoyance, we get along quite nicely with only a few basic terms—snow, slush, and sleet—and a number of adjectival modifiers. Richard Mitchell has described a certain primitive society where the main preoccupation is banging on tree-bark to harvest edible insects, and this particular people has developed a large, specialized vocabulary for talking about the different kinds of rocks and trees that are involved in this process. In each of these cases, the language in question is well adapted to the
10   needs of its speakers. Each language allows its speakers to easily talk about whatever it is important to discuss in that society.

35. The primary purpose of this passage is to

(A) suggest that some languages are superior to others
(B) show that each language adapts to its society
(C) compare how different cultures talk about snow
(D) show the way languages remain constant over time
(E) contrast primitive and modern languages

36. According to the passage, why do some Inuit languages have several words for "snow?"

(A) They have been influenced by other foreign languages.
(B) Inuit want more variety in their language.
(C) Inuit are more educated than other cultural groups.
(D) Snow is an important part of Inuit life and culture.
(E) Inuit languages change more quickly than other languages.

37. The word "preoccupation" in line 7 most nearly means

(A) frustration
(B) activity
(C) education
(D) anxiety
(E) distraction

38. Which of the following questions is answered by the information in the passage?

(A) How many different languages are there in the world?
(B) Who recorded all the different Inuit terms for snow?
(C) Where did the tree-banging primitive society live?
(D) What is the most commonly-used language?
(E) Why does Chicago have relatively few words for snow?

39. The author mentions which of the following influences on language?
   I.   Climate and weather
   II. Food and survival
   III. Education

(A) II only
(B) III only
(C) I and II only
(D) II and III only
(E) I, II, and III

I wanted to be a cauliflower,
all brain and ears,
thinking on the origin of gardens
and the divinity of him
5   who carefully binds my leaves.

With my blind roots touched
by the songs of the worms,
and my rough throat throbbing
10 with strange, vegetable sounds,
perhaps I'd feel the parting stroke
of a butterfly's wing . . .

Not like my cousins, the cabbage,
15 whose heads, tightly folded,
see and hear nothing of this world,
dreaming only on the yellow
and green magnificence
that is hardening within them.
20
            --John Haines

40. In this poem, being a cauliflower would include all of the following EXCEPT

(A) thinking great thoughts
(B) contemplating one's existence
(C) cutting oneself off from others
(D) being in tune with the world
(E) being involved with one's surroundings

41. The main literary technique used in this poem is

(A) metaphor
(B) rhyme
(C) irony
(D) sarcasm
(E) repetition

42. As used in line 4, "divinity" most nearly means

(A) sacrifice
(B) ignorance
(C) godliness
(D) concentration
(E) sweetness

43. The contrast between cauliflower and cabbages in this poem can best be described as the difference between

(A) happiness and sadness
(B) hearing and seeing
(C) poetry and prose
(D) faith and doubt
(E) awareness and isolation

44. With which of the following statements would the narrator be most likely to agree?

(A) We should focus on studying ourselves.
(B) Cauliflower is better to eat than cabbage.
(C) We should open ourselves up to experience the world.
(D) Too much thinking is a dangerous thing.
(E) People are not very different from vegetables.

"Look at me well! I am still alive and by the grace of God I shall yet prove victor!" His harsh voice rising above the din of battle, William pushed back his helmet and bared his face to his retreating troops who thought him slain. Inflamed by their leader's ardor, the Normans then surrounded their pursuers and rapidly cut them down so that not one escaped.

5   This episode marked the turning point of a blood-splashed October day nine centuries ago—a day which so changed the course of events that it is impossible to reckon our history without those few furious hours. For when darkness fell on Senlac Hill, near the seaside town of Hastings on the southeast coast of England, William, Duke of Normandy, had earned the lasting sobriquet of "Conqueror." And a flow of concepts began that would influence men's lives for centuries to come. William's victory at Hastings made England once more a part of Europe, as it had

10 not been since the better days of the Roman Empire. The Scandinavian influence on England began to give way to the political and cultural ideas of the Latin world. Besides feudalism and a new aristocracy, the Normans implanted in England much of their law, architecture, and social customs. Ultimately, the Conquest would affect the New World. Such terms as "justice," "liberty," and "sovereign" crossed the English Channel with William. Indeed, the Conquest left its mark forever on the language you are now reading.

45. In line 1, the purpose of William's speech was to

(A) calm the din of battle
(B) persuade retreating troops to take him with them
(C) inspire his armies to continue fighting
(D) leave a last statement before his death
(E) frighten his enemies into retreating

46. Which of the following best describes the main idea of this passage?

(A) William the Conqueror was a great fighter.
(B) The Norman Conquest changed the course of English history.
(C) The Normans drove the Scandinavian influence out of England.
(D) English history consists of many bloody battles like Hastings.
(E) The Roman Empire continued in England much longer than in other countries.

47. A "sobriquet" (line 8) is probably a kind of

(A) medical treatment
(B) fuel for cooking
(C) curse
(D) payment
(E) nickname

48. The author would most likely agree that

(A) The Norman army was victorious in spite of William's weak leadership
(B) William's greatest strength was his desire for peace at any cost
(C) Unlike most Europeans, William did not believe in God
(D) William was a passionate and effective military leader
(E) The Normans were displeased with William as a leader

49. According to the passage, the Conquest had which of the following effects?

 I. Restored England's ties to the rest of Europe
 II. Replaced Latin culture with Scandinavian political and cultural ideas
 III. Stopped the development of English society and language

(A) I only
(B) II only
(C) I and II only
(D) I and III only
(E) I, II, and III

SUMMIT
EDUCATIONAL
GROUP

Writing

- General Information
- What Are Your Readers Looking For?
- Creative or Formal?
- Preparing a Creative Story
- The Setup
- The Confrontation
- The Resolution
- Preparing a Formal Essay
- The Introduction
- The Body
- The Conclusion
- Notes on Style
- Evaluating Your Writing
- Examples of Student Writing
- Writing Practice

General Information

❑ The SSAT gives you 25 minutes to develop a clear and focused writing sample.

❑ You will have a choice between two writing prompts.

Middle Level tests have two creative prompts. These prompts give you the first sentence to be used in a story.

> *Nobody could have guessed that this would have happened to him.*

Upper Level tests have a creative prompt and a formal prompt. The formal prompt asks a question that usually relates to your own thoughts or opinions.

> *What are the best qualities of a person you admire?*

❑ **Note:** Your writing is not scored, but is sent directly to the schools to which you apply. Even though individual readers may have differing opinions on what makes a good writing sample, most readers are looking for clear, correct writing and a logical response to the topic.

❑ Directions are as follows:

Middle Level

> Schools would like to get to know you better through a story you tell using one of the ideas below. Please choose the idea you find most interesting and write a story using the idea as your first sentence. Please fill in the circle next to the one you choose.

Upper Level

> Schools would like to get to know you better through an essay or story using one of the two topics below. Please select the topic you find most interesting and fill in the circle next to the topic you choose.

SUMMIT
EDUCATIONAL
GROUP

SSAT Structure

Writing Sample – 25 minutes

Quantitative – 30 minutes

MATHEMATICS																								
1	2	3	4	5	6	7	8	9	10	11	12	13	14	15	16	17	18	19	20	21	22	23	24	25
EASY → MEDIUM → DIFFICULT																								

Reading Comprehension – 40 minutes

READING PASSAGES																																							
1	2	3	4	5	6	7	8	9	10	11	12	13	14	15	16	17	18	19	20	21	22	23	24	25	26	27	28	29	30	31	32	33	34	35	36	37	38	39	40
NOT IN ORDER OF DIFFICULTY																																							

Verbal – 30 minutes

SYNONYMS																													
1	2	3	4	5	6	7	8	9	10	11	12	13	14	15	16	17	18	19	20	21	22	23	24	25	26	27	28	29	30
EASY → MEDIUM → DIFFICULT																													

ANALOGIES																													
31	32	33	34	35	36	37	38	39	40	41	42	43	44	45	46	47	48	49	50	51	52	53	54	55	56	57	58	59	60
EASY → MEDIUM → DIFFICULT																													

Quantitative – 30 minutes

MATHEMATICS																								
1	2	3	4	5	6	7	8	9	10	11	12	13	14	15	16	17	18	19	20	21	22	23	24	25
EASY → MEDIUM → DIFFICULT																								

What Are Your Readers Looking For?

❑ The SSAT writing sample is not scored, but copies of the writing sample will be sent to the admissions offices of schools to which you are applying.

Make sure that your penmanship is clean and clear. Remember that it will be read by someone who is unfamiliar with your handwriting.

❑ Typically, writing sample readers are checking that your writing is focused and well-organized. Make sure that you express your thoughts clearly. Strong writing is more important than length; however, don't be too brief or else you won't have time to explain your thoughts.

The writing sample is an opportunity for you to show something about yourself. Your writing sample may show your knowledge, experiences, interests, or personality. Admissions offices are interested in learning about you, so the writing sample is a great opportunity to show your interests, personality, and strengths.

❑ Different schools have different standards when judging writing samples. Contact the admissions offices of the schools you are applying to and ask about what they look for in SSAT writing samples.

Creative or Formal?

❑ For the Upper Level writing sample, your first decision is whether you choose the creative prompt or the formal prompt.

❑ The **creative** prompt is for a short story. This may be a good option if you know how to create an interesting narrative and if you enjoy descriptive writing.

> *It was the most embarrassing moment of his life.*
>
> *She had never seen something so beautiful.*
>
> *They were all waiting for me to speak.*
>
> *She had always been a hard worker, but she had never faced such a difficult challenge.*

❑ The **formal** prompt is for an essay. This may be a good option if you are skilled at defending arguments and enjoy logic and reason.

> *What class or subject in school do you enjoy most? Why?*
>
> *Who is someone you respect? Explain why you feel this way.*
>
> *Explain a hobby you have that makes you special.*
>
> *Which two historical figures would you like to meet and why?*

❑ Try writing with both types of prompts. You may feel more comfortable with one type, which is important to know when preparing for the official test.

Preparing a Creative Story

❑ Most stories have three essential parts: setup, confrontation, and resolution.

The **setup** is used to introduce characters, describe settings, and establish situations. This usually comes first because it is needed in order to understand the rest of the story.

The **confrontation** is the main source of drama and tension in the story. Stories need some type of problem or conflict. This can be a personal desire, a disagreement, a difficult challenge, etc.

The **resolution** shows the outcome of the story. This is where the characters make important decisions, where relationships break apart or come together, where heroes succeed and problems are finally resolved.

❑ Before you begin writing your story, make sure that you know what will happen.

Take some time to plan and outline your story. This will ensure that your writing is focused and your time is managed effectively.

Prompt: *Nobody could have guessed that this would have happened to him.*

Nobody could have guessed that this would have happened to him. Just a week before, Frank had shoved him into the cold, dark depths of his own locker. For years, Frank had teased and tormented Kyle. Now, Kyle had the chance to play on the same team as Frank, the star quarterback of the school football team.

The coach of the football team had explained a few days earlier that one of their star players wasn't able to play anymore. The wide receiver had been injured in a recent practice, severely damaging his ankle, and wouldn't be returning for the rest of the season. Kyle was the wide receiver on the junior varsity team, and now the coach needed him to help fill the position on the varsity team.

> SETUP

Kyle's mind was filled with worries. Would he be able to play well enough? Most of the players were at least a year older than him, so they were more experienced. Would Frank bully him? He was tired of Frank calling him names and pushing him around. However, the situation could also be a great opportunity. Maybe he could show his skills, succeed, and have more of a chance to get an athletic scholarship. He had accepted the coach's offer because, more than anything, he wanted to prove to himself and to Frank that he was a strong player.

On the night of his first varsity game, Kyle nervously watched his teammates play. He sat on the hard bench on the sidelines and awaited his chance to shine. After the other team fumbled the ball early in the game, Kyle was able to get on the field with the offensive team. The players gathered in a huddle and Frank started barking out orders.

"Are you sure you can handle this, rookie?" Frank said, looking harshly at Kyle.

"Just get the ball to me," Kyle said with confidence. "I'm faster than anyone on the other team."

> CONFRONTATION

The players gathered on the line of scrimmage. Frank called the play, the linebacker snapped the ball, and Kyle was off running. His jersey waved in the cool air. He looked back and saw Frank look up toward him. For a second, he doubted that Frank would pass to him, but then the ball was launched, spiraling tightly toward him. Kyle sprinted on and snatched the ball out of the air. The other players were already far behind him, and he ran with the bright lights shining on him and the crowd cheering.

At the end zone, Kyle stood triumphant. Frank ran up to him and patted him on the back.

"Wow, I didn't know you were that fast," Frank said.

Kyle knew that he had earned Frank's respect. He had been afraid to join the varsity team, but he knew he could prove that he was as good as anyone.

> RESOLUTION

The Setup

❑ Use the beginning of your story to describe the characters and situation.

Think about what kind of person your main character is. It is more important to describe your character's personality or relationships than his/her appearance.

Your character should be dealing with a problem, difficulty, or choice. The setup explains what this situation is <u>before</u> the character faces this problem and takes an action.

Consider what happened before the confrontation of the story. What events led to the main tension? How did it all begin?

❑ Your setup should show who the characters are and explain the situation they are in. A great setup will make your reader want to keep reading to find out how the characters handle the situation.

> That moment changed everything. In an instant, my whole social life was undone, and it was years before I found my place in the world again.
>
> It all started back in the fourth grade. If I could do anything over again, I would change that year. I became friends with a group of people who were considered the "cool kids" in the school. Although these people were nice to me, they were cruel and condescending to many of the other students. They regularly bullied, teased, and gossiped about my classmates, and I am ashamed to say that I also took part in this. The unofficial leader of the group, Leslie, was a small girl whose greatest talent was criticizing others, usually the people who were unusual or unique in any way. As terrible as we were, there was a feeling of respect that we got from the rest of the students. Eventually, however, it all fell apart.

TRY IT OUT

Write a setup for a short story using each of the following prompts:

1. *It seemed like it was going to be an ordinary day.*

_____

_____

_____

_____

_____

_____

_____

_____

_____

_____

2. *It was over almost as soon as it started.*

_____

_____

_____

_____

_____

_____

_____

_____

_____

_____

The Confrontation

❑ Usually, the biggest piece of a story focuses on the problem or conflict that the main character faces.

Something should happen to your character. If he/she wants to accomplish something, maybe something gets in the way or tries to stop him/her; if he/she disagrees with someone, maybe they get in an argument; if he/she is afraid of something, maybe he/she finally his to face this fear. There should be an event that creates tension and drama in your story.

Your character should make a decision or take an action.

❑ Your confrontation should show what happens to the character and how he/she responds to it.

> Although the outcasts were her usual prey, Leslie sometimes went for some of her friends, me included. One day during the lunch hour, Leslie asked me if I was rich. I had never considered this before, and my family has never seemed to struggle with money, so I said yes, that my family was wealthy. Leslie then smiled mischievously and told me, "Well, you don't look like it. You dress like a homeless person." Although now I can see that this comment was just a shallow attack, it hit me hard back then. I was humiliated, and for a long time I worked extra hard to get Leslie's approval, because I didn't want her to criticize me again.
>
> Finally, after months of worrying about my clothes, I realized that I didn't need to please Leslie. I liked the clothes I wore, and that was all that mattered. My clothing style was unique, and that wasn't a bad thing. I finally decided that I liked being a bit different, and I wasn't going to let anyone make me feel bad about it. So, I stopped associating with Leslie and all of her friends. This was difficult at first, because I was losing most of my friends, but I knew it would be better for me, because I didn't like the person they were turning me into.

TRY IT OUT

Continue your short stories by writing confrontations:

1. *It seemed like it was going to be an ordinary day.*

_____

_____

_____

_____

_____

_____

_____

_____

_____

_____

_____

_____

2. *It was over almost as soon as it started.*

_____

_____

_____

_____

_____

_____

_____

_____

_____

_____

_____

_____

_____

The Resolution

❑ The end of a story shows what happened as a result of the character's actions.

   Something should have changed since the setup at the beginning of the story. In resolutions, characters often have a new realization or understanding. If the character has learned something, describe how he/she has changed or what he/she has learned. If the character has handled an issue, explain how the situation has changed.

❑ Your resolution should make the story feel complete, with no loose ends.

> Looking back, I sometimes regret the time I spent being Leslie's friend. I wish I hadn't been a bully and that I hadn't lived with such low self-esteem because of her. I have a hard time accepting that I let myself be such a close friend to her. However, although I wish I could change my past, it has made me the person I am today. Because of what I have gone through, I have learned to be more accepting of others and of myself. I never judge or criticize my peers, and I also have more confidence in myself because I don't worry about the opinions of others. In the end, it has become one of my life's most important lessons.

TRY IT OUT

Complete your short stories by writing resolutions:

1. *It seemed like it was going to be an ordinary day.*

_____

_____

_____

_____

_____

_____

_____

_____

2. *It was over almost as soon as it started.*

_____

_____

_____

_____

_____

_____

_____

_____

Preparing a Formal Essay

❑ Most essays have three essential parts: introduction, body, and conclusion.

The **introduction** establishes the main idea and focus of your essay. It includes your thesis, which is your essay's central argument or point.

The **body** is used to explain your argument and describe how your examples support that argument.

The **conclusion** summarizes your essay and connects it back to your main idea.

❑ Before you begin writing your essay, make sure that you know what your thesis and examples will be.

Take some time to plan and outline your essay. This will ensure that your writing is focused and your time is managed effectively.

Prompt: *Describe an experience that has inspired you.*

When I was eleven years old, I saw a group of boys harassing a girl in the hallway at my school. I pretended not to notice, as did most of my fellow students. However, one student, a fellow sixth-grade boy, stepped between the girl and her harassers and told the other boys to leave the girl alone. After making a couple of threats and insulting the boy, the group of boys walked away. The girl was upset, but okay, and when the boy verified that she was all right, he went back to his locker to get his things and head to class. Most people went back to their conversations and forgot all about it, but I was deeply affected by what had happened. This simple event made me change who I am so that I can be the type of person who will also stand up for others.

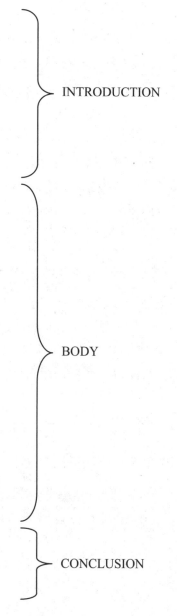

INTRODUCTION

This experience inspired me for a few reasons. One reason was that the boy who helped this girl wasn't friends with her. They didn't hang out in the same groups at all. He stepped in because it was the right thing to do, and for no other reason. It showed me that there are people who care about others even when they have no specific reason to do so. In our society, we often seek to protect and help those only in our "group," which is why major problems in other countries so often go ignored. This boy's attitude showed that he was willing to get involved to help people who had little in common with him. I was impressed by this selflessness, and since then I have tried to be the same way.

Another reason that this experience moved me was that it showed real character for him to step in between the girl and several boys (some of whom were known for getting into fights) when no one else had shown a willingness to get involved. I was too scared to get involved. I was worried about being beaten up, but also just of being made fun of in front of everyone. I allowed my fear to paralyze me and prevent me from stepping up and doing the right thing. I knew, though, that this other boy also would have been afraid of the same things, but he helped the girl anyway. I realized that there was nothing stopping me from also doing the right thing in a situation that scared me. Since then, I have tried to face my fear so that I won't be intimidated by people who need to be stopped.

BODY

Because of this single experience years ago, I have changed myself. In my memory, the boy who tried to help that girl is a great hero. He showed me a type of courage that I'll never forget. Now, I also try to help out people who need it, even if it scares me. It's the right thing to do.

CONCLUSION

The Introduction

- ❑ The purpose of the introduction is to state the main idea of your essay. In the introduction, you define and limit what you are going to discuss.

  The introduction is like a preview of your whole essay. It should mention the example you'll be discussing and it should state your thesis.

- ❑ **Basic Introduction:** The simplest way to begin your essay is to state your thesis, which is usually an answer or response to the essay prompt. Continue your introduction by describing your example and how it connects to your thesis. You don't need many details or specifics yet; these will be covered in the essay body.

  > A hobby I have that makes me special is rock climbing. This sport has taught me a lot about myself, because it has made me aware of my physical and mental strengths. It has also made me stronger and braver, and it has been an inspiration for how I live my life.

- ❑ **Inverted Funnel:** A more advanced method for writing an introduction is to begin with a general statement about the topic, then narrow the topic until you end with a statement of your thesis, specifically identifying the examples.

  > I grew up playing basketball, swimming, and attempting to play softball. All of these sports gave me an appreciation for healthy competition and team camaraderie, but I never felt a special connection with any of these. Rock climbing is different. It's individualistic, which means you have to trust and rely on your own strength and intelligence. Because of this, it teaches you a lot about your strengths and your limits. Climbing has taught me more about myself than any team sport I've played and it continues to do so.

TRY IT OUT

Write an introduction for an essay using each of the following prompts:

1. *Describe an experience that has inspired you.*

    _____

    _____

    _____

    _____

    _____

    _____

    _____

    _____

    _____

    _____

    _____

    _____

2. *Discuss a problem in the world that you would like to solve and how you would solve it.*

    _____

    _____

    _____

    _____

    _____

    _____

    _____

    _____

    _____

    _____

    _____

    _____

The Body

❑ In the body of your essay, you should explain how your examples support your main idea. Only include the details and descriptions that you need in order to prove your point.

Don't write everything you know about an example or try to impress your reader with the depth of your knowledge. If you're writing about a book, for example, don't recount the whole plot, but stick to the relevant details that support your main idea.

> Rock climbing makes me special because it helped me overcome a fear. For much of my life, I was frightened by any tall heights. After my first few attempts at rock climbing, I went from a girl who never went on roller coasters or ferris wheels or looked over the edge of a hill to someone who can climb up the side of a mountain and look around in appreciation and awe at the beauty of nature below her. I was terrified when I first pulled myself up the side of a tall cliff and looked down at the long drop back to the ground, but I overcame that fear. Now what I feel is pride for what I have accomplished and appreciation for the new strength I have found in myself.
>
> Of course rock climbing is physically challenging, but it is mentally challenging as well. With no two climbing routes being the same, the challenge is to figure out how to do the climb using both skill and strength. Along the same line, everyone has a different climbing style. That's what makes each climber unique. While I like to backstep and stem, another person may prefer to dyno and smear up the wall. I climb with people of all ages and backgrounds. Climbing does not discriminate. Sure, there is a lingo that everyone speaks and you have to learn, but it only adds to the thrill of the climb. Once you hear the word "crux" and you find yourself right in the middle of it on a climb and conquer it, you will truly know the meaning of the word.

TRY IT OUT

Continue your essays by writing the body paragraphs:

1. *Describe an experience that has inspired you.*

    _____

    _____

    _____

    _____

    _____

    _____

    _____

    _____

    _____

    _____

    _____

    _____

2. *Discuss a problem in the world that you would like to solve and how you would solve it.*

    _____

    _____

    _____

    _____

    _____

    _____

    _____

    _____

    _____

    _____

    _____

    _____

The Conclusion

❏ The conclusion wraps up your essay. It should not introduce any new ideas and is essentially a restatement of your main idea.

❏ When possible, it is a good idea to end with a general statement about your main idea. For example, if you wrote about past events, you can finish your conclusion by describing what is happening now and how this confirms your main idea.

> Rock climbing has provided some of the greatest challenges I have ever faced, and this has made me stronger. It has helped me to become braver and it has taught me about myself. This sport has inspired me to fearlessly work to achieve greater things and reach higher and higher. I've learned that, although life has many struggles, the best view can only be seen from the top.

TRY IT OUT

Complete your essays by writing conclusions:

1. *Describe an experience that has inspired you.*

    _____

    _____

    _____

    _____

    _____

    _____

    _____

    _____

    _____

    _____

2. *Discuss a problem in the world that you would like to solve and how you would solve it.*

    _____

    _____

    _____

    _____

    _____

    _____

    _____

    _____

    _____

    _____

    _____

Notes on Style

- Be clear.

- Be simple and direct.

- Don't use slang.

- Avoid fancy words, especially if you're not sure what they mean.

- Be natural. Don't be rude, arrogant, or breezy.

- Use transitions to connect your thoughts.

- Avoid qualifiers (e.g., very, so).

- Write neatly. Avoid cross-outs.

- Watch spelling and punctuation.

- Avoid incomplete or run-on sentences.

- Don't ramble or go off topic.

Read through the following essay and make edits. Note how the essay could be improved.

Prompt: *What are the best qualities of a person you admire?*

What does it mean to admire? I guess we all know what it means, but have you ever really looked past the simple six-letter word and tried to really understand why we do it? What are the qualities that make you admire someone? Of course, a person you admire must be a good person. But beneath that, deep down to the core of this phenomenon, there must be certain qualities. A person that is admired would have to have these qualities. They would have to be giving, successful, and humble. These really are the best qualities of a person I admire. I admire my uncle, and these are the qualities he has.

Humans, by nature, are very selfish beings, but an admirable person will go past their inner coding to something more. They will go past their own well-being for that of another. A good person has got to understand that as easy as it could be to run ahead of a slower person in life who has fallen, you must instead take the time to stop, dust them off, and give encouragements, even though that makes the whole run harder. Would you respect a person who is always greedy? Would you want to be friends with someone who only takes and takes? Wouldn't you rather be around a person who is generous and tries to help other people? I look up to my uncle very much because of all the great things that he does for people that he doesn't even know. There are a lot of examples of this.

Second, I am going to talk about how my uncle gives a whole lot to charities and always helps others, but he also is very successful. He manages his own construction company, which is a lot of hard work. A person you really admire should have this quality. Someone you can hope to become. Someone with good ethics. Someone who worked hard to earn all of his success and still gives to others. Can you believe that some people don't care about that? They are rich and do everything for more money, but they don't do anything to make the world better. That is why giving is also a quality in people I admire. People that you can trust and respect. You sure can't count on a person that is doing everything for themselves. That is my second reason I admire my uncle and wanna be more like him.

The last important quality is the simplest, yet still often forgotten. A person worth admiring is humble. Someone who doesn't think they're better than everyone else. One of the most amazing things about my uncle is how he never judges people or looks down on them. My uncle used to always say, "Not everyone is born as privileged as you and me." That is something that never really crossed my mind until now. It really makes you think. Is it fair that some people are so lucky that their family has a lot of money and security but other people are poor and have to struggle to get anything at all? Too many people take this for granted. I can't imagine how difficult that could be. How scary life could get. Thinking of this now makes me feel lucky to appreciate all the advantages I have had in life.

In conclusion, these are my main reasons I admire my uncle.

Prompt: *What are the best qualities of a person you admire?*

Margin note (left): A lot of this introduction is not necessary. It's better to be direct than to ramble.

~~What does it mean to admire? I guess we all know what it means, but have you ever really looked past the simple six-letter word and tried to really understand why we do it?~~ What are the qualities that make you admire someone? Of course, a person you admire must be a good person. But beneath that, ~~deep down to the core of this phenomenon, there must be certain qualities.~~ A person that is admired would have to ~~have these qualities. They would have to~~ be giving, successful, and humble. These ~~really~~ are the best qualities of ~~a person I admire. I admire~~ my uncle, ~~and~~ ← whom I greatly admire. ~~these are the qualities he has.~~

Margin note (left): This paragraph would be much stronger if it focused on one or two examples of how the uncle gives to others. Specific examples help create strong essays.

Humans, by nature, are very selfish beings, but an admirable person will go past their inner coding to something more. They will go past their own well-being for that of another. A good person ~~has got to~~ ← must understand that as easy as it could be to run ahead of a slower person in life who has fallen, you must instead take the time to stop, dust them off, and give encouragements, even though that makes the whole run harder. Would you respect a person who is always greedy? Would you want to be friends with someone who only takes and takes? Wouldn't you rather be around a person who is generous and tries to help other people? I look up to my uncle very much because of all the great things that he does for people that he doesn't even know. <u>There are a lot of examples of this.</u>

Margin note (right): Rhetorical questions can be effective, but don't use too many of them. Usually, a strong statement is more effective than a question.

Margin note (left): This paragraph would be stronger if it explained **why** hard work is an admirable trait in a person. Even if it seems obvious to you, it's important to explain in an essay.

~~Second, I am going to talk about how~~ my uncle gives a ~~whole~~ lot to charities and always helps others, but he also is very successful. He manages his own construction company, which is a lot of hard work. A person you really admire should ~~have this quality~~. .be Someone you can hope to become. ~~Someone~~ with good ethics. and ~~Someone~~ who worked hard to earn all of his success and still gives to others. ~~Can you believe that some people don't care about that? They are rich and do everything for more money, but they don't do anything to make the world better. That is why giving is also a quality in people I admire. People that you can trust and respect. You sure can't count on a person that is doing everything for themselves. That is my second reason I admire my uncle and~~ ~~wanna~~ be more like him.

Margin note (right): Try to avoid describing the organization of your essay ("Second, I am going to talk about…" or "In conclusion…"). Your reader can easily tell if you are moving on to a new example or if it's your conclusion by looking at your paragraphs.

Margin note (left): The quote from the uncle is a strong detail. This paragraph could be improved by an explanation of **why** humility is worth admiring.

~~The last important quality is the simplest, yet still often forgotten.~~ A person worth admiring is humble. ~~Someone who doesn't think they're better than everyone else.~~ One of the most amazing things about my uncle is how he never judges people or looks down on them. My uncle used to always say, "Not everyone is born as privileged as you and me." ~~That is something that never really crossed my mind until now. It really makes you think.~~ Is it fair that some people are so lucky that their family has a lot of money and security but other people are poor and have to struggle to get anything at all? Too many people take this for granted. I can't imagine how difficult that could be. or How scary life could get. Thinking of this now makes me feel lucky to appreciate all the advantages I have had in life.

Margin note (left): The conclusion should do more. For example, it could explain what the student has learned from his or her uncle.

~~In conclusion,~~ these are my main reasons I admire my uncle.

Evaluating Your Writing

❑ In general, your readers will consider five aspects of your writing sample: content, format, style, mechanics, and appearance. These five elements contribute to the reader's overall impression.

❑ Content

Does your answer make sense?

Do your ideas connect logically?

Are your examples appropriate?

❑ Format

Does your writing have clear body paragraphs with one topic in each?

❑ Style

Is your writing clear?

Does your writing flow smoothly?

Do you vary your sentence structure?

Do you use standard written English and good vocabulary?

❑ Mechanics

Does your writing have spelling errors?

Does your writing contain grammatical or usage errors?

❑ Appearance

Is your writing neat?

Are your paragraphs clear?

Are there cross-outs?

Do you stay in the margins?

Examples of Student Writing

TRY IT OUT

Read through the following writings and note strengths and weaknesses.

Mark any issues such as run-on sentences, incomplete sentences, misspelled words, or slang.

Describe any mistakes that have been made, such as off-topic rambling, repetition, or weak writing.

Offer suggestions for improvement.

Formal prompt: *What class or subject in school do you enjoy most? Why?*

Out of all the subjects in school, I would say that I enjoy my English classes the best. I would not say that the English classes are better, because I am lucky to have great teachers in all my classes, but I personally enjoy English the most. I am the kind of person who likes creativity and possibilities, and my English classes provide these.

It's important for every student to explore different subjects and determine which ones suit them best. Some students enjoy the subjects like math and science because the rules are very rigid and there isn't very much room for interpretation on answers. For some students, it is reassuring to know that 5+5 will always be 10 and the atomic number of carbon will always be 6. For me, however, there is no excitement in these absolute rules. I prefer questions with no definite answers. In my English classes, you can have lively debates involving some great literature. One classmate's interpretation of a Robert Frost poem might be completely different than my own, and they could both be valid. I've also been exposed to a wide variety of some great writers such as Shakespeare, Orwell, Fitzgerald, and many more. I may never have thought to read *1984* if I hadn't been assigned it in school, but now I'm glad that I have as it has opened my eyes to many new ideas. Most of what I've learned in English class is not about learning facts but learning different viewpoints and ways to think. I think this is what makes life interesting.

Most students that I know do not like writing assignment, but I enjoy my assigned papers, and hope to continue this in college one day by studying journalism. I enjoy the challenge of trying to communicate an idea or event in writing. It still amazes me that we are even able to share such complicated thoughts and details with series of words. Writing has been my passion for years, and I plan to make it my profession. I can be confident that I will always enjoy it because writing is an art that you can never be perfect at. You will always be learning, becoming a stronger writer, so it is a skill that will always be interesting.

I've learned a lot of interesting things in my math and science classes, but overall English is the subject for me.

Notes: _____

_____

_____

_____

_____

SUMMIT
EDUCATIONAL
GROUP

Creative prompt: *They didn't know if they would be able to do it.*

They didn't know if they would be able to do it. After a full six years of fighting the mighty Gauls, Julius Caesar and his men finally had reached the fort of Alesia where Vercingetorix, the "Great Warrior King," was based. The powerful Gallic leader had led his tribes to victory against the Romans before, but Caesar had grown more determined and desperate to conquer the Gallic forces.

The Galls were strongly fortified in Alesia, and Caesar knew he didn't have enough of a force to successfully attach the stronghold. In a display of his military genius, Caesar decided to build a wall and ring of trenches around Alesia. This would prevent anyone from leaving the city, and eventually the Gauls would starve.

It was a brilliant plan, but before the siege was ready a scout got out of Alesia and contacted other Gallic tribes to help fight the Romans. In order to defend his troops, Caesar ordered them to build another wall around them. This way, the inner wall would prevent the Gauls in Alesia from escaping and the outer wall would protect the Romans from any other Gallic tribes that might come attach them. Unfortunately, this meant the Romans were as trapped as the Gauls in Alesia.

Another problem for the Romans was a cliffside where they couldn't build a wall, and this created a weak point in their defenses. The Gauls discovered this weakness and knew it was their best chance to defeat Caesar's army.

After weeks of fighting, the Gauls organized a massive attack on the weak point in the Roman defense. Thousands of Gallic warriors from Alesia attacked the inner walls. At the same time, an even greater Gallic army came and attacked the outer walls in the same area. With a little fighting force left, the Romans were weary and their morale was low. Outnumbered and exhausted, the Romans had little chance of winning the battle.

Caesar, with his skills of oratory and strategy, managed to give his troops confidence and strength. When all hope seemed to be lost, Caesar personally led a small group of soldiers in a surprise attack against a large Gallic force.

"Those Gaulish pigs are the only things getting in the way of our victory!" said Caesar. "After we kill his barbarians, Vercingetorix will be marched all the way back to Rome for a public execution, and all of you will be heroes!" The legionnaires were shouting and talking amongst themselves in agreement. "Now, form ranks and seal the doom for any that stand in our way!"

Suddenly, the Romans were ready for battle again. They felt courageous, strong, and restored.

Julius Caesar was at the front with his horse, Maximus. "CHAAAAARGE!" screamed Caesar. Then, from the legion came an even louder cry that shook the heavens.

The Gauls were terrified to see the Romans suddenly charging them, led by the mighty Caesar. Even though the Gauls outnumbered the Romans ten to one, they became so afraid of the legionnaires that they ran away. Caeasar and his men chased the Gauls down and slaughtered them all. Seeing this victory, the rest of the Romans were encouraged and they defeated the rest of the Gallic forces.

Through his courage and intelligence, Caesar became an eternal symbol of power. He will always be remembered as an incredible leader, and his legendary ingenuity and bravery will forever inspire others.

Notes: _____

_____

_____

_____

_____

Chapter Review

❏ Format/Directions

"Schools would like to get to know you better through an essay or story using one of the two topics below. Please select the topic you find most interesting and fill in the circle next to the topic you choose."

The writing sample is not scored, but is sent directly to admissions committees.

Typically, writing sample readers are checking that your writing is focused and well-organized. Make sure that you express your thoughts clearly.

The writing sample is an opportunity for you to show something about yourself.

❏ Creative or Formal?

The Middle Level SSAT will let you choose between two creative prompts.

The Upper Level SSAT will let you choose between a creative and a formal prompt.

❏ Preparing to Write

Plan before you begin writing. Create an outline to guide you through the writing and make sure you manage your time.

❏ Creative

The setup is used to introduce characters, describe settings, and establish situations. This usually comes first because it is needed in order to understand the rest of the story.

The confrontation is the main source of drama and tension in the story. Stories need some type of problem or conflict. This can be a personal desire, a disagreement, a difficult challenge, etc.

The resolution shows the outcome of the story. This is where the characters make important decisions, where relationships break apart or come together, where heroes succeed and problems are finally resolved.

❏ Formal

The introduction establishes the main idea and focus of your essay. It includes your thesis, which is your essay's central argument or point.

The body is used to explain your argument and describe how your examples support that argument.

The conclusion summarizes your essay and connects it back to your main idea.

Writing Practice - Creative

❑ Creative prompts

1. *Nobody could have guessed that this would have happened to him.*

2. *It was over almost as soon as it started.*

3. *It was the most embarrassing moment of his life.*

4. *She had never seen something so beautiful.*

5. *They were all waiting for me to speak.*

6. *It seemed like it was going to be an ordinary day.*

7. *She had always been a hard worker, but she had never faced such a difficult challenge.*

8. *They didn't know if they would be able to do it.*

Use this page to plan your writing, and then use the next two pages to write.

Prompt: _____

Characters and source of drama: _____

_____

Outline:

Setup

_____

_____

_____

_____

_____

Confrontation

_____

_____

_____

_____

_____

Resolution

_____

_____

_____

_____

_____

Writing Practice - Formal

❏ Formal prompts

1. *What are the best qualities of a person you admire?*

2. *What class or subject in school do you enjoy most? Why?*

3. *Who is someone you respect? Explain why you feel this way.*

4. *Describe an experience that has inspired you.*

5. *Discuss a problem in the world that you would like to solve and how you would solve it.*

6. *Explain a hobby you have that makes you special.*

7. *Which two historical figures would you like to meet and why?*

Use this page to plan your writing, and then use the next two pages to write.

Prompt: _____

Thesis and examples: _____

_____

Outline:

    Introduction

_____

_____

_____

_____

_____

    Body

_____

_____

_____

_____

_____

    Conclusion

_____

_____

_____

_____

_____

SUMMIT
EDUCATIONAL
GROUP

Answer Key

TEST-TAKING FUNDAMENTALS

Pg. 7 – BEATING THE SSAT

1. correct answer: D. attractor: B
2. correct answer: D. attractor: A, E

Pg. 10 – USING THE ANSWER CHOICES

1. B

QUANTITATIVE

Pg. 19 – PLUGGING IN

1. D
2. D
3. C
4. E

Pg. 21 – SOLVING BACKWARDS

1. E
2. B
3. A

Pg. 23 – CHOOSING NUMBERS

Put It Together

1. A
2. A
3. D
4. D

ARITHMETIC

Pg. 31 – ADDITION, SUBTRACTION, MULTIPLICATION, AND DIVISION

Try It Out

1. 100,700
2. 11,000
3. 1,150
4. 6,020
5. 11,110
6. 3,813
7. 0
8. 1,000
9. 13,000
10. 85
11. 21
12. 621
13. 28,900
14. 0
15. 999.9
16. 22
17. 412
18. 0
19. 347.76
20. 1

Put It Together

1. B
2. B
3. B
4. C
5. C
6. B
7. D

Pg. 35 – ODD AND EVEN INTEGERS

Try It Out

1. 4, 6, 400
2. 0, 12, 18, 100
3. 1, 3, 11, 21

Put It Together

1. C
2. E
3. D

Pg. 37 – POSITIVE AND NEGATIVE NUMBERS

Try It Out

1. −3
2. 1
3. 7
4. 0
5. 1
6. −1
7. −12
8. −5
9. 23
10. −4
11. 8
12. −15
13. −10
14. 12
15. 4

Put It Together

1. A

Pg. 39 – DIVISIBILITY AND REMAINDERS

Try It Out

1. yes
2. no
3. 2
4. 0
5. 7

Put It Together

1. B
2. E
3. D

Pg. 41 – MULTIPLES AND FACTORS

Try It Out

1. 1, 32, 2, 16, 4, 8
2. 1, 63, 3, 21, 7, 9
3. 2, 4, 6, 8, 10
4. 12, 24, 36
5. 2, 2, 2, 3   2, 2, 3, 7   2, 2, 5, 5

Put It Together

1. E
2. E
3. D

Pg. 43 – FRACTIONS

Try It Out

1. $\frac{5}{4}$

2. $\frac{20}{3}$

3. $\frac{41}{7}$

4. $1\frac{1}{2}$

5. $2\frac{2}{3}$

6. $4\frac{3}{4}$

7. 10
8. 12
9. 14
10. 5
11. 70
12. 450

Put It Together

1. E
2. D
3. C
4. B
5. B
6. E
7. D
8. D

Pg. 47 – REDUCING FRACTIONS

Try It Out

1. $\frac{2}{3}$

2. $\frac{13}{15}$

3. $\frac{9}{20}$

4. $\frac{4}{9}$

5. $\frac{1}{3}, \frac{3}{8}, \frac{4}{3}$

6. $\frac{3}{8}, \frac{2}{5}, \frac{3}{4}$

7. $\frac{1}{6}, \frac{7}{30}, \frac{8}{15}, \frac{4}{5}$

8. $\frac{3}{7}, \frac{1}{2}, \frac{2}{3}, \frac{4}{5}$

Put It Together

1. B
2. C
3. A
4. E

Pg. 51 – ADDING AND SUBTRACTING FRACTIONS

Try It Out

1. $\frac{2}{3}$

2. $\frac{5}{6}$

3. $\frac{2}{3}$

4. $\frac{3}{4}$

5. $1\frac{2}{15}$

6. $\frac{17}{18}$

7. $1\frac{1}{2}$

8. $7\frac{5}{6}$

9. $\frac{1}{3}$

10. $\frac{1}{4}$

11. $\frac{3}{10}$

12. $\frac{1}{12}$

13. $\frac{5}{14}$

14. $6\frac{2}{3}$

15. 1

16. $1\frac{1}{2}$

17. $2\frac{2}{5}$

Put It Together

1. E
2. D
3. E
4. A
5. B

Pg. 55 – MULTIPLYING AND DIVIDING FRACTIONS

Try It Out

1. $\frac{2}{21}$

2. $\frac{1}{5}$

3. $\frac{2}{5}$

4. $\frac{2}{5}$

5. $\frac{2}{5}$

6. 12

7. $4\frac{1}{6}$

8. 21

9. $1\frac{1}{2}$

10. 2

11. $\frac{4}{5}$

12. $\frac{2}{3}$

13. $5\frac{1}{5}$

14. 4
15. 30
16. 49

Put It Together

1. B
2. E
3. D
4. E
5. A
6. B

Pg. 59 – DECIMALS AND PLACE VALUE

Try It Out

1. 8
2. 5

Put It Together

1. C
2. D
3. D
4. B

Pg. 61 – ROUNDING AND ESTIMATION

Try It Out

1. 2
2. 1.5
3. 2.23
4. 23
5. 400
6. 350
7. 100.0
8. D
9. C

Put It Together

1. B
2. A
3. D
4. E
5. B

Pg. 65 – DECIMAL OPERATIONS

Try It Out

1. 18.8203
2. 83
3. 7.65
4. 150.01
5. $\frac{19}{20}$ or 0.95
6. 9.8
7. 0.98
8. 25.29
9. 0.0014
10. 2,900
11. 3.294
12. 90
13. 40
14. 40
15. 2.01
16. 160
17. 30.2

Put It Together

1. C
2. D

Pg. 67 – PERCENT-DECIMAL CONVERSION

Try It Out

1. 63%
2. 207%
3. 4%
4. 12.56%
5. 0.05%
6. 0.73
7. 1.19
8. 0.075
9. 0.0075
10. 0.021

Put It Together

1. E

Pg. 69 – PERCENT-FRACTION CONVERSION

Try It Out

1. $\frac{2}{5}$
2. $\frac{17}{25}$
3. $\frac{2}{25}$
4. $1\frac{2}{5}$
5. $10\frac{1}{100}$
6. 10%
7. 25%
8. 60%
9. 120%
10. 71%

Put It Together

1. B
2. B
3. A

Pg. 71 – SOLVING PERCENT PROBLEMS

Try It Out

1. 4.8
2. 62.5
3. 1.28
4. 45
5. 50
6. 75
7. 125
8. 33.$\overline{3}$
9. 200
10. 6.25
11. 30
12. 2

Put It Together

1. C
2. E
3. C
4. B
5. C
6. A
7. D

Pg. 75 – RATIOS

Try It Out

1. 4:7
2. 2:5
3. 5:18
4. 3:2
5. 10
6. 30

Put It Together

1. A
2. A
3. B
4. C
5. B
6. D

Pg. 79 – PROPORTIONS

Try It Out

1. 8
2. 10
3. 12
4. 16
5. $8\frac{1}{3}$
6. $480
7. 60
8. 25 miles
9. 4

Put It Together

1. A
2. B
3. C
4. A

Pg. 83 – EXPONENTS

Try It Out

1. 1
2. 2
3. 4
4. 8
5. −2
6. 4
7. −8
8. 16
9. 1
10. −1
11. $\frac{1}{9}$
12. $\frac{8}{27}$
13. 3 or −3
14. 4
15. −2
16. −1
17. $\frac{1}{10}$
18. 3

Put It Together

1. D

Pg. 85 – MULTIPLYING AND DIVIDING EXPONENTS

Try It Out

1. 2^5 or 32
2. x^7
3. 7
4. x^{10}
5. 6^6
6. x^{44}
7. $16x^6$

Put It Together

1. E

Pg. 87 – ROOTS

Try It Out

1. 4
2. 7
3. $\frac{1}{3}$
4. $\frac{2}{3}$
5. x
6. x^2
7. $2x^5$
8. 10
9. 4
10. −1
11. −5
12. $\frac{1}{2}$
13. $2\sqrt{2}$
14. $2\sqrt{3}$
15. $4\sqrt{5}$
16. $4\sqrt{2}$

Put It Together

1. D
2. C

Pg. 89 – ORDER OF OPERATIONS

Try It Out

1. 37
2. 7
3. 196
4. 1

Put It Together

1. D
2. A

Pg. 91 – AVERAGES

Try It Out

1. 16
2. 100
3. 9
4. 39
5. 5
6. 2
7. 18
8. 52
9. $170
10. 11

Put It Together

1. E
2. D
3. B
4. D
5. E
6. E

Pg. 95 – PROBABILITY

Try It Out

1. $\frac{1}{2}$
2. $\frac{5}{8}$
3. $\frac{2}{3}$

Put It Together

1. D
2. C
3. E

Pg. 99 – ORDERING AND SEQUENCES

Try It Out

1. 0.00936, 4.1937, 4.23, 33.01, 33.1
2. $\frac{5}{12}, \frac{3}{5}, \frac{2}{3}, \frac{7}{10}$
3. Fred
4. 19

Put It Together

1. E
2. B
3. A
4. B
5. C

Pg. 103 – CHARTS AND GRAPHS

Try It Out

1. 6
2. 3
3. $1.28
4. April
5. 15
6. 40

Put It Together

1. A
2. C
3. D
4. D
5. C
6. B

ARITHMETIC PRACTICE

Pg. 108

1. E
2. B
3. D
4. C
5. A
6. C
7. D
8. B
9. A
10. A
11. C
12. D
13. D
14. B
15. A
16. D
17. C
18. C
19. D
20. E
21. D
22. D
23. E
24. D
25. C
26. A
27. E
28. C
29. A
30. D
31. C
32. E
33. C
34. E
35. C
36. B
37. B
38. D
39. D
40. B
41. A
42. D
43. D
44. B

ARITHMETIC MIDDLE LEVEL PRACTICE

Pg. 120

1. D
2. B
3. D
4. A
5. D
6. B
7. D
8. D
9. D
10. B
11. E
12. E
13. B
14. A
15. A
16. C
17. E
18. D
19. E
20. E
21. C
22. E
23. A
24. C
25. A
26. C
27. C
28. E
29. B
30. C
31. E
32. B
33. C
34. A
35. D
36. D
37. D
38. D
39. D
40. D
41. A
42. B
43. D
44. A
45. B
46. B
47. B
48. B
49. A

ARITHMETIC UPPER LEVEL PRACTICE

Pg. 134

1. B
2. C
3. E
4. A
5. B
6. A
7. D
8. C
9. D
10. D
11. C
12. C
13. C
14. A
15. D
16. D
17. A
18. C
19. D
20. E
21. D
22. C
23. A
24. C
25. E
26. E
27. D
28. D
29. C
30. C
31. D
32. D
33. B
34. B
35. C
36. A
37. A
38. D
39. D
40. D
41. D
42. B
43. E
44. E
45. D
46. C

ALGEBRA

Pg. 151 – ALGEBRAIC EXPRESSIONS

Try It Out

1. $17+3x$
2. $12+x$
3. $-4x$
4. $3x^2+3$
5. $-3x^2+5x+12$
6. $3x+10$
7. $x+1$
8. $3x+1$
9. $-14x+7$
10. $2x+6$
11. $8x+28$
12. $-4x-3$
13. $-3x-18$
14. $35x-42$
15. x^2+x
16. $2x^2-12x$
17. $-5x^2-20x$
18. $8x^2+18x$
19. $22x+2$
20. $5x^2-12x-2$

Put It Together

1. A
2. A
3. D
4. B
5. C

Pg. 155 – ALGEBRAIC EQUATIONS

Try It Out

1. 11
2. 5
3. 0
4. 1000
5. 50
6. 1
7. 20
8. 125
9. 10
10. 13
11. 20
12. 100
13. 60
14. 12
15. 4
16. 18

Put It Together

1. D
2. D
3. D
4. E
5. A
6. C

Pg. 159 – TRANSLATING

Try It Out

1. $\frac{50}{100} \cdot (24) = x$, $x = 12$
2. $y - 6 = 17$, $y = 23$
3. $\frac{1}{2} \cdot (28) = x$, $x = 14$
4. $9 + u = a$
5. $1 + z = x$
6. $u + v + w = 9$
7. $7 \times 4 = y$, $y = 28$
8. $-5 = \frac{a + b + c}{3}$
9. $S = F - 2$
10. $2N + 1 = 11$, $N = 5$

Put It Together

1. D
2. D

Pg. 161 – WORD PROBLEMS

Try It Out

1. 9
2. 54
3. 10
4. 11
5. 13

Put It Together

1. B
2. A
3. C
4. D
5. C
6. E
7. B

Pg. 165 – SSAT FUNCTIONS

Try It Out

1. C
2. B
3. C
4. C
5. A

Put It Together

1. C
2. D
3. B
4. B
5. D
6. A

Pg. 169 – INEQUALITIES

Try It Out

1. 3, 4
2. 1, 3, 5, 7
3. -2, -1
4. $n > 4$
5. $x \le 18$
6. $x < 2$
7. $s \ge 1\frac{1}{2}$
8. $x < -4$
9. $r > -3$
10. $m < 3$

Put It Together

1. D
2. E
3. C
4. E
5. D

ALGEBRA PRACTICE

Pg. 174

1. D
2. B
3. E
4. A
5. A
6. D
7. D
8. C
9. E
10. D
11. B
12. C
13. C
14. D
15. D
16. B
17. D
18. E
19. E

ALGEBRA MIDDLE LEVEL PRACTICE

Pg. 180

1. C
2. E
3. C
4. C
5. D
6. C
7. B
8. E
9. E
10. D
11. C
12. E
13. B
14. B
15. C
16. C
17. D
18. B
19. D
20. E
21. B
22. D
23. C
24. D
25. C

ALGEBRA UPPER LEVEL PRACTICE

Pg. 186

1. B
2. E
3. B
4. C
5. C
6. E
7. B
8. B
9. C
10. D
11. E
12. B
13. E
14. E
15. C
16. E
17. B
18. C
19. B
20. D
21. A
22. B
23. C
24. E
25. E

GEOMETRY

Pg. 198 – ANGLES

1.

2.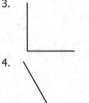

3.

4.

5. 45°
6. 90°
7. ~150°
8. ~170°
9. 90°
10. 90°
11. 90°, 120°
12. ~50° and ~40° (sum is 90°)
13. 60°
14. 145°
15. 45°
16. 360°

Put It Together

1. C

Pg. 201 – PAIRS OF ANGLES

Try It Out

1. 145°
2. a=95, b=85, c=95

Put It Together

1. A

Pg. 203 – PARALLEL LINES

Try It Out

1. Angles are 30° and 150°

Put It Together

1. D

Pg. 205 – TRIANGLES

Try It Out

1. 60°
2. 105°

Put It Together

1. A
2. B
3. B

Pg. 207 – ISOSCELES AND EQUILATERAL TRIANGLES

Try It Out

1. 45° and 45°
2. 46° and 46°
3. Sides = 4, and angle = 60°

Put It Together

1. B
2. C

Pg. 209 – RIGHT TRIANGLES

Try It Out

1. Sum of all angles in a triangle is 180°. The sum of the two non-right angles must be 90° so that the sum of these angles and the right angle will be 180°.
2. 60°

Put It Together

1. A
2. C

Pg. 211 – AREA AND PERIMETER – RECTANGLE AND SQUARE

Try It Out

1. Perimeter = 8, Area = 4
2. Area = 21, Perimeter = 20

Put It Together

1. D
2. B
3. C
4. C
5. A
6. E
7. E

Pg. 215 – AREA AND PERIMETER – TRIANGLE

Try It Out

1. 12
2. 6
3. 6
4. 7.5
5. 3

Put It Together

1. B
2. D
3. B

Pg. 219 – CIRCLES

Try It Out

1. 8π
2. 6π
3. 16π
4. 9π

Put It Together

1. C
2. C

Pg. 221 – ESTIMATING FIGURES

Try It Out

1. D

Pg. 223 – VOLUME

Try It Out

1. 64
2. 48

Put It Together

1. C

Pg. 225 – COORDINATE PLANE

Try It Out

1.

2. K: (0, 4) L: (2, 3) M: (4, 2)
   N: (−1, 1) P: (3, 0)
   Q: (−3, −2) R: (−1, −2) S: (2, −2)

Pg. 227 – SLOPE

Try It Out

1. 1
2. 3
3. -3
4. $\frac{2}{3}$
5. $-\frac{1}{3}$
6. S
7. T

Pg. 229 – GRAPHING LINES

Try It Out

1.

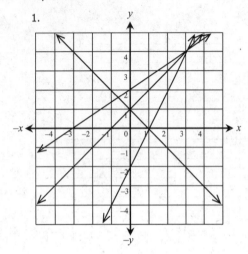

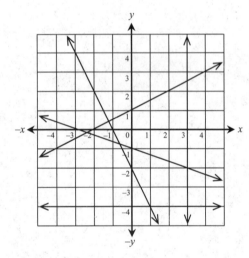

2. A: $x = -4$
    B: $y = x - 3$

    C: $y = \frac{1}{2}x - 2$

    D: $y = -x + 4$

    E: $y = -2x + 2$

3. $y = x + 4$

4. $y = -3x + 2$

5. $y = -\frac{2}{3}x - 1$

GEOMETRY PRACTICE

Pg. 232

1. B
2. D
3. D
4. C
5. C
6. C
7. C
8. D
9. C
10. E
11. D
12. E
13. C
14. D

GEOMETRY MIDDLE LEVEL PRACTICE

Pg. 238

1. D
2. A
3. C
4. D
5. C
6. C
7. A
8. B
9. C
10. A
11. D
12. C
13. D

GEOMETRY UPPER LEVEL PRACTICE

Pg. 244

1. D
2. E
3. D
4. A
5. C
6. B
7. C
8. C
9. E
10. B
11. E
12. C
13. B

SYNONYMS

Pg. 255 – ANTICIPATE THE ANSWER

Try It Out

1. A
2. D
3. D

Pg. 257 – SECONDARY DEFINITIONS

Try It Out

1. A
2. A
3. B

Pg. 259 – POSITIVE OR NEGATIVE

Try It Out

1. –
2. –
3. +
4. –
5. –
6. –
7. +
8. +
9. –
10. +
11. C
12. E
13. E

Pg. 261 – ATTRACTORS

Try It Out

1. D
2. B
3. C

Pg. 263 – ROOTS

Try It Out

1. I
2. H
3. A
4. D
5. G
6. F
7. B
8. C
9. J
10. E

Try It Out

1. B
2. C
3. E
4. D

SYNONYMS MIDDLE LEVEL PRACTICE

Pg. 282

1. C
2. E
3. C
4. D
5. B
6. E
7. C
8. D
9. E
10. E
11. C
12. C
13. B
14. B
15. D
16. D
17. A
18. A
19. D
20. C
21. C
22. A
23. A
24. E
25. D
26. C
27. B
28. E
29. A
30. D
31. E
32. B
33. B
34. B
35. B
36. B
37. E
38. D

SYNONYMS UPPER LEVEL PRACTICE

Pg. 286

1. D
2. C
3. C
4. D
5. B
6. C
7. A
8. B
9. C
10. B
11. C
12. B
13. E
14. D
15. D
16. A
17. C
18. E
19. A
20. A
21. A
22. D
23. B
24. A
25. C
26. E
27. D
28. A
29. A
30. A
31. E
32. A
33. E
34. A
35. D
36. D
37. B
38. B
39. B

ANALOGIES

Pg. 295 – DEFINING THE RELATIONSHIP

Try It Out

1. A key opens a padlock.
2. A pyramid is a 3D triangle.
3. A sculptor makes a statue.
4. A playwright makes a script.
5. Reign is what a king does, or a reign is a period in which a king rules.
6. Cumulus is a type of cloud.
7. A melodious sound is a nice, pleasant sound.
8. A pancake is made from batter.
9. A sonnet is a type of poem.
10. A neurologist is a type of physician.

Pg. 297 – APPLYING THE RELATIONSHIP

Try It Out

1. An eye chart is used to measure vision.
   C
2. A poem is divided into stanzas.
   C
3. An apple is a type of fruit.
   C

Pg. 299 – REFINING THE RELATIONSHIP

Try It Out

1. A judge presides over a courthouse.
   E
2. Goggles are used to protect welders.
   B
3. A rhinoceros uses its sharp horn for defense.
   D

Pg. 301 – COMMON ANALOGY RELATIONSHIPS

Try It Out

1. Person/Tool – A carpenter uses a hammer.
2. Characteristic – A globe is spherical.
3. Person/Creation – A sculptor makes a statue.
4. Part/Whole – An atlas is a collection of maps.
5. Function – A mask covers a face.
6. Action/Result – Stress makes one agitated.
7. Type – A mouse is a type of rodent.
8. Degree of Intensity – A ripple is a tiny tidal wave.
9. Synonym or Degree – Furious means very angry.
10. Function – A scalpel is used to dissect.

Pg. 303 – FIRST AND THIRD ANALOGIES

Put It Together

1. B
2. A
3. C

Pg. 305 – ATTRACTORS

Try It Out

1. Attractors: "farm," "earth," "ground," "property"
   E
2. Attractors: "swamp," "forest," "grass"
   D
3. Attractors: "blade," "target," "bullet"
   C

Pg. 307 – BEING AN ANALOGY DETECTIVE

Try It Out

1. None
2. A hurricane is a type of storm.
3. None
4. None
5. Goggles are used to protect eyes.
6. None
7. Quartz is a type of rock.
8. A ticket is used to gain admission.
9. A shoe is made of leather (but not necessarily, so this is a rather weak analogy)
10. A nightmare is a bad dream.
11. None
12. None
13. Common is the opposite of rare.
14. None
15. Wheat is used to make flour.
16. (A) None
    (B) None
    (C) YES
    (D) YES
    (E) None
17. (A) YES
    (B) None
    (C) YES
    (D) None
    (E) None

Pg. 309 – SOLVING BACKWARDS

Try It Out

1. C
2. E

ANALOGIES MIDDLE LEVEL PRACTICE

Pg. 312

1. B
2. E
3. C
4. B
5. B
6. A
7. E
8. D
9. C
10. A
11. C
12. B
13. C
14. E
15. A
16. E
17. C
18. E
19. A
20. D
21. B
22. D
23. A
24. C
25. D
26. B
27. D
28. D
29. B
30. E
31. B
32. A
33. A
34. B
35. D
36. A
37. C
38. E
39. B
40. E
41. E
42. C
43. D
44. C
45. C
46. C
47. B
48. E
49. D
50. D

ANALOGIES UPPER LEVEL PRACTICE

Pg. 317

1. E
2. B
3. A
4. A
5. C
6. E
7. C
8. B
9. B
10. B
11. D
12. B
13. A
14. B
15. C
16. A
17. D
18. B
19. A
20. D
21. E
22. A
23. D
24. E
25. A
26. C
27. A
28. B
29. C
30. E
31. D
32. A
33. A
34. C
35. E
36. B
37. B
38. A
39. A
40. B
41. B
42. C
43. A
44. B
45. B
46. E
47. A
48. D
49. C

READING COMPREHENSION

Pg. 327 – ACTIVE READING

Try It Out

1. They are symbols of "natural forces, elements, animals, or ancestors", and they also represent tradition and a source of profit.
2. The dolls have become more complex and refined. Also, they have become a source of revenue, in addition to a traditional practice.
3. Preserving tradition and making money.
4. He became very interested in photography.
5. Something that is difficult to describe.
6. He liked his mother's photos and the anticipation of how an image would develop.
7. New and old technologies
8. He does not like digital as much as older cameras. It goes against his interest in photography, so he still uses older types of cameras and film.

Put It Together

1. B
2. C
3. A
4. B

Pg. 331 – MAPPING THE PASSAGE

Try It Out

1. Slash-and-burn agriculture
2. Fact
3. Slash-and-burn agriculture, which is the technique of clearing sections of forest to make farm land, has been practiced for a long time.
4. In recent times, this practice has grown to become unsustainable and very destructive.
5. Slash-and-burn agriculture has been used sustainably for many years, but on a large scale it is too destructive.
6. To explain the practice of slash-and-burn agriculture and show the potential danger of how it is being used today.

Pg. 334 – ANTICIPATE THE ANSWER

Put It Together

1. E
2. C
3. B
4. A

Pg. 336 – PROCESS OF ELIMINATION

Try It Out

1. (A) no mention of "investing"
   (B) too broad; the passage is about waster and biodegradability
   (C) too narrow and off-topic; the passage is about the problem, not the process
   (D) too broad; the passage is about a particular problem
   (E) CORRECT
2. (A) incorrect; passage lists materials that are biodegradable (paper, food scraps, natural materials), but doesn't say which is the most biodegradable.
   (B) too broad; only focuses on one aspect of modern society
   (C) incorrect; doesn't explain why
   (D) CORRECT
   (E) incorrect; never specifies how much
3. (A) incorrect; he likely already knew this
   (B) incorrect; he likely already knew this
   (C) incorrect; he already knew this
   (D) CORRECT
   (E) incorrect; this is linked to modern consumers
4. (A) CORRECT
   (B) incorrect; no evidence of this
   (C) incorrect; changing traditions doesn't mean people are unaware
   (D) incorrect; no evidence of this
   (E) incorrect; passage is not focused on plane meals

Pg. 341 – MAIN IDEA QUESTIONS

Try It Out

1. Africa's impressive art serves multiple purposes.
2. E
3. B
4. C
5. A

Pg. 343 – DETAIL / SUPPORTING IDEA QUESTIONS

Try It Out

1. he believed it was a fundamental formula for peace
2. D
3. B

Pg. 345 – VOCABULARY QUESTIONS

Try It Out

1. connection / relation
2. A
3. C
4. C

Pg. 347 – TONE / ATTITUDE QUESTIONS

Try It Out

1. D
2. B
3. C

Pg. 349 – INFERENCE QUESTIONS

Try It Out

1. track (running)
   "asphalt track"
2. city
   "chain-link," "asphalt," school is "massive"
3. twenties
   Bang was twenty-five, and the rest are probably of similar age.
4. gloomy, dark, tense, harsh
   Descriptions are dark, landscape is "wounded" and seems cruel and crumbling, and there is violence and danger.
5. to show that the area is going to waste
6. 11
   "my eleven years"
7. to be freed from slavery
   Margaret's will can set her free.
8. her owner who recently died
   Her will is going to be read, and if she can set Harriet free then Harriet is currently owned.
9. She loves the idea of freedom so much that the word feels physically good to her.

Put It Together

1. B
2. E
3. D

Pg. 353 – APPLICATION QUESTIONS

Try It Out

1. the current or future advancements of computer technology
2. growing more efficient and powerful
3. A
4. B

Pg. 355 – EXCEPT/LEAST/NOT and ROMAN NUMERAL QUESTIONS

Try It Out

1. D
2. D
3. C

READING COMPREHENSION MIDDLE LEVEL PRACTICE

Pg. 359

1. D
2. C
3. B
4. A
5. A
6. C
7. A
8. D
9. D
10. B
11. B
12. A
13. D
14. B
15. B
16. C
17. C
18. D
19. B
20. D
21. A
22. E
23. C
24. D
25. B
26. E
27. D
28. D
29. A
30. D
31. E
32. D
33. B

READING COMPREHENSION UPPER LEVEL PRACTICE

Pg. 367

1. B
2. C
3. D
4. B
5. B
6. D
7. C
8. A
9. D
10. C
11. D
12. B
13. A
14. A
15. E
16. A
17. D
18. D
19. D
20. C
21. A
22. C
23. E
24. C
25. A
26. C
27. E
28. E
29. C
30. E
31. B
32. E
33. D
34. C
35. B
36. D
37. B
38. E
39. C
40. C
41. A
42. C
43. E
44. C
45. C
46. B
47. E
48. D
49. A